"THE STORIES OUR PARENTS FOUND TOO PAINFUL TO TELL"

"THE STORIES OUR PARENTS FOUND TOO PAINFUL TO TELL"

by RAFAEL RAJZNER & Henry R. Lew

adapted with the voluntary assistance of 22 righteous translators

from "THE ANNIHILATION OF BIALYSTOKER JEWRY BY RAFAEL RAJZNER," previously published in one small Yiddish edition, by the "Bialystoker Centre," 19 Robe Street, St. Kilda, Melbourne, Australia in 1948.

AMCL PUBLICATIONS

First published in Australia in 2008,
by AMCL Publications
338 Balaclava Road,
Caulfield North ,
Melbourne, Victoria 3161.
Tel. 613-9509-9977 Fax 613-9509-7605

Book designed by Alexander M. C. Lew and Henry R. Lew.
Cover designed by Joelle Rault from the oil painting "The Jewish Bride 1914" by Abraham Behrman (1876-1942) who perished in the Bialystoker ghetto.

Printed and bound in Australia,
by White's Law Bindery,
802-804 Glenhuntly Road,
Caulfield South,
Melbourne, Victoria 3162.

National Library of Australia, cataloguing - in - publication data

Rayzner, Refa'el.
Der umkum fun Byalistoker Yidntum, 1939-1945. English.
The Stories Our Parents Found Too Painful to Tell / authors, Rafael Rajzner, Henry R. Lew.
2nd printing 2008.
Caulfield North, Vic. : AMCL Publications, 2008.
ISBN 978-0-646-48473-0 (pbk.)
Includes index.

1. Jews – Poland – Bialystok.
2. Holocaust, Jewish (1939-1945) – Poland.
3. World War, (1939-1945) – Jews - Poland.
4. Bialystok (Poland) – Ethnic relations.

Lew, Henry R.

940.5318

IN MEMORY OF MY PARENTS,

LEO (LONEK) LEW
(Bialystok 11/08/1907 - Melbourne 2/06/2002),

AND

EUGENIA (GENIA) LEW nee BASZ
(Bialystok 26/01/1916 - Melbourne 4/05/1992).

Henry R. Lew
(Born Melbourne 2/02/1948, whilst his parents were resident in the Bialystoker Centre.)

TABLE OF CONTENTS

FOREWORD TO THE ENGLISH EDITION BY HENRY R. LEW.

1. PROEM.

Rafael Rajzner's personal memoir "The Annihilation of Bialystoker Jewry" occupies a unique place in Holocaust history. It is one of a dearth of personal Holocaust memoirs which were written and published immediately after the war. This was at a time when survivor-victims still suffered the severe mental anguish of post-traumatic stress syndrome when reminiscing their terrible ordeals. Sufficient time for a degree of healing to occur had not yet passed. These people were also troubled by other pressing demands. They had new families and they often had to learn new languages, in strange foreign countries, in order to work and support their families. They had to think to their childrens' futures and try, as best as possible, to put their own past to a side. They couldn't even tell their children exactly what had happened. It was too painful to do so. **These were the stories our parents found too painful to tell!**

The reason that Rajzner's book, unlike others, was largely forgotten, probably relates to his premature death, aged 56 years, in 1953. This was well before the capture of Adolf Eichmann, one of the major architects of Nazi Jewish genocide, in Buenos Aires on May 11th 1960 and the commencement of his subsequent trial in Jerusalem on April 11th 1961. These events generated such enormous worldwide publicity, as a result of the "new television age," that horrors of the Holocaust were now presented to vast audiences in ways never seen or heard of before. More victims were encouraged to tell their stories, but it often took decades for them to eventually face their ghosts and do so. Rajzner was simply not available to retell his.

Two of the earliest writers of personal Holocaust memoirs remain the two best known. These are the Nobel Laureates Primo Levi and Elie Wiesel. Levi's first book, *"Se questo è un uomo,"* was published in Italian in a print run of 2000 copies on October 11th 1947. Levi's publisher was an amateur, Franco Antonelli, who undertook to publish the book because of anti-fascist sympathies. It is in all probability in the first score of Holocaust memoirs published after the war. Wiesel's first book, *"Un di velt hot geshvign,"* was published in Yiddish by the "Central Union of Polish Jews in Argentina" in 1956. Wiesel admits it took him ten years to recover sufficiently to write it. Levi's first book did not become well known until after it was published in English as *"If This Is a Man"* in 1958. It was renamed *"Survival in Auschwitz"* in the United States. Levi's next book of memoirs *"The Truce"* in English, renamed *"The Reawakening"* in the United States, was only published in 1963, well after the Eichmann case. Wiesel's first book likewise only became well known after it was first published in three volumes in English, and again, in its entirety, only after the Eichmann case. *"Night"* first appeared in 1958, before Eichmann's capture, but *"Dawn"* 1961 and *"Day,"* previously *"The Accident,"* 1962 were published after it.

Rafael Rajzner's memoir was first published in Yiddish by "The Bialystoker Centre" of Melbourne, in Australia, in 1948. Like Levi's *"Se questo è un uomo"* it is probably in the first score of Holocaust memoirs published after the war and portrays events still fresh in the author's mind. To be able to read it in English for the first time should therefore be a rare experience.

2. CONCEPTION.

I remember, many years ago, hearing someone make the comment that writing a book is like having a child. From the perspective of a parent, I cannot bring myself to agree with this. For a parent every child nurtured is irreplaceable, a book like any other work of art is not. It can be re-done. Yet for some inexplicable reason this statement remains fixed in my mind. It was explained to me at the time that a writer is inspired to create a book by an act of love. The manuscript grows out of nothing into a form with a future. It is cared for along the way, emotionally and financially, by its creator. And finally it develops an independent life and propels itself into the future.

With all this in mind I can clearly remember the evening that this English version of Rafael Rajzner's "The Annihilation of Bialystoker Jewry" was conceived. It was during the summer of 2001-2002. I was driving home from work and, as was often the case, I decided to look in on my elderly father. He was in his ninety-fifth year and not particularly well. I let myself into the house. I always carried a key from that day thirty years earlier when I first left home. I walked the entire length of the building for the kitchen, in which he was most often located, was at its rear. Lonek was sitting at the table, as usual, reading his newspaper. He looked up at me and smiled. His eyes always radiated a genuine pleasure whenever he saw me. *"Sit down Harry,"* he beckoned, *"and share a cup of tea with me."* He always wanted to share something with me. *"I wanted to ask you whether we had ever discussed Rafael Rajzner's book?"* We hadn't! *"I picked it up today,"* he continued, *"and re-read some of its pages. I hadn't done this for more than fifty years. Rajzner tells us the story about how Jewish Bialystok was destroyed. I knew Rajzner well from the Bialystoker Centre. I bought the book directly from him, when the*

Bialystoker Centre published it, in a small Yiddish edition, in 1948. It is an extremely valuable book. This is not because Rajzner was a writer, an intellectual or a historian. He was none of these things. In fact he was quite a simple man and he wrote in a rather simple Yiddish. He does not analyse and discuss or offer opinions and explanations. The real importance of his book lies in the fact that he was a survivor of the ghetto; he was there; he was an eyewitness. That is why his book is so important and deserves to be preserved. No academic or historian can ever hope to compete with him, no matter who they are. It was Rajzner who told me how most of the members of my own family perished. If it were not for him I probably would never have found out. This book needs to be published in an English edition to allow it to be brought to a new and wider audience. There are many details mentioned in this book that should not be allowed to disappear, particularly in this new era of Holocaust deniers. This could well happen if such books are never translated into English. It is probably the first ethnic book about the Holocaust to be published in Australia, at a time when Australians were little interested in ethnic writings. In today's multicultural Australian society people deserve the opportunity to access it, if not for any other reason that Bialystokers and their descendants, although small in numbers, have contributed more than their fair share to the post-war development of this wonderful country."

"You would have been the ideal man to translate this book," I told him. *"Your Yiddish is excellent as is your English, and you have been retired for nearly thirty years."* But as I looked into his eyes I was suddenly aware of a profound sadness entering them. He nodded his head from side to side. *"Unfortunately this was never a job for me,"* he sighed. He became silent for a while and then he moved on to other matters. I always knew that Lonek could have translated a Yiddish book like Rajzner's effortlessly, as easy as pie. The language would never have been an issue. It was the contents that was the

problem, a nightmare for him, and simply too painful to dwell on. It dealt with the destruction of the centre of his universe. Lonek's method of coping had always been to put such issues aside as best as possible, and to concentrate, instead, on the rest of his life. And he did this admirably, even to the extent of repeatedly saying there are no evil nations only evil people, and that the good people of all nations deserve his respect.

I feel a need at this point to make special mention of the "Bialystoker Centre." A significant number of Bialystoker Jews had migrated to Melbourne during the nineteen twenties and thirties in search of a better life. Many of them became highly successful businessmen and prospered. Leslie Rubinstein, Michael Pitt and Leo Fink readily come to mind, but there were many more. When World War II finally ended a group of these Bialystokers combined resources and founded the Bialystoker Centre. The Committee included such names as Michael Pitt, Abrasha Zbar, Abraham Sokol, Misha Merkel, Judel Slonim, Abram Serry and Wolf Davis, all well known to me as a child. Others, who I don't remember, include Messrs. Lapin, Hamery, Glagowsky, Gibgot, Silver and Dorevitch. These gentlemen purchased a beautiful Italianate mansion on Robe Street St. Kilda and made it their centre's headquarters. When refugees such as my parents, Leo and Eugenia Lew, arrived in Melbourne in 1947 they were met with at Spencer Street Station and taken straight to the Bialystoker Centre, where free accommodation was available. I was born whilst my parents were still resident at the centre, and I was a baby there when the centre first published Rafael Rajzner's book. It was all this nostalgia which sparked my positive feelings for the creation and publication of an English version of Rafael Rajzner's book.

I am sure that my father would never have expected me to have been involved in the production of an English edition of Rajzner's book. It simply would never have occurred to him. He knew that my Yiddish was limited and that in my wildest dreams I could never have translated a Yiddish book. Indeed during the few remaining months left to him, we never again broached the subject of Rajzner's book. It was not until after Lonek's death that I began to ponder the feasability of re-editing Rajzner's book in English.

I was in my father's house sorting through his library, when I suddenly came across it. It was one of a number of foreign language volumes, written in the numerous foreign languages, which Lonek both read and wrote. I managed to find new homes for most of them. Some went to the Makor Library, some to the Kadimah Library. Others were placed with organisations, which collected foreign language books and distributed them to new immigrants. However Rajzner's book became one of a select group, and was added to my own library.

At first I looked for a suitable Yiddish translator. I made enquiries and even went as far as getting a reasonable quote of $12,000 for the job. I also thought about how to finance it. I could either pay for it myself, or I could to try to raise the money in pledges, of $500 each, from twenty-four surviving Bialystokers. I gave some thought to both these options, but in the end neither seemed suitable. So like my father, I pushed all thoughts of Rajzner's book to one side, and simply got on with the rest of my life.

I dropped the idea of employing a single proficient translator, expert in both Yiddish and English, because I didn't want to limit myself to being a financial backer of the project. Now please don't get me wrong. I am in no way belittling the role of philanthropists. Philanthropists play an important part in the lives of many people, much more than I could ever hope to play. But I believe that philanthropy is better spent on the living than the dead, and in this instance I felt a need to put my own sweat and tears into the project, not just my money! Also when it comes to raising funds, I have never felt comfortable asking others for money for such an intensely personal project, a tribute to the dying wishes of my father.

3. FRUITION

The real breakthrough came one day when my wife Sandra asked me to take her shopping to the supermarket. *"Do I have to?"* I replied. Her response was, *"Be a friend and keep me company. While I'm shopping I don't mind if you go across the road to the Sunflower Bookshop."* The Sunflower Bookshop specialises in books of Jewish interest.

While I was in the bookshop I picked up a volume entitled ***"Outwitting History"*** by Aaron Lansky. It was subtitled ***"How a Young Man Rescued a Million Books and Saved a Vanishing Civilisation."*** This book grabbed me from its very first page. I strongly recommend it to anyone who wishes to experience an incredible read. By the time Sandra came to collect me I had already devoured a number of its fascinating pages.

It told the story of Aaron Lansky, an eighteen-year-old, first year student at Hampshire College Massachusetts who, in 1973, enrolled in a course of *"Holocaust Studies."* He came from a secular Jewish family and had never heard Yiddish spoken at home.

Within a short time, Lansky was becoming less interested in the Holocaust as an event, and progressively more interested in the people whom the Holocaust had sought to destroy. He transferred his interest to what he calls 'a sociological viewpoint of Jewish History,' a fascination not with Judaism but with Jews. And it soon became obvious to him, that if he wished to continue to pursue his journey, he needed to seek out original source material. And to do this he needed to learn the language in which this source material was written. He needed to enrol in a course to study Yiddish.

One thing led to another and Lansky started to look for Yiddish books to help him improve his language skills. He soon became aware that many older Yiddish speakers were dying and that their extensive Yiddish libraries were being thrown out into dumpsters and being buried in ground-fills. If these procedures were allowed to continue Yiddish would gradually die out and eventually become extinct. This realisation transformed Lansky's life. It caused him to stop his formal Yiddish studies and to become, instead, the man he is today, the man who has devoted the rest of his working life to the rescue of Yiddish books.

Lansky now started to lay the groundwork for what eventually became the "National Yiddish Book Centre." This centre would serve as a storage point for the collection of unwanted Yiddish books. If asked the centre was happy to distribute any duplicate copies of its books to anywhere in the world, wherever individuals or institutions, such as schools or universities, might happen to want them. To facilitate all of this Lansky mobilised a small army of friends and acquaintances who were willing to help. He started to write many letters to prominent Jews, to writers and intellectuals, to leaders of the American Jewish community, and to numerous Jewish agencies, seeking support. He was looking for funding and, as is usually the case, it was proving difficult to find. It is certain that his dream would never have survived, except for the generosity of a small number of early interested benefactors. Lansky, however, was a man of perseverance and before long he had convened a board and managed to find six thousand square feet of floor space, the whole second floor of an old dilapidated warehouse, at a modest rental of nine thousand dollars per annum.

Lansky also issued press releases to more than three hundred newspapers. Newspaper publicity followed and people started to develop an awareness of the book centre's existence. Articles appeared in the Boston Globe, the New York Times, numerous Jewish publications, and eventually even in Time Magazine. All this media attention stimulated more and more Yiddish readers to offer their libraries to the centre or to volunteer as active "zamlers" (local district collectors) for the centre. Lansky became an invited speaker and was asked to make television appearances, on one occasion together with Leo Rosten, the best selling author of *"The Joys of Yiddish."* After the fall of communism he delivered Yiddish books in person to Russia. He was granted a MacArthur Foundation Fellowship, worth nearly a quarter of a million dollars, and received an offer to relocate his National Yiddish Book Centre, free of charge, to the Mount Holyoke College Campus in New England. Instead he decided to purchase a block of land adjacent to his former alma mater, Hampshire College in Amherst, Massachusetts. He saw the independent purchase of property as the only means of providing the centre with permanence. A $7,000,000 institution was designed to be built on the block. In appearance this building was to be based on the old wooden synagogues of eastern Poland and Russia. More appeals were held, but now that Lansky was well-known the funds were eventually raised.

Today the National Yiddish Book Centre is one of the foremost and best known Jewish institutions in the United States. And all this is due to the whim of a dedicated penniless persistent young idealist, truly an example of a miracle in our own times.

I bought "Outwitting History," took it home, and devoured it in forty eight hours. It was inspirational. I immediately emailed Aaron Lansky and asked him if he could supply me with a list of names of Yiddish translators. He sent me fifty-nine names. I wrote this letter to each and every one of them:-

Dear Sir/Madam, My name is Harry Lew and I am writing to you with a most unusual request. There is a book published in Yiddish, in Melbourne in 1948, by a Holocaust survivor Rafael Rajzner titled "The Annihilation of Bialystoker Jewry." I want to get this book translated into English, to make it available to a wider audience. I am therefore writing to everyone on the National Yiddish Book Centre's register of prominent Yiddish translators asking for a mitzvah (good deed). If I send you ten pages of this book would you be kind enough to translate it into English for me. When the whole book is translated I will edit and publish it, mention each contributor, and send each contributor a personal copy to donate to the Holocaust Museum or Library of his or her choice. Please reply to this letter and tell me if you can help me.
Yours sincerely,
Harry Lew.

I also approached some local people. Rajzner's book contained three hundred and twenty-four pages. I needed thirty-three translators.

I got less than the thirty-three required takers, but at least we had a start. A number of the translators wrote back to say that they would be pleased to do the work for a fee, usually in the vicinity of $US 500, but these people were rejected. This book would be translated gratis by 22 "Righteous Human Beings" who gave of their hearts. The English translations varied considerably, but this was to be expected. Some of them required more work, others less, but they were equally appreciated. My job was to try to give them a single voice, to try to create the feeling that the translations had been done by a single person. It is left to the translators themselves and to my readers to tell me if I have been successful. I will gladly accept their verdict whatever it may be.

To give this book a single voice was not an easy task. Rajzner, himself, is quite variable. Some parts of his book read like a best selling thriller, other parts are quite parochial. He mentions many people by name, who would not normally be considered to be historically significant, the sort of people who might not be mentioned anywhere else. Rajzner might be the only surviving record of their existence. I am reminded of the numerous foot soldiers who gave their lives for a cause, only to be forgotten forever. Generals tend to be remembered by history, not the nameless privates who do the brunt of the dirty work.

I therefore decided against deleting any of the names. I wanted everyone mentioned in the Yiddish text to appear in the English one. I even added a few more, my grandparents Hersz and Raya Leah Lew; my uncles Fishel Lew and Hillek Basz; and my cousin David Lew; about whose fate Rajzner had informed both my parents way back in 1947. I made no attempt to upgrade Rajzner's language, to transform it into high literature. For one I am not the person sufficiently talented to do so. I am neither a poet nor a man of letters. My aim has been simply to re-create this book in English as Rajzner originally intended it to be, a frank eye-witness account of a terrible human tragedy.

Some of my 22 translators, on completing their pieces, volunteered to do more. I always accepted their offers. In some instances it enabled me to get the same pages translated twice. I found these dual translations particularly helpful. At other times when I experienced difficulties I turned to Mr. Israel Kipen, a fellow Melbournian and a former Bialystoker, for help. Israel was one of my translators and nobody could have been more obliging. He is a wonderful man, a gentleman and a scholar, who was at all times ready and willing to offer me help.

And then one day, lo and behold, the whole book was translated.

4. THE TRANSLATORS.

I would now like to personally mention and thank all my translators:

Miriam Dashkin Beckerman of Toronto, Canada.

Miriam has a Diploma in English Literature with Honours from York University. She is a well-known translator of numerous Yiddish and Hebrew works into English. In 1998 she shared the Dora Teitelboim Foundation Prize for translating *"The Return of Noah Amshel"* by David Katz from Yiddish into English

Jack Berger of Mahwah, New Jersey, U.S.A.

Jack is a graduate of the Cooper Union for Advancement of Science and Art and has a Ph.D. in Chemical Engineering from the University of Illinois. He is a former Vice-President of Citibank, for whom he worked for thirty years, and as a hobby he has done a number of Yiddish translations for Yizkor (Remembrance) Books pertaining to the Holocaust.

Helen Burstin of North Caulfield, Melbourne, Australia.

Helen survived the war as a young girl together with her mother in Russia. She and her husband Simcha were accountants for most of their working lives in Melbourne. Prior to that, Simcha had worked for the Yiddish section of the Melbourne Jewish News, for several years, during the 1950s. Helen, Simcha and their daughter Ena are well known identities in local Yiddishist circles. When Helen first came to Melbourne she lived in the Bialystoker Centre together with my parents and Rafael Rajzner. When I visited her home to pick up her translation, she asked me if I knew a lady named Genia Lew who lived in the Bialystoker Centre in 1948. Genia, of course, was my late mother.

Anna Clarke of Ottawa, Canada.

Anna survived in Poland from 1939-1944, first in the east under the Soviets, later as an internee of the Warsaw Ghetto, and finally in hiding, with documents stating she was a gentile. In 1944, she was sent to Germany as a Polish slave labourer and worked as a housemaid until liberation. After the war she acted as an interpreter for the British Government. It was in this capacity that she met her husband, an intelligence officer with MI5. They remained in Germany until 1954, then migrated to Canada. In Canada Anna graduated M.A. from the University of Ottawa, did some freelance broadcasting for the Canadian Broadcasting Commission, and also taught at college.

Victor Cohen of Elizabeth, New Jersey, U.S.A.

Victor's schooling was at a Yeshivah. He obtained an M.A. degree from New York University, majoring in Jewish Studies and Philosophy. His working life was spent in education, as a teacher in the New Jersey Public School system, as an adjunct Professor of Philosophy at a county college, and as an administrator in the field of Jewish Education. He is the author of "The Soul of the Torah - Insights of the Hasidic Masters on the weekly Torah Portions," and during his retirement is currently working on another book.

Meir Fass of Rego Park, New York, U.S.A.

Meir was born in Israel after its independence. He moved to New York where he had a career in import/export shipping services. He has recently retired and heard of this project second hand. He therefore differs from my other translators in that he approached me, not vice-versa. His brilliant translation of the last fourteen pages of Rajzner's book helped complete the project.

Luba Goldberg of South Yarra, Melbourne, Australia.

Luba, a fourteen year old girl, and a recent graduate of the ORT Girl's School in Bialystok, had just returned to her small home town of Ciechanowiec, when war broke out in September 1939. She remained there under Soviet occupation until Germany attacked Russia in June 1941. She was then relocated to the ghetto at nearby Sokoly, until the commencement of its liquidation. She was fortunate enough to escape from the ghetto and after a number of harrowing experiences managed to survive with partisans in the Bransk Forest.

Ruth Fisher Goodman of Wilmington, Delaware, U.S.A.

Ruth was born in New York City. She graduated from the Workman's Circle Yiddish School in 1945, got a Bachelor's Degree in Elementary Education from the City University of New York in 1949, and a Master's Degree in Reading from the University of Delaware in 1968. She has been both a teacher and a professional translator. She is widely traveled. Her publications include the video *"How to Teach Reading to Adult Illiterates through the Language Experience Approach."*

Beni Gothajner of Elsternwick, Melbourne, Australia.

Beni is a former teacher, whose specialties were Yiddish, English and History. These skills proved to be the perfect combination for this project. Thank-you Beni for suggesting that I divide this foreword into segments.

Mindle Crystel Gross of Boynton Beach, Florida, U.S.A.

Mindle graduated from the Sholem Aleichem School in Brooklyn, New York and Brooklyn College and she also attended a Jewish Teachers Seminary in Manhattan. Her various occupations include having been a bilingual secretary in Yiddish and English, teaching Yiddish both at Sunday School and at Adult Education, and working as an Ophthalmologist's technician and office manager. She plays classical piano for recreation. If I could present a special medal as an "Honorary Bialystoker" to one of my translators I would award it to Mindle. I think of her as my personal ***"Oliver Twist."*** Every time she completed a translation she would ask, ***"Could I please have some more."*** In all Mindle did six translations of ten pages each and they were all great. Mindle also proof-read the entire original completed version of the translation. Good on you Mindle.

Israel Kipen of North Caulfield, Melbourne, Australia.

Israel was born into an Orthodox family of Jewish manufacturers in Bialystok. He survived the Holocaust by taking the eastern escape route through Russia, Japan and the open port of Shanghai, where he resided for 6 years, prior to arriving in Australia in 1946. Israel has involved himself in a wide variety of Jewish communal activities and has made significant contributions to organised Jewish life in Melbourne. He has played a most important role in the establishment, growth, and consolidation of Melbourne's Jewish day-school system. This has recently been recognised by his having been awarded a Doctor of Letters Honoris

Causa from Melbourne University. His autobiography "A Life to Live" was published in 1989.

Ruby Kohn of Kingston, New York, U.S.A.

Ruby was born in Canada into a Hebrew and Yiddish speaking family. As a ten year old Ruby visited relatives in Poland, all of whom except for a solitary first cousin later perished in the Holocaust. She has a Bachelor's degree in Sociology and a Master's degree in Social Work, both from the University of Toronto, and a Masters degree in Library Sciences from Queen's College at Long Island. She worked for twenty years as a social worker and later on as a librarian for a number of years prior to retirement.

Ben Korman of Dianella, Perth, Western Australia.

Ben grew up in Melbourne, where he attended the I. L. Peretz Yiddish School, first as a pupil and then as a student of its Teacher Seminar. He graduated from the University of Melbourne with the degrees of B.Sc. in 1969, M.B. B.S. in 1971 and M.D. in 1996. Nowadays he works as a practising anaesthetist in Perth. He has been the President of the Holocaust Institute of Western Australia since its inception in 1990.

Don Marejn of Toorak, Melbourne, Australia.

Don, a Bialystoker, studied Chemistry in France during the early nineteen-thirties, after which he returned to Bialystok to work in his family's tannery business. When the Soviets invaded Bialystok in 1939 he was forced, as a capitalist, to flee first to Lithuania and later, clandestinely, into the Soviet Union. After the war he was repatriated back to Poland and left for France a few months later together with his wife

Sonia. They migrated to Melbourne in 1950. Don and Sonia are well-known philanthropists in Melbourne. They have provided more than fifty scholarships to post-graduate students at Tel Aviv University, have endowed a Day Care Centre at the Melbourne Montefiore Homes for the Aged, and have been supporters of the Melbourne Sholem Aleichem Yiddish School.

Shifra Pollard of Boca Raton, Florida, U.S.A.

Shifra was raised in Brooklyn, New York, learned Yiddish at school, and graduated from Brooklyn College. She taught English and American Literature at High School for twenty-five years and in retirement also taught Yiddish at a local college.

Jacob Rosenberg of North Caulfield, Melbourne, Australia.

Jacob was a teenager living in Lodz on September 1st 1939. *"The war finished my primary schooling," he says, "the ghetto was my high school, Auschwitz was my university, and Mauthausen was my institute of post-graduate studies."* Jacob was liberated in May 1945, arrived with his wife Esther in Melbourne in 1948, and worked for many years in the clothing trade. On retirement Jacob returned to his childhood love of writing. He is a recognised Australian poet and writer, both in Yiddish and in English; and his most recent book, "East of Time," won the prestigious 2006 Douglas Stewart Prize at the New South Wales Premier's Literary Awards and the 2007 National Biography Award. "East of Time" was also shortlisted for the Australian Literary Society's 2006 Gold Medal.

Murray Sachs of West Newton, Massachusetts, U.S.A.

Murray has a B.A. from the University of Toronto and an M.A. and Ph.D. from Columbia University in New York. He has taught French language and literature at various universities, and from 1960-1996 was Professor of French and Comparative Literature at Brandeis University in Waltham, Massachusetts. He is now Emeritus Professor. He is the author of four books and more than thirty articles in professional journals, and he has also served on the Editorial Advisory Board of six professional journals.

Berek Segan of Toorak, Melbourne, Australia.

Berek, a native Yiddish speaker from Lida in Poland, emigrated to Australia after obtaining his Matriculation Certificate in 1938. Berek has had a profound love of music since early childhood. He studied violin from the age of 6 and attended the Vilnius Conservatorium as a schoolboy. In Melbourne he became a successful businessman and an early supporter of the Melbourne Symphony Orchestra and Opera Australia. In 1975 he established the biennial Castlemaine Festival of the Arts. For his contribution in promoting a relationship between business and the arts he was presented with a "Business and the Arts Award" from the University of Sydney in 1975, an O.B.E. in 1975, and an A.M. in 1980.

Michael Silver of East Brighton, Melbourne, Australia.

Michael survived the Holocaust first as a prisoner of the Soviet Government for one and a half years, and then, after his release, as a refugee in Central Soviet Asia. He was repatriated to Poland in 1946 and migrated to Australia in 1958. He worked for many years as an auditor with the Commonwealth Public Service. I first met Michael in 1976, when we climbed Mount Sinai together.

Simcha Simchovitch of North York, Canada.

Simcha survived the Holocaust in Poland by escaping to the Soviet Union. He emigrated to Canada in 1949. He has a B.A. in Humanities from the University of Toronto and a Masters in Hebrew Literature from the Jewish Theological Seminary of America in New York. Until his retirement in 1998 he was Librarian and Curator of the Beth Tzedec Museum in Toronto. He is a poet, writer, and translator. He won the Dr. Hirsh and Debra Rosenfeld Award for Yiddish Literature from the I.J. Segal Cultural Foundation in Montreal in 1991 & 2004; the Zhitlowski Award for Writers of High Quality from the Yiddish Cultural Association of New York in 1998; the Izzy and Betty Kirshenbaum Award for Excellence in Yiddish Writing from the Book Committee of the Jewish Federation of Greater Toronto on six occasions, in 1992, 1993, 1995, 1998, 2000 and 2002; the Harry and Florence Topper & Milton Shiel Award for Creative Yiddish Writing from the Book Committee of the Toronto Jewish Congress in 1990 & 1997; and the Nachman Sokol, Chaim Joel and Mollie Halberstadt Prize in Yiddish and Yiddish Translation, Canadian Jewish Book Awards, at the Koffler Centre of the Arts, Toronto in 2004.

Nathan Sobel of Long Beach, New York, U.S.A.

Nathan, a child survivor of the Holocaust, and the only member of his family to survive, is from Luboml, formerly in Poland, now in Ukraine. His family managed to hide for a long time in a dugout his father built under an apple tree in their yard. A crawl tunnel from the kitchen provided access to it. Nathan's father and sister were murdered in 1943. In January 1944, he saw his mother, two brothers, and ten other Jews machine-gunned by Polish resistance fighters in a barn. Nathan miraculously managed to hide away in the hayloft, but then had to escape a blazing inferno, when the barn was set alight. He served in the Palmach during Israel's War of Independence, emigrating to the United States in 1951. An urban planner, Nathan also edited the English translation of "Luboml: Memorial Book of a Vanished Shtetl (New York: KTAV, 1997)." In my first printing run I inadvertently omitted Nathan from the list of translators and had to add him as a postscript. When I rang Nathan to say sorry he replied, "What's new, everyone forgets me!" You are definitely not forgotten Nathan and your efforts are most appreciated.

Edward Zerin of San Francisco, California, U.S.A.

Edward was ordained as a Rabbi at the Hebrew Union College in 1946 and received a Ph.D. from the University of Southern California in 1953. After serving as a congregational rabbi for twenty-eight years, he and his wife Dr. Marjory Zerin founded the Westlake Centre for Marital and Family Counselling in 1974. He is the author of eight books and numerous professional articles; has served as a Jewish consultant in the preparation of numerous Catholic textbooks; and has been a faculty member at Boston University, U.C.L.A., Grinnell College and Drake University.

I would also like to take this opportunity to thank Dr. Leon Slonim, who read the manuscript and offered valuable suggestions, and also to thank Danuta and Renata Schnall for their help with the epilogue. They have become valued friends.

Henry R. Lew.
North Caulfield,
Melbourne, Australia. (October 2007).

ORIGINAL PUBLISHER'S NOTE.

It might seem strange that the book of Rafael Rajzner's memoirs, "The Annihilation of Bialystoker Jewry," is published by the newly formed Bialystoker Centre in Melbourne, Australia.

We originally hoped that the Bialystoker Centre in New York, the largest of its kind in the world, would perform this task. New York greeted Rajzner's manuscript enthusiastically, thought it worthy of publication, and promised to help pay for it. And then for financial reasons, they regrettably reneged on their offer. The money was needed to house three hundred elderly citizens in their old people's home instead.

In Melbourne, former Bialystokers found it inconceivable that such a unique and valuable document should not be published.

Rafael Rajzner helped manage the co-operative printing plant, which produced "Undzer Leben," (Our Life), the largest daily Yiddish newspaper in Bialystok, under the long-standing editorship of the renowned journalist, Pesach Kaplan.

Rajzner lost his wife and his two children to the Nazis. He was interned in the Bialystoker ghetto, imprisoned in the Bialystok Gaol, and transported to numerous concentration camps. During this time he used his intense powers of observation and his phenomenal memory, to store numerous facts relating to many tragic events in exquisite detail. He was driven by an iron will to survive so that he could, one day, inscribe these observations and memories onto paper, and this he began to do immediately after his liberation. He decided not to limit himself to personal experiences, but in the interests of a more total historical picture, also collected eyewitness reports from other surviving Bialystokers.

The most remarkable feature of Rajzner's writing is that he managed, despite heart breaking and mind numbing experiences, to restrain his feelings and emotions. He doesn't allow words to exaggerate the gruesome facts he describes. His memorable text is entirely trustworthy.

Abrasha Zbar. (Melbourne 1947).

ORIGINAL FOREWORD.

AN EYEWITNESS FROM HELL.

I have never felt so unworthy when writing an introduction to a new book. I feel like a scribe who is about to pick up a pen and start a new Torah. I am about to set foot on holy ground. I feel an urge to undergo penance, to purify my soul, to immerse myself in water. Perhaps I should have fasted.

Rafael Rajzner was a printer. He helped manage the co-operative printworks, which produced the daily newspaper "Undzer Leben." He was never a journalist or a writer. To his credit he has not now tried to become one. His book is simply an eyewitness account, a chronicle of the final destruction of the Bialystoker ghetto.

Rajzner is in no way a pretentious man. He is merely a miraculous survivor, who felt a moral need to tell the world what Bialystok and its people went through. Future historians should be grateful to him for this testimony. For even though it is essentially an account of the destruction of a single town, it is also an important strand in the total fabric of the bestial destruction of European Jewry by Hitler's Germany. It leaves us with no doubt as to what the Nazis and their collaborators could accomplish.

As I read Rajzner's book I shuddered with painful nausea. I was overcome by every form of human emotion. I felt endless pity - burning love - searing anger - a poisonous thirst for revenge. And then suddenly I stopped believing. I told myself that such a story can only be a perverse fantasy of a sick mind - that no people can be so gruesome - so heartless - so wildly inhuman. And then I returned to reality.

I realised that this story was indeed true, but worse still it was not the whole truth, only a small part of it. And I realised that when victims start talking about revenge, about wiping all Germans off the face of the earth, they too are starting to sink into the dark void of a similar horror.

Rajzner's simple writing style enhances his text and adds to its literary merit. This is because the events he writes about defy the concept of art in literature. No words can adequately describe them, no expressions can hope to encompass them. These are happenings which don't lend themselves to poetic embellishment, they can only be described in naked simplicity. There is no wordsmith alive, whose pen can adequately capture the horrors that people endure - when they peer through small cracks in prison walls - watching thousands of naked human beings - their most beloved family members and friends among them - being herded through falling snow into gas chambers. Such pain is as endless as the sky over sand dunes, as vast as the ocean which drowns a solitary swimmer. Rajzner immortalises suffering simply. That is his great strength. Literature can always be forgotten. Rajzner's chronicle should never be allowed to!

Yehoshua Rapaport (Melbourne 1947).

CHAPTER 1.

THE MOOD IN BIALYSTOK IN THE MONTH BEFORE THE WAR.

In August 1939 an ominous mood loomed over Bialystok. All ears were glued to the radio. Negotiations were taking place in Moscow. It was hoped that England, France, Poland and the Soviet Union could come to an agreement, that a crisis might be averted! Would hope prevail - or would despair? Then we heard the news that the German Foreign Minister, Joachim von Ribbentrop, had flown into Moscow and signed a friendship pact with the Soviet Union. All hopes of peace suddenly seemed dead.

Poland mobilised immediately. It was as if everyone's worst fears were suddenly realised. No one had more to fear from the outbreak of war than the Jews. Hitler's intention towards them was perfectly clear. Many of the young Jewish men called up for military service were of two minds. On one hand they saw themselves as victims of rampant Polish anti-Semitism, on the other hand they had to do their best to thwart a German victory.

And then it happened! Germany attacked Poland! Two hundred thousand Jewish soldiers fought valiantly in the Polish army, and thirty-two thousand of them died for it.

THE SUDDEN GERMAN OFFENSIVE.

At 5 a.m. on Friday September 1st 1939 the Polish radio started broadcasting strange messages. *"Attention! Attention!"* it said, *"They are coming! They are flying!"* Initially people found these pronouncements confusing, but one thing was certain, they bore an ill wind. It did not take long for the situation to clarify itself. The radio now clearly announced that German planes had started attacking Polish cities. Danzig had fallen to the Germans. Hitler's main advance was centred on Poland's west. East Prussia, close to Bialystok, was not yet being used as a springboard for attack.

It took two weeks for the German invaders to reach the outskirts of Warsaw. During this time Bialystok was subject to daily air attacks. The bombings were mainly centred on the railway lines and on military barracks and stores, but some civilians were also killed. Jewish refugees started to trickle into Bialystok from the west, bringing with them the first eyewitness accounts of German atrocities. This trickle rapidly swelled into a flood of broken humanity. Bialystok became overcrowded. Everyone became very nervous. People were fearful of a German occupation and, as yet, not even one German soldier had been sighted.

Friday September 15th 1939 was the second day of Rosh Ha-Shanah (the Jewish New Year). At 10 a.m. we heard that the Germans were at the edge of town. People stopped praying and ran out of the synagogue. They scattered so as to hide from incoming troops.

By midday the first detachments of German soldiers entered Bialystok along Mazowiecka and Danbrowskiego Streets and before long the city's empty streets were teeming with them. They pulled out machine guns and started shooting at windows. Many people, mostly Jews, were killed or wounded.

A curfew was immediately declared. People were not allowed on the streets between 8 p.m. and 5 a.m.

Nazi soldiers started entering Jewish homes and robbing them. There were instances of Jewish women being shot and killed for refusing to part with their rings. All resistance was immediately met with shooting.

Jews stayed off the streets even during the permitted hours. There were instances where people who ventured out to buy bread and potatoes were killed.

On Monday, the third day of the occupation, rumours started that the Germans would soon hand over Bialystok to the Soviets. Before the day was out these rumours were confirmed by the German command. Radio Moscow had announced the previous day that the Soviet Union was about to liberate its former forfeited Polish territories of Belarus and the Western Ukraine.

This news was welcomed by the Jews. The Soviets were preferable to the Germans.

On Thursday afternoon September 21st 1939 three Soviet aircraft flew over Bialystok. They dropped leaflets, in the White Russian language, to the effect that Soviet troops were on their way to liberate the town.

Then on Friday morning, only hours before the start of Yom Kippur (the Day of Atonement), the Germans packed up and withdrew from the town. They headed back in the direction from whence they had come, towards Warsaw and East Prussia.

A joint welcoming committee of Jews and Gentiles was rapidly convened to greet the incoming Soviets. Some committee members had been in contact with them and expected the first troops would march into Bialystok that afternoon. This information was passed on to the people.

Thousands of people started to crowd Bialystok's streets in expectation. Working people waved red flags and carried flowers. Some Jewish youth, embittered by their short taste of German occupation, were unable to control themselves. They started throwing stones at the last German soldiers to leave. Fortunately the Germans did not respond to these acts of defiance.

A week of German occupation had caused well over a hundred Jewish deaths and even more businesses and homes had been plundered.

CHAPTER 2.

THE SOVIET ARMY MARCHES INTO BIALYSTOK.

Large numbers of Soviet troops started arriving in Bialystok on the afternoon of Yom Kippur eve. Townsfolk massed in the streets in order to greet them. Everybody was present, individuals, professional groups, political organisations. The mood was warm, friendly and enthusiastic. Red flags were waved, flowers were abundant. Large numbers of Jewish youth decided to boycott the "Kol Nidrei" service. They could not bear to drag themselves away from their liberators. The Soviet troops likewise responded cordially. They told of good conditions back home. *"Only in the Soviet Union could all people live out their lives as free citizens."*

The next morning the Soviet Command cancelled the special conditions that had been imposed by the German Army. The city started to breathe easier. Normal life with its characteristic hustle and bustle started again. But all did not remain rosy!

The Soviet occupation brought new economic and social values with it. This made life harder, not easier, for most Bialystokers. Winter was on its way and many necessities were in short supply.

Queueing for bread was introduced. Hungry Bialystokers would stand in freezing frosts of -30 degrees Celsius from 2 a.m. onwards, for 24 hours. When they finally reached the shop front they would learn that everything had been sold. Life had become very hard.

Initially there was also much unemployment, but before long, the Soviets established numerous government agencies and enlarged the factories. Several months later, by the beginning of Spring 1940, lack of employment had ceased to be an issue.

BIALYSTOKERS AND REFUGEES ARE SENT INTO DARKEST RUSSIA.

With near full employment life began to normalise. Food supplies improved. Bit by bit people adapted to the new way of life. Conditions became more bearable.

That first winter housing was a significant problem. Factories had been enlarged in preference to building dwellings. Thousands of Soviet officials had arrived from greater Russia to commandeer a substantial number of existing dwellings, and tens of thousands of Jewish refugees had poured into Bialystok from the west, mainly from Warsaw and Lodz. These men, women and children had walked hundreds of kilometres, in ferocious weather, to escape the hell which the Hitlerites had created. They surreptitiously and illegally slipped across the border into Soviet territory. Bialystok, a city of 100,000 people before the war, more than doubled its population. Private housing became grossly overcrowded. The overflow had to be accommodated in synagogues, in houses of study, and in community centres. Conditions became poor and hygiene suffered.

Bialystoker Jewry did their best for the refugees. Those who could be accommodated in private homes were. But under the Soviets, the Bialystokers were no longer masters of their own homes. People had been forced to downsize their living space and many apartments no longer had room for new inhabitants.

Many of these Jewish refugees had been people of means before the war, and they found the current miserable conditions unbearable. Some even returned home to the west, failing to strike an appropriate balance between the threat of death in the Soviet versus the Nazi sector.

The Soviet authorities did not want the Jewish refugees to remain in Bialystok. Their policy was to drive them deeper into Russia. The Soviet security forces started serving the refugees with permits, which required they translocate themselves to the eastern side of the old Polish-Russian border. However, the majority of the refugees seemed keen to remain in Bialystok and showed no signs of moving on. For a little while the Soviets tolerated this.

Then, one appointed night, late in April 1940, the NKVD secret police pounced. They surrounded the buildings where most of the refugees were housed, conducted mass arrests, transported prisoners to the railway station, and loaded them onto freight cars. But these refugees were not alone. A few thousand Jewish and Gentile Bialystokers were transported with them. These townsfolk were "the undesirables," capitalists not communists, and included in their number were factory owners and prominent merchants. All of these people were sent to the farthest reaches of the Soviet Union. At the time their deportation was deemed tragic, but in reality many of them survived because of it.

These events impacted strongly on the majority of Bialystokers. They worried about the fate of the deportees. Everyone wondered whether he or she would be next. Several months later people started receiving letters from the deportees. They complained that they were starving and begged for food rations. The Bialystokers responded strongly to their requests and, thanks to the many food parcels sent, the situation of the deportees improved.

NORMALISATION OF LIFE IN BIALYSTOK.

With the passage of time life in Bialystok began to normalise. Established factories were working two to three shifts a day. New ones were being built. New state-owned shops opened daily and people could soon buy enough to satisfy their basic needs.

Social institutions prospered under the Soviets. Elderly residents of the Jewish poorhouse and the Jewish old people's home were generously provided for. Initially they even managed to retain their kosher kitchen. However later on it was decided to merge these Jewish institutions with Christian ones, and their inhabitants were moved to newer cleaner premises in Suprasl. These arrangements were not to the liking of many of the elderly Jews. They had lost their kosher kitchen and they felt uncomfortable living intimately with gentiles. Those who were strictly orthodox, felt a need to leave.

The three Bialystoker orphanages were similarly amalgamated into a single institution, under the directorship of Simon Brodie. They were re-located into a large handsome building on Wesola Street. The children enjoyed the best of everything under the Soviets. They were given plenty to eat and they were well dressed.

The Soviets also accomplished much in the field of education. Because of the excessive numbers of students, existing schools worked two to three shifts a day and plans were drawn up for the building of new schools.

Cultural life in Bialystok continued on a high level. Well-known Polish, Russian and Jewish theatre companies visited the town. Abraham Morevskin established a Jewish National Theatre. Moshe Broderzon, a poet, writer and playwright from Lodz, opened a Jewish Miniature Theatre. The Yiddish comedians Shimon Dzigan and Israel Schumacher were its star attractions. A city choir was founded. The well-known Warsaw chorister Mr. M. Schnayur was appointed as its director. Eddie Rosner brought his famous Warsaw jazz orchestra to Bialystok. A community folk house was opened to encourage people to engage in such activities as theatre, music, singing and painting. Large factories formed their own musical ensembles and professional artists were engaged to manage them. The city's cinema houses were expanded. Prices were affordable and these venues were always playing to packed houses.

It was at this time that the two famous Jewish artists Landoy and Zishe Katz died.

Landoy was performing Shakespeare's "The Tempest" to a packed Palace Theatre. All of a sudden he suffered a heart attack and dropped dead. The impact was overwhelming. The performance was cancelled, but Landoy's dead body continued to lie on stage. The next morning the artists' union issued an obituary notice to the effect that Landoy's body would lie in state on the stage for the entire day. His fellow artists would form a guard of honour by his casket, and theatregoers who admired him were invited to come and pay their last respects. A huge crowd attended his funeral and after it the theatre closed for several days as an act of respect.

Katz was suffering from depression, because some of his closest friends had been deported to the farthest reaches of

Russia. In a moment of extreme grief he penned a suicide note and hanged himself with a pair of suspenders. His death had a profound effect on people in artistic circles.

Both men were buried in the Bagnowka Cemetery.

THE SOVIET AUTHORITY'S ATTITUDE TO JEWISH RELIGIOUS NEEDS IN BIALYSTOK.

The Soviets made no attempt to cater for Jewish religious needs. Nearly every Jew in Bialystok was now a public servant, working either for a government factory or a government instrumentality. All workers were required to start work early, while it was still dark, even on the Sabbath. There was little opportunity to attend organised early morning prayers, a situation compounded by the fact that most Jewish prayer houses had been commandeered for other purposes. They were being used as military quarters, sports clubs, granaries and store houses.

Jewish religious institutions were heavily taxed and none more than the Great Synagogue. Its land tax bill was five roubles per square metre, which amounted to 4000 roubles per month. All religious institutions were made to pay five roubles per kilowatt hour for electricity; nearly fifteen times the normal rate of 35 kopecks. This forced the few prayer houses which remained open to be very frugal with their lighting, even on important holy days. This high cost of lighting was a deliberate Soviet ploy. It was designed to trivialise the importance of these institutions and to demoralise their membership.

A religious Jewish carpentry cooperative was established. Its members were not required to work on the Sabbath or on Jewish holidays. Some of them slaughtered their own meat to ensure it was kosher. They were happy to supply kosher meat and other religious priorities to strictly observant Jewish families.

The Mikveh, the Jewish ritual bath-house, where religious Jews and their wives immersed and purified themselves, was also commandeered by the state. The members of the religious Jewish carpentry cooperative responded by collecting money for a new Mikveh. They re-built it inside a private dwelling. It was very popular. Many people came and visited, from nearby and faraway.

Some very religious Jews refused jobs where they had to work on the Sabbath. Skilled tradesmen, capable of earning 600 roubles a month, took lesser jobs, at 130 roubles a month, as security guards or night watchmen. If one walked past locked shops, in the early hours of the morning, they could be seen wearing prayer shawls and phylacteries and praying with devotion. It was a heart-rending sight.

THE FEAR THAT NAZI GERMANY WOULD ATTACK THE SOVIET UNION.

The winter of 1940-1941 ushered in a return to a more or less normal life. Then rumours began circulating regarding a war with Germany. By early summer these rumours started to acquire some substance. Large convoys of Soviet military transports were seen driving westwards through Bialystok towards the German border.

The threat of war caused the Soviets to act against people who they saw as possible fifth columnists. Early on Thursday morning June 19th 1941 the Soviet police swooped. They raided many homes, Jewish and non-Jewish, looking for people who had been politically active during the previous Polish regime (1919-1939). This included Zionists, Bundists, Revisionists, clergy of all denominations, prominent businessmen, wealthy landowners, indeed anyone who could have been interpreted as being anti-Soviet. The men were arrested and imprisoned. The women and children were trucked to the railway station and loaded onto freight trains destined for the farthest reaches of the Soviet Union. Chance had it that many of the women and children survived. The men were not so lucky. When the Germans arrived a week later they were released from prison. Those who were Jews were eventually gassed and incinerated with their fellow Bialystokers.

The cruelty of the Soviet police generated fear and terror among the townsfolk. But its duration was short lived. Two days later war broke out and what followed was so gruesome that Soviet atrocities were soon forgotten.

CHAPTER 3.

NAZI GERMANY BRUTALLY ATTACKS THE SOVIET UNION.

At 4 a.m. on Sunday June 22nd 1941 Bialystok awoke to a symphony of explosions. People opened their doors. They were clearly frightened. The town was being attacked from the air. This was the real thing, war! One could watch dog fights between German and Soviet aircraft in the skies. One could see bombs being dropped onto residential areas. Many Jews were clearly being killed or wounded.

People turned on their wireless sets to listen to Radio Berlin. Hitler was heard raving over the airwaves. He had ordered an attack on the Soviet Union.

It was not long before we had heard where bombs had fallen and who the victims were. Houses in Piotrkowska Street had taken direct hits. Yechiel Isaac Inditski, the former bookseller and newsagent, was severely wounded and died shortly afterwards. His wife was killed instantly. Nearby neighbours were also counted among the dead and wounded. More bombs had fallen on Wojskowa Street, close to the park. Here Zalman Wejnrajch, the well-known, long-serving municipal council treasurer, died together with his wife and daughter.

For a while many of the Soviet officers thought they were watching training manoeuvres. When they realised this was the war they suddenly fell into a heap, at a loss as to what to do. And then retreating divisions started to arrive in town from the border to the west. They told of the Soviet Union having been attacked at 4 a.m. along the entire length of its border with Germany, both by land and by air. Air Force divisions stationed at the border had been completely destroyed.

Chaos started to ensue. Soviet officers packed their wives and children into military vehicles and set out along the roads to the east. These roads became very congested very quickly.

That evening Molotov spoke on the radio. First he accused Hitler of having brutally attacked the Soviet Union in the same month that Napoleon had attacked Czarist Russia. Then he added that Hitler and his Nazis would be crushed to an extent, which would make Napoleon's defeat pale into insignificance.

Jews in Bialystok were very frightened. Many ran to ask friends what they should do. A few young men and women followed the Soviets and set out eastwards along the Baranowicka Road, but most of the townsfolk stayed put and hoped that the Germans would be repelled.

It was hard to sleep on Sunday night. The rolling movements of heavy tanks were heard everywhere. At first we thought these were Russian tanks coming to the rescue, but at dawn we realised our mistake. The tanks were Russian alright, but they were not attacking. They were retreating eastwards from Bialystok towards the Soviet Union.

THE PRISONERS SET FIRE TO THE GAOL.

At 10 a.m. on Monday June 23rd 1941 the prison guards deserted their posts. More than 2000 prisoners were suddenly free to escape. Within minutes they had set fire to the prison and groups of them were converging upon the town. Many of them looted Soviet shops and storehouses. You could see them carrying bottles of vodka and dragging sacks of sugar and other wares along the ground. Soviet troops, who had remained behind, opened fire on these ex-prisoners and killed some of them.

Many Jewish prisoners, who had been arrested four days earlier for subversive political activities, were now free again. This group included Yaacov Goldberg, a Zionist activist; Bunim Farbsztejn, the Agudat Israel leader in Bialystok; Michel Kanczypolski, a representative of the left-wing faction of the Labour Zionists; Hersz Szwec, the leader of the right-wing faction of the Labour Zionists; and Aaron Breszinski, a writer, and Josef Rubinlicht, both of whom worked for the Yiddish newspaper Unzer Leben.

A few weeks later Mordechai Chmelnik, a member of the right-wing faction of the Labour Zionists, arrived back in Bialystok from Brest (Brest-Litovsk). He had been a political prisoner there for about a year and had managed to free himself under similar circumstances.

A month later another group of Bialystokers, who had been prisoners in Minsk, returned home. This group included Samuel Finkel, the former textile manufacturer, and his son and Cybulkin, the longtime Chairman of the Pajen Bank. Cybulkin died shortly afterwards. They informed us that the youngest son of Oswald Trilling, a well-known Bialystoker textile manufacturer, died in the Minsk prison.

SOME JEWS START TO FLEE BIALYSTOK.

Many Bialystokers were disturbed by the Soviet retreat. A throng of young people crowded the streets that entered into the roads that led to Russia. They didn't know what to do. They just stood there waiting for some news.

The roads to Russia were inundated with automobiles, tanks and marching foot soldiers. Reasonable passage along them was impossible. Every 15 minutes or so a German plane would swoop down over a road to shoot at the fleeing hordes. This converted the landscape into a horrible tangled mess. Human bodies lay scattered among overturned vehicles and dead horses.

When messengers relayed this terrifying news back to Bialystok many people changed their minds about leaving. Nevertheless there were a small number of daring young Jewish men and women who were prepared to take the risk. Some wandered the roads for more than a month and then, exhausted and defeated, finally dragged themselves back to Bialystok. Others became victims of the German military machine. A small number eventually broke through and escaped into deepest Russia and from these a significant proportion survived.

POLES RANSACK THE TOWN.

The lack of authority that prevailed served as a catalyst for many Bialystoker Poles, men, women and children, to commence looting. They broke into the fully stocked Soviet shops and warehouses and soon emptied them of everything they contained. Not satisfied the worst of them started to plunder orphanages and Jewish homes. The few armed Soviet troops who remained behind no longer seemed to deter them. The looting continued for a week until the Germans arrived. A small number of Bialystoker Jews were also involved in the rampage. Most were connected to the underworld, like Chana Yolkeshe, the sister of Yolke the drayman, who was shot dead robbing a tobacco shop on Lipowa Street.

THE ONWARD MARCH OF THE GERMAN ARMY.

The German army did not march straight into Bialystok. It chose to bypass Bialystok to the south and advance east of it through Brest to Kobrin and on to Slonim.This enabled the Germans to bomb the bridges over the Shchara River. This was a manoeuvre calculated to cut off retreating Soviet troops and force them back into Bialystok. The initial reappearance of these Soviet troops on the streets of Bialystok sparked us up. We thought they were reinforcements. But our hopes were short-lived. It soon became apparent that these were retreating troops who were surrounded with nowhere to go. With this realisation all expectations that our situation would improve evaporated. The days of Soviet rule in Bialystok were clearly numbered and the town lapsed into a depressive mood.

JEWISH BIALYSTOK ON THE THIRD DAY OF THE WAR.

By Tuesday June 24th 1941, the third day of the war, Jews in Bialystok were in a daze as to what to do. They knew full well what was happening on the roads to the east and that to attempt to escape along them was very dangerous.

THE FINAL TWO DAYS OF SOVIET RULE IN BIALYSTOK.

Over the next two days one noticed a sharp decline in the number of visible Soviet military personnel in town. The few who remained scurried frantically from one side of town to the other constantly looking for a means of escape.

By Thursday night there was hardly a Soviet soldier left. Nobody knew where they had gotten to. One man who remained behind seemed frightened of his own shadow. He continued to shoot blindly into the dark. At dawn there was an expectation on the streets that the Nazis would arrive soon.

CHAPTER 4.

NAZI ATROCITIES AGAINST THE BIALYSTOKER JEWS UP TO THE TIME THAT THEY WERE HERDED INTO THE GHETTO.

THE NAZI MURDERERS ENTER BIALYSTOK.

At 9 a.m. on Friday June 27th 1941, the overnight silence was temporarily broken by the rattle of gunfire, and then there was silence again. Hitler's leading troops entered Mazowiecka Street and moved on into the densely populated Jewish area. This included such streets as Piaskowa, Senders, Suraska, Sucha and the Fish Market and the adjacent lanes and alleyways. It was here that some Nazis threw grenades and incendiary bombs into Jewish houses and set them burning furiously. Other Nazis entered houses, which had not yet caught fire, and started dragging the menfolk out. These men were ordered to raise their arms, and then they were forcefully herded, under a hail of heavy blows, towards and into the Great Synagogue.

THE FIRST MARTYRS DIE IN THE FLAMES OF THE GREAT SYNAGOGUE.

Once the synagogue was fully packed the Nazis surrounded it with a thick cordon of heavily armed troops. Within seconds these killers had thrown gas canisters and grenades into the synagogue and it had burst into flames. This hellfire became the scene in which heart-rending tragedies played themselves out. The choking odour of the burning gas was intolerable and people felt an immediate need to end their suffering. A son hanged his father from a menorah with a trouser belt at the father's request. Others cut each other's arteries. One energetic young man climbed up onto a window, knocked out some glass, and entered into a heated verbal exchange with the Nazis. He was shot in the hand and fell down to the ground drenched in blood.

As the fire became more intense and belched off thicker smoke the cordon of Nazi murderers backed away from the building. This provided Bartoczko, the Polish watchman, with an opportunity to open the synagogue's back door. By risking his life Bartoczko gave ten Jews the opportunity to escape. Included among them was the young man who had climbed up onto the synagogue's window.

Meanwhile other Nazi murderers were combing the back yards of nearby properties looking for more men. Those they managed to drag out were shot in full view of their wives and children.

Among those who perished in the synagogue were Dr. Krakowski; Note Jacobson, an accountant; Kaplan, a merchant-manufacturer from Kupiecka Street; Aron Zabludowsky, the son of Chaim-Zvi and a well-known chess player in Bialystok; Poliak, who owned the pharmacy by Rabbi's Street; Alter Steinberg, also known as Alter Chalele, a beloved Bialystoker comedian; Isaac Brenner; Radzinower, the proprietor of the Aquarium Restaurant; Jamnik, the cork manufacturer; Michel Grodzenski and his son and son-in-law; Kaplan, a restaurant proprietor; Byspucki, a merchant; Fuksman, the son of the furniture manufacturer Fuksman; Isaac Lach, a well-known soccer player; Abraham Spektor and his two sons; David Wysocki; and David Lew, the son of Fishel Lew, the Chief Accountant of the Jewish Kehilla or Jewish Community Services in Bialystok.

Among those found shot dead in the streets were the widow and daughter of the former Labour Zionist activist Berel

Jaszynowski; the lawyer Gottlieb; and the son-in-law of the pharmacist Kurycki. The body of another lawyer Tespoya, the brother-in-law of the well-known Bialystok real estate owner Baruch Gewin, was found in a garbage bin on Lipowa Street.

THE FEARLESS DEDICATION OF MRS. GITEL CHAJKOWSKI-PLAC.

Sixty little Jewish children were living at the new orphanage on Wesola Street. With little regard for her own safety, and ignoring the fact that it was dangerous for Jews to be on the streets, the long-time Orphanage Director, Mrs. Gitel Chajkowski-Plac, put her life on the line and fought her way through to the orphanage.

Along the way Nazis were rounding up Jews and setting fire to their homes. Close to two thousand Jews were incinerated or shot this day, and despite this, Mrs. Gitel Chajkowski-Plac, fearing no evil, ventured through a valley of the shadow of death to seek out and comfort her charges. When she learnt that the orphanage's Polish watchman had gone to the Germans to tell them that the orphans were children of hardened Jewish communists, Mrs. Chajkowski-Plac hid them in a cellar up to their necks in water and saved their lives.

Mrs. Chajkowski-Plac was the only person, who did not abandon the orphans at this most critical time. Her dedication to the children, at risk to her own life, deserves prominent extolment as an exceptional act of humanity.

THE TRAGEDY OF THE FIRST TWO DAYS OF NAZI RULE.

The Nazi army used the minor resistance put up by a small group of Red Army soldiers as an excuse to shower every house in its path with gas and incendiary bombs. Entire streets disappeared into mountains of ash.

This conflagration, which engulfed the Jewish section of the city, continued for twenty-seven hours. When it finally ended at midday on Saturday nearly two thousand Jews had been brutally murdered and over thirty streets, containing a third of the Jewish dwellings in town, had been flattened to the ground. The streets destroyed included Suraska, Kosciuszko Square past Baruch Gewin's building, Senders up to the front of the Roman Catholic Church, Szkolna with its surrounding lanes and byways, and the area surrounding the Fish Market. The devastation was so horrendous that people standing by the clock tower could suddenly see distant forests beyond the ruins.

And even though their burning homes had been surrounded by cordons of heavily armed Nazi troops, there were some Jews who miraculously managed to escape from them.

The toll of these first two days of Nazi rule was the beginning of a series of tragedies, which were to engulf Bialystoker Jewry over the next two and a quarter years.

THE NAZI COMMANDANT ORDERS THE CREATION OF A JUDENRAT.

On Sunday June 29th 1941, the Nazi Commandant of the city summoned Chief Rabbi Dr. Gedalja Rozenman and Engineer Ephraim Barasz, the last Director of the Jewish Kehilla. They were considered to be the titular heads of Bialystok's Jewish community. At the meeting Rozenman and Barasz were ordered to form a Judenrat (Jewish Council) to which

German authorities would issue directives pertaining to the Jews.

When the meeting was over Rozenman and Barasz conveyed its minutes to other Jewish leaders. A large consultative meeting was called and the following men were elected to the Judenrat : Chief Rabbi Dr. Gedalja Rozenman; Engineer Ephraim Barasz; Dov Subotnik; Mendel Kaplan; Dr. M. Katzenelson; a Mr. H. Liman from Slonim; Yaacov Goldberg, a Zionist activist; H. Glickson, the former Director of the Merchant's Guild; Pesach Kaplan, the former Editor of the Yiddish newspaper Undzer Leben; Mordechai Chmelnik, a leader of the right-wing Labour Zionists in Bialystok; Motel Rubinstein, the Headmaster of the Mendele School and the brother-in-law of the Bundist activist Yaacov Pat; Samuel Punianski, a member of Mizrachi a religious Zionist movement; Rabbi Baruch Eliyahu Halpern, also a member of Mizrachi; Rabbi Pinje Ajzensztat; Yaacov Lifszyc, the former Chairman of the Merchant's Guild; Abe Furman; Moshe Szwif; Issac Markus, a former Commandant of the Volunteer Fire Brigade; Abram Tyktin, the former owner of a dispatching business; Zvi Wider, the former leader of the Artisan's Union; Pesach Chmelnicki, the former leader of the Dispatcher's Association; and Samuel Polonski, a longtime member of the leadership of the Great Synagogue. Pesach Kaplan was also elected Secretary to the Committee.

The Committee then elected an Executive Group, which consisted of Rabbi Gedalja Rozenman, Ephraim Barasz, Dov Subotnik, H. Liman and Yaacov Goldberg. Rafael Gutman was appointed Secretary to the Executive Group. Gutman was a well-known writer of Hebrew textbooks. He and his wife had come to Bialystok as refugees in late 1939 and had decided to stay.

Chief Rabbi Dr. Gedalja Rozenman was the official Chairman of the Judenrat in name only. In practice Engineer Ephraim Barasz served as a de facto chairman. Barasz tended to be dictatorial in manner and often opposed the opinions of the other four members of the Executive. But to be fair to him he was a very decent man, extraordinarily energetic, and trying to act for the common good as he saw it.

At one of the early Judenrat meetings Mendel Kaplan suffered a heart attack and dropped dead. The news of this sent reverberations throughout the community.

THE NAZIS ISSUE CONTEMPTUOUS DIRECTIVES TO THE JUDENRAT.

From day one the Nazis issued contemptuous directives to the Judenrat. Their first directive was for thousands of Jewish slave labourers, men or women! These workers were forced to work under frightful conditions and were frequently beaten and tortured.

Another directive was that the Judenrat must supply the Nazis with certain Jewish valuables within 48 hours. Items demanded included jewellery, fur coats, leather jackets, satin covers, top grade feathery pillows and thousands of kilos of shoe leather. If they failed to meet these targets severe sanctions would be imposed.

Each day the Gestapo would seize Jews off the streets. This was supposed to be conscription for slave labour, but in reality many of these Jews were simply beaten and tortured.

The Gestapo would forcefully enter Jewish homes to confiscate valuables. Large trucks would be driven into streets which were then sealed off. These trucks would be loaded up with stolen Jewish goods. No item was sacrosanct. If it might have a value it was deemed suitable for expropriation.

MORE THAN TWO THOUSAND HUNGRY JEWS VOLUNTEERED TO WORK FOR THE NAZIS.

More than two thousand Bialystoker Jews had no means of support and were starving. Any valuables they previously owned had already been forfeited to Nazi arson and robbery. These men and women volunteered to work for the Nazis. The work was arduous and performed under the most gruelling of conditions. But such people were desperate and would perform any work for a small quantity of food. The food given them came from abandoned Soviet stores and, with a bit of luck, they sometimes managed to smuggle some of it back home. Some of these people were actually working in the stores and one such group deserves special mention. The two foremen of this particular group, Yudel Gurewich and Alter Ginsberg, the son-in-law of the well-known Bialystoker printer Meir Pruzhansky, decreed that their two hundred workers should donate one day's rations each week to help feed the hundreds of hungry orphans in Bialystok. Thanks to this noble deed the orphans were sustained for a longer period of time.

THE NAZIS MURDER THREE HUNDRED JEWISH INTELLIGENTSIA.

Early Thursday morning July 3rd 1941, under cover of darkness, Nazi murderers closed off the following streets:- Przejarz, Grochowa, Krakowska, Dambrowski, Kupiecka, Zamenhof, Bialystoczanska, Ruzanski, Zydowska, Bronska, Gieldowa and Lipowa. The villains drew their revolvers and forced their way into Jewish homes. Their mission was to collect, beat, and forcefully drag 1000 Jewish men, aged 16-60 years, to the Municipal Square. At the square these men were humiliated. They were made to perform a leaping song and dance with their arms held high in the air.

Then two dead-drunk senior Gestapo arrived and ordered the men to fall into rows. Each man was asked what work he did prior to the war. Three hundred of them, professionals and intelligentsia, were detained. The rest were told to scoot or be shot. They scattered quickly into the darkness of the surrounding streets. Beaten and broken they dragged themselves back to their houses.

The three hundred detainees were then beaten and tortured for several hours. With the stuffing knocked out of them, they were loaded half-dead onto trucks and driven out of town. These men were never seen or heard of again. They were driven two kilometres in the direction of Wasilkow, then detoured to a field in the Pietrasze Forest, where they were machine gunned to death.

Included in among these ***"Thursday victims"*** were Dr. Yaacov Rajfer; Gutman, a lawyer from Piaskowa Street; Reuven Sklyut, who worked for Undzer Leben; Wajnszel and Orlowski, teachers at Druskin's High School; Aron Murkis, a teacher at Zeligman's High School; Rotsztejn, a merchant, and his son; Berel Zabludowsky; Herschel Maze, a dairy owner; Becalel Frenkl, a Maccabi sportsman and Hillek Basz, a law graduate employed as an administrative officer at the Bialystok Electric Company.

BESTIAL MURDERS OF THREE THOUSAND MORE JEWS.

Then at 5 a.m. on Saturday July 12th 1941 a similar Nazi action took place, but on a much greater scale. Large numbers of Gestapo, in more than thirty trucks, surrounded a significant part of the remaining Jewish district. By now Bialystoker Jews were accustomed to having their houses searched and their valuables plundered. Many thought this was more of the same but they were wrong.

This time the Nazis were much more sinister. They forced Jewish men out of their homes into the cordoned-off streets and loaded them onto trucks. The trucks then headed off for an unknown destination, but not for long. They drove back and forth all morning and by midday more than three thousand Jewish men and boys had been taken away. These Jews never returned, but it was not long before we learnt what happened to them.

Some Polish peasants from the district soon told us that a large number of Jewish men had been shot and buried in a field in the Pietrasze Forest. The peasants painted a gruesome picture. They told us that the earth with which the Nazis had covered the men wriggled for a while, because many of them had been buried alive.

These victims became known as the ***"Sabbath Martyrs."*** They included Dr. Boris Pines, an ophthalmologist and son of the famous ophthalmologist Dr. Leon Pines; Dr. David Kagan, a well-known paediatrician from Zamenhoff Street; Leon Gdanski, a prominent lawyer and the son-in-law of Zionist activist Hersz Lew; Tilleman, also a lawyer; Dr. Tapicer, the son of the pharmacist Tapicer; Rev. Eliyahu Wolocki, cantor, shohet (ritual slaughterer), and moihel (circumciser); Moshe Zabludowsky, a well-known teacher at the Hebrew Gymnasium (High School); Phillip and Simon Kuriansky, the sons of community activist Moshe

Kuriansky, and their brother-in-law, a shoe merchant on a large scale; Joseph Seligsohn, a printer, and his son and nephew Munia Seligsohn; Aaron Breszinski and Joseph Rubinlicht, employees of Undzer Leben; Yaacov Shapiro, the former Chairman of the Esperanto Society and a correspondent for "The Daily Illustrated Courier," a prominent newspaper in Krakow; Wilenczyk, a tailor; Khessin, the Shammash or Beadle of the Synagogue Choir; and Asher Messer, the well-known ticket master at the Palace Theatre.

THE NAZI MURDERERS DEMAND AN INDEMNITY FOR THE THREE THOUSAND SABBATH MARTYRS.

Immediately after the three thousand ***"Sabbath Martyrs"*** were brutally murdered, and before we were notified as to their fate, the Nazi Commandant informed the Judenrat that a ransom of 5 kilos of gold, 100 kilos of silver and two million Soviet roubles would secure their release.

The Judenrat responded by calling an immediate meeting of its Council. Without much ado the Council voted that the only option was to collect the ransom.

The mothers and wives of the seized men were immediately targeted. These women parted with all their jewellery and also large sums of money. Over the next three days collectors visited every Jewish home in Bialystok and everyone dug deep and donated as best as they could.

When the entire ransom was collected Engineer Barasz led a delegation of the Judenrat leadership to the Commandant. They received a cold reception. The Commandant made them stand in a corridor for a long while before he agreed to see them. Then he told them that the detainees would not be released. They were already working in a labour camp in Germany. The ransom would merely insure against more men being taken away.

This response stunned the Judenrat leadership into silence. They walked out of the Commandant's office with heads bowed. Back at headquarters, the former old people's home at 32 Kupiecka Street, they called a immediate plenum of the entire membership. The full assembly was notified as to the Commandant's words. These matters were discussed for a while and then the Judenrat panicked. They decided to suppress the Commandant's communication, to maintain the illusion that the prisoners would soon be released.

The wives and mothers of the abducted men immediately sensed that they were being lied to. They organised daily demonstrations outside the Judenrat building. These demonstrations were stormy. Tempers frayed. Some of the ladies even took to assaulting Judenrat members.

Before long these angry ladies had appointed community activist Moshe Kuriansky as the spokesman for their cause. Kuriansky was commissioned to establish a special committee to attempt to secure the release of the men. Kuriansky's committee collected much more money but it never managed to achieve anything else. After several months Kuriansky's committee was disbanded. The money which it collected was returned to the original donors.

JEWS ARE COMPELLED TO WEAR A YELLOW BADGE.

The Gestapo issued daily directives which imposed increasing demands on the Judenrat. One of the earliest and most degrading was the ***'Directive of the Yellow Badge.'*** It stated that every Jewish man, woman and child over the age of ten years must wear a yellow Star of David over their hearts and on their backs.

Some Jews insisted they would not allow themselves to be branded in this way. Others started rumours that in a few days the Jews of Bialystok would be herded into a ghetto.

CHAPTER 5.

LIFE IN THE BIALYSTOKER GHETTO TILL THE SLAUGHTER OF FEBRUARY 5TH 1943.

It did not take long for the Bialystoker ghetto rumour to be confirmed. The Nazis notified the Judenrat that a ghetto was about to be established. Every Jew would be required to start moving into it on July 25th 1941. The living space for every Jew would be confined to three-quarters of a square metre and the fencing in of the ghetto had to be completed by August 7th 1941.

The Judenrat expressed regrets as it passed this information on to the Jewish population. Jews who already had relatives living in the prescribed ghetto area were asked to move in with them. A 'Housing Commission' would be formed to allocate space to those families who were unable to find accommodation.

It proved to be a most stressful time. Bialystokers visited relatives and friends who lived in the ghetto district seeking accommodation. Close people were heard arguing heatedly over the provision of rooms for their families. Some wealthy Jews offered poor Poles living inside the ghetto an exchange of homes. Expansive five-room apartments with all modern conveniences were swapped for tiny dwellings without running water.

The prescribed ghetto area included streets such as Rosenberg (a small street), Polna, Nowy Swiat, Bialystoczanska, Jurowiecka, Kupiecka, Zamenhof, Gieldowa, Fabryczna, Ciepla, Czysta, Czenstochowska, Linas Hatzedek, Lipowa, Zydowska, Nowogrodzka, Chmielna and the numerous laneways running in between them. *(Linas Hatzedek was a charitable organisation whose members cared for and stayed with the sick. It also founded Bialystok's first Ambulance Service in 1928. The Jews called 'Rozanska Street' where Linas Hatzedek's headquarters was situated, 'Linas Hatzedek Street.')*

Jews who lived outside the ghetto started moving belongings in immediately. They stored them in the homes of relatives and friends. People worried that on July 25th the Nazis would suddenly announce all moves had to be completed in one day. They didn't want to have to suddenly leave possessions behind to be confiscated by the Nazis.

On Sunday July 25th the Jews started vacating their houses. A few Jews managed to acquire wagons for the move. It did not prevent them from having possessions stolen.

A large proportion of the Jews were women and children and they bore their heavy packs on already burdened shoulders. Thousands of them had husbands and fathers who had been incinerated in the Great Synagogue and machine-gunned at Pietrasze during the Thursday and Sabbath slaughters. Many of the men who were still alive were frightened to show their faces. They feared death, torture and immediate consignment to slave labour units.

Polish hooligans took advantage of the situation. They attacked the defenceless Jewish women and children. If the Jews dropped their packs the hooligans were quick to grab them. Whenever Jewish boys resisted and put up a fight Nazis came to the rescue of the hooligans. Many a poor, bloodstained, beaten up Jewish boy could be seen dragging his feet towards the ghetto.

The Nazis guarding the ghetto compound were totally lacking in sympathy. They heckled and ridiculed the Jewish women and children lugging heavy packs on their backs. They humiliated them by scornfully photographing them. The Jewish relocation lasted nearly a week and these heart-rending scenes were re-enacted daily.

Conditions inside the ghetto were dreadful. Many families had nowhere to go and simply wandered the streets. Others had been forced to flee burning homes with just their clothes on. The Judenrat's 'Housing Commission' was overrun. It suddenly had to find accommodation for 50,000 destitute souls.

THE GHETTO CEMETERY.

A site, which became known as the Zabia Street Cemetery, was immediately set aside for burials. It was located behind Katok's mill on Polna Street.

COLLECTIVE HOUSING.

Hundreds of homeless families were taken to empty factories and school houses and told to re-settle there. To have to live in one of these collective houses or "kolhozen" was at best appalling, the most oppressive experience a person had to endure during the first six months of ghetto life. Families, many formerly well off, were crammed together like sardines in a can. Dirt and filth abounded. Arguing, cursing and yelling became the norm. The most trivial of situations could easily erupt into a fight. There was nowhere to prepare food. There were no cooking appliances or utensils. People would light a fire to heat up watery soup, either inside the building or out on the street.

Twelve months later there were no ghetto dwellers living in kolhozen. A few of them, the fortunate ones, had found better accommodation. The rest had been deported and, at that time, nobody knew whereto.

THE GHETTO FENCE.

The relocation of Bialystoker Jewry to the ghetto was completed on Friday July 31st 1941. On Sunday August 2nd the Judenrat was ordered to commence erection of a surrounding three-metre-high wooden fence. This fence had to be completed by Friday August 7th or else! The scene which evolved was reminiscent of Pharoah's ancient Egypt. Jewish slaves of all ages participated. These slaves had to find their own materials: wooden boards, branches, twigs, nails, etc. Different slaves from different streets were allotted different segments of the fence. Different groups would fight over little things, a pale of wood or a nail, but despite such hiccups work progressed at a fast and furious rate. Everyone feared the consequences if the fence was not finished on time. When Friday arrived the Gestapo extended the deadline to Saturday. They needn't have bothered. The fence was completed late on Friday night.

THE GHETTO GATES.

On Sunday August 9th 1941, the ghetto was locked up for the first time. There were two gates in the fence, the first at the corner of Jurowiecka and Sienkiewicza Streets, and the second at the corner of Kupiecka and Pilsudskiego (formerly Lipowa) Streets. The second gate was eventually sealed and replaced by a new one at Czysta Street by the railway line. Each gate was manned by two Gestapo and two Jewish guards. The Jewish guards were Judenrat appointees, but this did not prevent them harassing and robbing their fellow Jews.

50,000 Jews were in an instant separated off from the world, without any means of support. They had no hospitals, no pharmacies, no medicines and no workplaces. Factories, which had operated within the ghetto walls, were now closed. Some people had brought food, mainly bread and potatoes. The unfortunates, whose houses had been burnt down, brought nothing. They suffered the most. They relied on the Judenrat to solve their problems. It is fortunate that need and will-power can sometimes be stronger than steel. Almost immediately the Judenrat began to rebuild itself.

THE JUDENRAT AT WORK - THE OFFICES IN THE GHETTO.

THE PROVISIONS OFFICE.

Yaacov Goldberg was chosen to run the Provisions Office. His job was to supervise the distribution of bread. The Nazis supplied him with 35 grams of bread per person per day and some other small items. Half of this was passed on to the populace. If people wanted more they had to show that they were expending more than the usual amount of energy.

THE HOUSING OFFICE.

Moshe Szwif headed the Housing Office. His job was to provide and manage housing and to collect rents. Thousands of people needed placement in a limited number of spaces. Szwif achieved this by adhering to the Soviet system of nationalization. He assumed jurisdiction over all privately owned homes. He complained continually about lack of fairness in housing. Some families had large quarters, others were squeezed into very tight spaces. This attitude continued to prevail right up to the commencement of the liquidation of the ghetto on August 16th 1943. This was well after Szwif's position had been handed over to the popular triumvirate of Moshe Wysocki, Aaron Albeck and Asher Truszanowicz.

Moshe Wysocki, a former editor of the weekly journal *"The Bialystoker Voice,"* had been prominent in small business associations before the war. Before moving to the Housing Office, he had supervised baking inside the ghetto for several months. He was pessimistic as to the future, convinced that Bialystoker Jewry could never survive the current hellish situation. He wrote a manual detailing how to engage in military action against the Germans and read excerpts from it at weekly Sabbath study sessions. No-one knows what became of his manual.

Aaron Albeck published *"Dos Naye Leben"* (The New Life) before the war. He suffered a devastating personal tragedy which left him deeply depressed. The Nazis murdered his only daughter. Bullets fired over the ghetto wall into Albeck's brother's apartment claimed the girl's life.

Asher Trushanowicz was a former editor of *"The Bialystok Jewish Courier."* He too suffered personal tragedy and was an even greater pessimist than Wysocki. His diary of daily life in the ghetto has also been lost.

THE FINANCE OFFICE.

Dov Subotnik headed the Finance Office. Mitkin the former owner of a dispatching business was his deputy. The Finance Office was the Judenrat's taxation office. It levied taxes on the Jews, the highest ones on those with the most assets. The monies collected paid the salaries of Judenrat executives and employees, and was also used to bribe high ranking Nazi officials. If wealthier Jews refused to pay, Jewish security guards were sent along to pressure them. A night or two in the ghetto gaol was usually sufficient to convince a tax avoider to pay. The Finance Office issued fines and made many enemies. But despite this the ghetto intelligentsia liked to meet in its premises.

THE INDUSTRY OFFICE.

The Nazis decreed that all Jews aged 15-60 years and all Jewesses aged 17-50 years had to work for the German war effort. Many people had physical disabilities, and were incapable of performing the heavy work carried out by slave labourers outside the ghetto. To enable such people to survive, the Judenrat created an Industry Office. Its job was to create factories and promote employment inside the ghetto. The factories needed to be properly equipped. This meant collecting broken down machines from Jewish owners and repairing them. Mr. H. Liman, the director of the Industry Office, was very energetic when it came to getting factories started. He was not beyond using force to get equipment, which made him many enemies. Despite this he had the people's own wishes at heart. By creating as many jobs as possible inside the ghetto, he hoped to spare them the dangers of having to work outside it.

THE CONSTRUCTION OFFICE.

The Judenrat established a Construction Office with Engineer Michael Zabludowsky in charge. All renovations and repairs were carried out under his supervision. Construction workers built a much needed bath-house inside Judenrat Headquarters at 32 Kupiecka Street. It was the only one of its type in the ghetto.

THE ECONOMIC OFFICE.

An Economic Office opened under the direction of Abe Furman. Its main role was to provide inexpensive clothing. Those most needy were given their clothing free of charge.

THE TWO JEWISH WORKERS' EMPLOYMENT OFFICES.

The Nazis demanded that the Judenrat establish a Jewish Workers' Employment Office. This office had to register all Jews and their occupations, and provide slave labourers whenever the Nazis asked for them. Severe consequences were threatened should the office fail to do so. The people hated this office and its management. This was because the Nazis always called for more slave labourers than the office could supply, and the office responded by making sick Jews become slave labourers. These draconian measures led to fiery incidents, and caused the office management to be seen as collaborating blood suckers who capitulated to the enemy

This disenchantment led to the office being divided into two entities. The first entity, an insiders' office, served the interests of Jews working inside the ghetto. The second entity, an outsiders' office, helped the Nazis manage Jews who worked outside the ghetto. The insiders' office was run for two long years by Samuel Polonski. He was unpopular but the inside workers tolerated him. On the other hand the outside workers were continually complaining to Engineer Barasz about the brutal treatment meted out to them. Barasz was forced to change the leadership of this office on at least three occasions.

THE SOCIAL SERVICES OFFICE.

The Judenrat established an office of Philanthropic and Social Services. Mordechai Chmelnik headed a committee of three. His assistants were Motel Rubinstein and Chanan Efros. The three of them provided aid to hundreds of people in dire straits.

THE HEALTH SERVICES OFFICE.

A Health Services Office was established under the directorship of Dr. M. Katzenelson. His charter was to provide medical services at a reasonable cost. Katzenelson was a compassionate and practical leader and his office always tried to help those who sought its services.

Katzenelson quickly organised a new in-patient hospital in a building that had previously been used as a hospital. He set up a separate out-patient clinic on Linas Hatzedek Street. Most doctors living in the ghetto worked there free of charge during the day. Katzenelson also opened two pharmacies on Kupiecka and Linas Hatzedek Streets, which operated on an ability to pay system. However those who genuinely couldn't pay, received their medications gratis.

Dr. Gurewich was appointed Head of Surgery, but his health was not good. He died of a heart attack a few months later and was buried in the ghetto cemetery. Many people attended his funeral. Gurewich was succeeded by Dr. Nunberg, one of the best surgeons in Warsaw. Nunberg stayed in the position until the ghetto was liquidated.

This office also opened an orphanage and an old people's home. There was a need for both. The orphanage at 7 Czenstochowa Street cared for more than 100 children. The old people's home cared for 60 residents. Its dedicated staff helped prolong their lives.

THE LAW AND ORDER SERVICES OFFICE.

The Gestapo ordered that a Law and Order Services Office be set up. Isaac Markus was appointed Commandant and Victor Bubrik Deputy-Commandant. A year later Moshe Berman, the son of the well-known director of the Music School choir, replaced Bubrik.

The Law and Order Services Office employed more than 200 people. Most were middle class people of integrity who risked their lives more than once for the overall good of the community. Some however didn't deserve to be called human beings.

Isaac Markus, a compassionate man with a good Jewish heart, never used his position for personal gain. He lived the life of an average middle class Jew in the ghetto. His nature can be gleaned from words he spoke to a group of Bialystoker printers being sent to Germany to work.

"Believe me," Markus said, *"it is not easy for me to tear you away from your families and hand you to these murderous robbers. But I honestly believe your chances of survival are better than ours."*

Shedding tears Markus said goodbye to each man separately and gave him a packet of cigarettes. When the men were seated in a wagon ready to leave, a security guard ran up to them. *"Isaac Markus sends you some warm bread, 200 German marks, and his very best wishes,"* he added.

This group of print workers included Leib Ziberski, the former owner of a large bicycle and radio shop on Gieldowa Street; Yekhiel Platz and Herschel and Moshe Kozak, who were all associated with Undzer Leben; Naum Zakrzewski, a print worker and the son of the book-binder Isaac Zakrzewski; and Isaac Sukenik. They were taken to Lodz Prison and tortured. Nazi guards terrorised them by marching them into the prison courtyard and ordering them to stand under the gallows for more than an hour. Then a guard yelled out, *"Who will be the first to go?"* Yekhiel Platz answered in a loud, clear voice, *"I am the eldest; I am prepared to die first."* He then bravely stepped forwards and marched towards the gallows. The Germans burst into laughter and beat and chased the men back to their cells. Miraculously Markus was right and all but one of them survived. The exception was Isaac Sukenik. He was shot dead on January 16th 1945, whilst in the final stages of tuberculosis.

Deputy-Commandant Victor Bubrik, the son of the long-term magistrate and writer Bubrick, was a suitable choice for such a responsible position. He helped many people under trying circumstances and maintained his good name till the end.

Moshe Berman was appointed Deputy-Commandant when Bubrik voluntarily resigned. Berman was an upstanding individual, exceptionally just and totally sincere. His reputation was never sullied and his conscience remained clear to the end.

THE FIRE BRIGADE.

A fire brigade was set up under Fire Chief Markus, the brother of Isaac Markus. Dozens of former Jewish firemen, who were well versed in fire-fighting activities, volunteered for it again.

THE CULTURAL OFFICE.

The Gestapo forbade the setting up of educational institutions inside the ghetto. The Judenrat disregarded this decree and set up a Cultural Office, whose prime purpose was to open up new schools.

Pesach Kaplan, the former Editor of Undzer Leben, was appointed Head of the Cultural Office and Shimshul Brotmakher, a former teacher, became his deputy. After many trials and tribulations they succeeded in opening up two schools. One was located in a former Business College at 37 Fabryczna Street, the other at 22 Nowy Swiat Street. Classes ran three shifts a day, six days a week, a mere drop in the ocean compared to what was needed. Jewish children could be seen walking aimlessly through the ghetto all day, juvenile victims of Hitler's infamous Nuremberg laws.

THE JUDICIAL OFFICE.

A Judicial Office was established to handle ghetto disputes. It employed the few surviving Jewish attorneys.

THE JUDENRAT OPENS TWO KITCHENS IN THE GHETTO.

The Judenrat responded to a dire need and opened two kitchens inside the ghetto. The first, "The People's Kitchen," provided a litre of 'thin soup' for a few groshen (cents). The second was almost a farcical kitchen. It couldn't provide enough food to feed a three-year-old. But one should not be too critical. The Judenrat faced overwhelming odds and all it could do was try its best.

THE JUDENRAT EMPLOYS MORE THAN 500 OFFICIALS.

These offices employed more than 500 people, all on minimal wages. Despite the poor wages some employees managed to accumulate significant sums of money. Perhaps some tax money collected to bribe Nazi officials got sidetracked into Jewish pockets.

JEWISH LAWYERS HAVE TO REPORT TO THE GESTAPO.

The Nazis issued terrible new decrees each day. On Thursday August 25th 1941 the Gestapo ordered all Jewish lawyers to attend an interview the following day. They needed to discuss important matters with them.

Nearly every lawyer decided not to go. The Gestapo responded by cruising through the ghetto in a car picking up suspects. 70 Jews were arrested. There were ten lawyers among them. The prisoners were taken to the Gestapo lock-up in the cellar of Ostrowski's Hotel on Sienkiewicza Street. None of the lawyers returned home. A later eye-witness report confirmed that they had been tortured in a terrible manner and then transported half-dead to Nowosholke to be shot. Glinka and the older son of Engineer Barasz were two of their number.

POLES KILL JEWS IN THE BIALYSTOKER DISTRICT.

Jews started to arrive in Bialystok from the small provincial towns of Tiktin, Trestin and Grajewo. They reported that local Poles were murdering Jews there. In Tiktin, the Poles forced the Jews to walk out of town to a large field, and then shot them with rifles stolen from retreating Russians. In Trestin, Poles forced Jews into pits and shot them. In Grejewo, most of the Jews were murdered in their own homes.

The situation was so dire that Jews from small towns, without a Nazi presence, sent delegations to beg Nazi Commandants of larger towns, to send troops to protect them.

PREPARATIONS FOR THE FIRST EXPULSION OF JEWS FROM BIALYSTOK.

Rumours started that the Nazis were about to ship some Jews out of the ghetto, destination unknown! It was explained that this was to reduce crowding before it caused an epidemic. The rumours were soon confirmed.

A fortnight before Rosh Hashanah (Jewish New Year) 1941, the Gestapo announced that 12,000 Jews were to be transported out of Bialystok. Motor vehicles would be used and the Judenrat was expected to cover the costs. Jews chosen would be permitted only a few belongings.

The Judenrat called a special meeting. It was a lengthy one because many painful decisions had to be made. How would the 12,000 Jews be chosen? Those who worked for the Judenrat were automatically exempted. Jews who worked were also marked down for special consideration.

The Judenrat issued the following edict. The poor and unemployed would go first. People who lived in collective housing (kolhozen) would be next. The remainder would be chosen from alphabetical lists.

Once this edict became common knowledge unemployed people started to look for ways to save themselves. Their best chance lay in obtaining an outside work permit. There were some outside employers of Jews who had bought such permits cheaply from the Nazis. They now offered to sell them to the Jews for 25 dollars each, a truly handsome profit. There were also some Judenrat officials trying to get into the act, offering to sell Judenrat permits for a similar amount.

Most poor Jews couldn't avail themselves of these offers. Thirty per cent of them had nothing, no way of obtaining 25 dollars. All they could do was express distaste for those who wished to profit out of their misery. In the end it was mainly the unemployed poor and their wives and children who were sent away.

FROM WYZWOLENIA PLACE TO PRUZHANY.

On Rosh Hashanah eve 1941, the Judenrat security guards served orders on those listed for the first transport. They had to present themselves to Wyzwolenia Place at 8 o'clock in the morning and await transportation to Pruzhany. They were allowed minimal hand luggage.

These people were distraught. Many thought the journey was a death sentence. Even if they arrived at their destination, they were sure the Nazis would starve them there. In Bialystok there was always a chance to sell something in exchange for a morsel of food.

The first transport to Pruzhany carried 500 people. Everyone received two kilograms of bread from the Judenrat. A Judenrat representative accompanied them. When he returned the following day, he reported what he had seen. It was horrific. The Nazis had stolen the transportees' belongings. Anyone who tried to resist was beaten mercilessly. Some were crippled permanently.

The news of this report flashed through the ghetto at the speed of light. Jews waiting to be taken now regarded their transportation orders as fait accompli death sentences. Some became sick with fear. Others, bolder, decided to hide. Searches ensued, but it was only the most hardened searcher, who would forcefully drag a family out of a hideout.

When listed Jews were counted for the transportation quotas, many were found to be missing. The Gestapo ordered the Judenrat to make up numbers by randomly picking up people off the streets. These tended to be poor Jews with nowhere to hide. Such tragic scenes were enacted daily for more than a week.

Meanwhile the Judenrat was trying to negotiate a reduction of numbers being transported to Pruzhany. On Sukkot eve (the Jewish festival of Tabernacles), it was announced that Barasz was about to address people in the courtyard of the Judenrat building. He told them that the Pruzhany edict had been lifted. His statement brought boundless joy. People started hugging and kissing each other. But this happiness was short-lived. A few days later the Pruzhany edict was reinstated.

The Judenrat entered into further long and difficult negotiations with the Gestapo. The devils' hearts were finally softened by promises of much money and many valuable gifts. An announcement was made that the Pruzhany resettlement would end with the 6,000 Jews already transported.

Again the joyous news spread through the ghetto like wildfire. People however were less inclined to believe it. They waited for the decision to be reversed. But this time the Gestapo announced that the Pruzhany edict would not be reinstated, and that Bialystoker Jews could continue working worry free at their jobs.

THE GHETTO BOUNDARIES ARE CONSTRICTED.

No time passed before the next setback. The pretext for sending 6000 Jews to Pruzhany had been "reduction of ghetto crowding." Now the Gestapo paradoxically decreed that since the ghetto population was less, its boundaries needed to be constricted. Panic set in. People worried they would be forced to vacate lodgings and forfeit possessions. It was mainly from the sale of their meagre possessions that most of them eked out a living.

It did not take the Gestapo long to implement the new policy. The ghetto was reduced in size. Hundreds of families once again suffered the anxieties of dislocation. Conditions were once again just as cramped as they had been prior to the Pruzhany expulsion.

JEWS FROM PRUZHANY FLEE BACK TO BIALYSTOK.

Most of the Jews sent to Pruzhany had no means of sustaining themselves there. So they risked the wicked winter weather and tried to return to Bialystok. A few more affluent ones returned by wagon, but the majority struggled home on foot. They dragged their feet through terrible frosts. They risked attack by Polish bandits after clothes and shoes. And when they eventually reached the ghetto gates, Gestapo guards refused them entry. Some wandered around the ghetto for a day or two, looking for a guard to take a bribe.

Others tried to re-enter the ghetto in among groups of returning Jewish slave labourers.

And even when they re-entered the ghetto, their worries were not over. The Judenrat didn't dare to report their return to the Germans. So they remained without documents, and this included ration cards. They had to cope with fear of detection and hunger as best as they could. And despite this, the exodus from Pruzhany continued until 60-70% of the transportees had returned.

LIFE IN THE GHETTO DURING THE WINTER OF 1941-1942.

Life in the ghetto was very difficult during the winter of 1941-1942. Each day yielded new edicts and tragedies. Gestapo incursions became a daily event.

On one occasion the Gestapo found an illegal radio at 40 Jurowiecka Street. Dozens of innocent people were arrested in connection with it. They were dragged to Gestapo headquarters, tortured for several days to within an inch of death, and then shot.

At another time the Gestapo arrested some butchers caught slaughtering a cow. These men were dragged to Gestapo headquarters, interrogated, and tortured mercilessly. They remained there for several months, before being transported to Nowosholke, a town that served as a mass grave for thousands of Jews.

Other Jews were arrested, tortured and murdered for smuggling small quantities of flour into the ghetto. Nowik, a former candle maker and the son-in-law of leather manufacturer Zuske Levine, perished in this way.

A Nazi guard supervising Jewish female railway workers, decided to have fun shooting near their heads. Two Jewish girls, driven into this inappropriate work by hunger, died as a result.

JEWS WERE FORBIDDEN TO WALK ON FOOTPATHS.

Jewish slave labourers risked severe punishment, even death, if they used the footpaths outside the ghetto. They had to contain themselves to gutters and roadways. As a consequence their shoes filled with water in bad weather. And then, without warning, a Nazi chauffeur could drive his vehicle into a work brigade and maim or kill several Jews at a time. Max Zbar, the son of Shlomo Zbar, the well-known printshop owner, and the brother of Abrasha Zbar, the Vice-Chairman of the Melbourne Bialystoker Centre, was maimed in this way. He suffered permanent injuries and lay in the ghetto hospital for a long while.

Such tragedies were a daily event and shattered people's nerves. The associated stress led to relatives and friends arguing and fighting, particularly if several families shared a single apartment.

THE GHETTO IS PLAGUED BY WIDESPREAD HUNGER DURING THE WINTER OF 1941-1942.

The winter of 1941-1942 saw widespread hunger in the ghetto. Food became very expensive, three times as much as outside. Clothing had become cheap in comparison and was no longer tradeable for food. This situation caused more Jews to seek work outside the ghetto. Contact with the outside world provided a better deal for those exchanging possessions for food. It offered them more hope of sustaining their families for a longer while.

By the end of the winter the number of Jewish slaves working outside the ghetto had increased to 5000.

THE JUDENRAT BUILDS FACTORIES.

Even though there were large numbers of Jews working outside the ghetto, the Nazis continued to put pressure on the Judenrat. They were not prepared to tolerate thousands of elderly men and women living idly in the ghetto. They had no place for people not working for Hitler's war effort. The Judenrat understood the implications of this and called an emergency plenary meeting. There was much debate and a decision was made to rapidly build new factories and workplaces, where the elderly could work.

To build new factories inside the ghetto was no easy task. There was simply no room. More people had to be evicted from living quarters, but their will to cling together and live helped them overcome these difficulties.

The Judenrat issued the following decree. **"It is absolutely necessary for every Jew to be employed. It is a matter of life and death. We ask every owner of hand tools and handwork machines to report to the Head of the Industry Office and to offer them to him. Those who refuse to recognise the importance of this appeal or decide to ignore it will have their equipment forcefully confiscated."**

Despite the situation it was still a lot to expect of a poor working man that he part with a machine, which might be his only chance of making a living. Nevertheless most people came to terms with this, and brought along machines which were literally their last means of support.

THE TYPES OF FACTORIES THAT WERE BUILT IN THE GHETTO.

Many different types of factories were created in the ghetto - a large tailoring shop - a knitwear factory - shoe factories, including one that specialised in felt shoes - a large wheelwright factory - a brush factory - a cardboard box factory - a saddle factory - a furniture factory - a lock factory - blacksmith's shops - electro-mechanical plants - and numerous other small undertakings.

In order to guarantee that the aged were qualified, the Judenrat opened several workshops, where electricians, mechanics, bricklayers, carpenters, tailors and blacksmiths were trained.

WAITING FOR THE CREATION OF FACTORIES.

Many elderly Jews, too weak to be slave labourers, were suddenly keen to commence work, now that **"work"** was synonymous with **"staying alive."** They started pestering the Industry Office for jobs. The Industry Office pointed out that first preference must be given to people who donated their personal machinery to community workshops. Qualified tradesmen were next in line. There were few jobs for unqualified people. Applicants outnumbered jobs two to one, so protection started to play an important role. Those who didn't know on which door to knock were likely to be left out in the cold. By mid-1942 most of the new factories had started production.

NAZI PARTY MEMBER STEFFEN'S FACTORY.

A prominent Nazi party member named Steffen opened a large factory inside the ghetto. It was a private factory and outside Judenrat jurisdiction. It was run by Samuel Finkel's son and it manufactured many fine goods. Its carpenters built magnificent furniture. Two hundred tailors of both sexes manufactured German military uniforms and luxury garments for the S.S. Shoemakers produced the finest footwear. Furriers made the best and most expensive fur coats. Jewish chemists also worked there and manufactured numerous products including soaps. The factory even had an art studio which employed renowned painters such as Yehoshua Rosenecki of Bialystok and Abraham Behrman of Lodz .

In all Steffen employed close to 500 people. These employees were remunerated with small quantities of food. It was still significantly more than they would have received in a Judenrat factory. Because Steffen's workers were better fed than those of the Judenrat, they were also more productive. To put things into perspective it is necessary to point out that the food, which Steffen gave to a qualified carpenter or tailor for a month's work, was equivalent to four days' pay in pre-war times. This enabled Steffen to extract enormous profits from his worker's efforts.

HOW THE JUDENRAT PAID ITS WORKERS.

The Judenrat was unable to pay its workers properly. The Nazis paid pitifully for the tens of thousands of jackets, pants, shoes and other products, which the Judenrat workers made for them. These workers felt they deserved extra rations of bread for their efforts but the Nazis refused them outright. The Judenrat compromised by rationing the bread available to it. The Judenrat received 35 grams of bread per person, per day. It halved the average daily ration down to seventeen and a half grams a day and used the rest as bonus payments for its staff and workers. Extra allocations were also put aside for those who performed hard physical labour outside the ghetto. This included tasks such as lifting and carrying heavy goods and loading coal.

In the beginning the Judenrat paid its qualified workers a kilogram of bread a day, but this was soon cut back to less than half. Unqualified workers and office staff were paid less. Once a month workers received a bonus of a small amount of cash. This was the flow on of the pitiful payments received from the sale of their products.

WORKERS SMUGGLE IN FOOD FROM OUTSIDE THE GHETTO.

Hunger was rife in the ghetto. If one member of a family of four received a kilogram of bread a day and the other three normal rations, hunger still prevailed. Bread and potatoes were the principal foodstuffs, but to buy extra was virtually impossible. Even if one had the money to pay the exorbitant prices, there was still a question of availability. The ghetto was cut off and not in contact with the outside world. But extreme hunger and despair have a way of overcoming obstacles.

To exchange clothing inside the ghetto for food outside the ghetto was to risk death. But it was a risk many of the 5000 Jewish outside workers were prepared to take. They left in the morning with extra layers of clothing on their bodies. At times during the day, while working, they would remove their yellow Star of David and try to venture inconspicuously through the streets of Bialystok. They would make contact with Christians they knew and try to barter clothes for food. This was a particularly risky ploy. They had to avoid the preying eyes of Gestapo and those of young Polish hooligans likely to turn them over to the Gestapo. If picked up on the way they were unlikely to survive. And when they returned to the ghetto, they faced the same risks again. A best case scenario if you were caught, was to be beaten and have the food confiscated. One needed nerves of steel to endure such conditions. And despite this many Jewish outside workers were successful in smuggling considerable quantities of food back into the ghetto.

THE HORSE-AND-CART OPERATORS ALSO SMUGGLE IN FOOD.

The hundred or so horse-and-cart operators (wagoners and coachmen) who lived in the ghetto were important in reducing hunger. They were permitted to drive their carts and carriages through the ghetto gates and used them to smuggle in food. Some of them took great risks, bribing Gestapo guards to look the other way, when they drove their wagons laden with food through the ghetto's gates. Some of these brave men eventually paid with their lives for such deeds, but there is no doubt they helped Jews in the ghetto cling to life. If it wasn't for the Nazi's 'Final Solution,' they would have played an important role in most of the Jews surviving.

THE TRADE TEACHING INSTITUTE.

Towards the end of 1941 Szloser, the last Principal of the ORT Girls' School, was chosen to head the new Trade Teaching Institute. By late January 1942, the school building was ready to accommodate several hundred students. The institute grew in leaps and bounds and soon became a significant undertaking with many heads of departments. Mens' clothing was manufactured under the tutelage of Granowicz; ladies' clothing under the experienced eye of ladies' fashion expert Plonski. The men's clothing section manufactured standard garments for Judenrat employees and special elegant items as gifts for the Gestapo. Included among the institute's employees were Zeligman, the part-owner of Zeligman's Jewish Secondary School; Motel Zabludowsky, a former teacher of mathematics at the Jewish Trade School; Prensky, a refugee from Warsaw who had been an electrical engineer; Mrs. Sonia Wainstat, the daughter of Pesach Kaplan the former editor of Undzer Leben; Bacer; and Miss Kanel, the sister of Dr. Kanel.

In time the institute evolved from school into industrial enterprise. This necessitated a change in administration. Joseph Lin, the former head accountant of Centos in Warsaw, was appointed new Managing Director. Szloser was demoted to First Deputy Director. Kindzelewski, a well-known accountant, was made Second Deputy Director. Sonia Wainstat became General Manager.

This factory now worked three shifts a day and employed a large number of women over 60 years of age. These exhausted women worked to survive. They sat in front of sewing machines with half-closed eyes, churning out tens of thousands of pairs of pants for the Nazi murderers.

THE INSTITUTE ORGANISES AN EXHIBITION.

At Pesach time (during the Jewish festival of Passover) 1942 the Institute put on an 'Exhibition of Wares.' A number of official guests of honour were invited to the opening ceremony. The list included Judenrat representatives, other public officials, and two high ranked Gestapo who were thought of as fairly friendly. The first speaker was Zvi Wider, the former leader of the Artisans' Union, who lamented the current tragic situation which existed in the ghetto. Next was Zalman Wainrajch, a highly regarded gentleman, whose poignant words brought everyone to tears. Wainrajch, almost eighty years old, had been a wealthy philanthropist before the war, but he was now living in a state of penury. The current Jewish tragedy depressed him greatly. He fell ill shortly afterwards and remained bedridden till he died. His dying words were a curse on Hitler's Germany. The two Gestapo accepted their invitations and one of them addressed the audience. He declared that *"Thanks to the work of the Trade Teaching Institute, Bialystoker Jewry would survive the war."* The assembled crowd received this declaration warmly, but they knew deep in their hearts not to store too much hope in it. When the formalities were over everyone received sausage sandwiches with tea and sugar, unheard of luxuries at the time. When the crowd dispersed their general consensus of opinion was that they had attended a *"wedding at a cemetery."*

THE BEHAVIOUR OF THE VARIOUS FACTORY MANAGERS.

The behaviour of the various factory managers warrants discussion.

Joseph Lin, the Managing Director, was demanding of his workers, but he was in essence a decent man.

Szloser was warm and friendly towards his workers and they loved him.

Joseph Waksman, the son-in-law of Pesach Kaplan, managed the largest clothing factory in the ghetto. It was located at the corner of Kupiecka and Jurowiecka Streets. This outlet produced large quantities of clothing for the military - tens of thousands of overcoats, jackets and pants per week. Waksman was good to his workers and they thought highly of him.

Liberman managed the large shoe factory in Gubinski's building at the corner of Nowy Swiat and Linas Hatzedek Streets. He was an honest man who did his best for his workers.

Goldberg, the son of the mechanic, managed a cardboard factory by the Biala Stream on Kupiecka Street. He was a difficult man who made life hard for his workers.

Engineer Farber managed the electro-mechanical workshop on Kupiecka Street. He treated his workers well and they regarded him as a true friend.

Krynski, the youngest son-in-law of Pesach Kaplan, managed a saddlery workshop in Cytron's building in Kupiecka Street. He was a man of infinite patience and his workers held him in high regard.

SECRET INSURGENTS FROM WILNO ARRIVE IN THE GHETTO TO APPEAL TO ITS INHABITANTS.

Around Purim time (the Jewish Festival in remembrance of Queen Esther) 1942 a number of Jewish partisans from Warsaw and Wilna (Vilnius), Edek Bodak and the Bialystoker Chaika Grossman included, were secretly smuggled into the ghetto. Their message to Bialystoker Jewry was that slave labour was not a salvation. Sooner or later Bialystok would suffer the same fate as the rest of European Jewry. *"You have only one avenue open to you. You have to arm up, leave the ghetto and join the partisans. This is the only way to heap revenge on the Nazis."* Because their mission was secret, these partisans only met with a small number of trustworthy contacts. Their ideas were never disseminated throughout the entirety of the ghetto. Many inhabitants were never privy to them. For those in the know, some couldn't bring themselves to desert their families considering the current circumstances. For others, proverbial city dwellers, the thought of an indefinite stay in the forest was difficult to accept. Only a few heeded the partisan's advice.

Had the partisan's thoughts been more widely disseminated, it is possible, despite misgivings, that more young people might have joined them and survived.

TWO SYNAGOGUES ARE RE-CREATED IN THE GHETTO.

During the winter of 1942 a group of orthodox Jews in Bialystok decided to take a risk and restore Samuel Cytron's Bet Midrash (Prayer House) in Polna Street. To do so was contrary to a Nazi directive forbidding the construction of religious institutions. Bunim Farbsztejn, the leader of Agudat Israel, a political fraternity of orthodox Jews, took charge of this project. At the time Farbsztejn was working outside the ghetto and he spent part of his working day scavenging through deserted, dilapidated Jewish houses looking for building materials. At nightime he would bring these materials back to the ghetto and use them to restore Cytron's Prayer House. Orthodox Jewry finally had a formal place inside the ghetto in which to pray and study together.

Next Puzhe's Prayer House on Fabryczna Street was re-opened. It was smaller than Cytron's and fewer people worshipped there. But its attendance numbers were greater than they had been pre-war.

In addition to the two prayer houses, a number of minyans were also established. (A minyan is a group of at least ten male worshippers above 13 years of age and constitutes the minimum quorum for Jewish public prayer). It is worth noting that many Jews attended these various services despite the poor conditions and the significant risks involved.

BUNIM FARBSZTEJN OPENS A KITCHEN AT CYTRON'S PRAYER HOUSE.

Bunim Farbsztejn also channelled his amazing energies into another area of need. This time he converted the ladies' section of Cytron's Prayer House into a soup kitchen. The Judenrat supplied some money, but Farbsztejn raised the lion's share himself. Within two months he had a working kitchen regarded as the best in the ghetto, where hundreds of needy people were provided with a sustaining kosher meal each day. This was a truly remarkable feat and probably ranks as the most outstanding of Farbsztejn's many and multi-faceted social endeavours.

THE JUDENRAT DECIDES TO TRANSFORM EMPTY LAND INTO VEGETABLE GARDENS.

Yaacov Goldberg, in his capacity as director of the Provisions Office, was responsible for the supply of vegetables in the ghetto. He conferred with Agronomic Engineer Shalit, a native of Wilna, and they decided it was necessary to use all vacant blocks and yards inside the ghetto for growing vegetables. Shalit was put in charge of the project and provided with assistants from among the city's best gardeners. His team included the brothers David and Berel Shlumiel, Shlomo Suchonicki, Moshe Janowicz and Gorfinkel. Due to their professional excellence and incredible dedication, all empty and neglected sites in the ghetto were transformed into blooming gardens by springtime. Shalit and his gardeners recruited young boys and girls who were members of Zionist Youth Organisations, such as He-Halutz. Although most of these young idealists had never worked a plough, it did not take them long to become productive gardeners in the Zionist pioneer spirit. Their produce included such vegetables as radishes, cucumbers, tomatoes and onions.

The Provisions Office sold these vegetables on to ghetto dwellers at a reasonable price. This helped keep the price of brought in vegetables down. As summer arrived, people were able to augment their meagre diets with fresh vegetables, and in many instances this helped them improve their health. After the difficult winter of 1942, these fresh vegetables made the early summer months easier to bear.

TRAGIC NEWS FROM WILNA, SLONIM, BARANOWICZ, LYDDA, WARSAW AND TREBLINKA.

The few Jews who managed to escape from Wilna to Bialystok were bearers of bad news. They told us that most of Wilna's Jews had been shot at Ponary and that Jews from Slonim, Baranowicz and Lydda had received similar treatment. A few escapees from the Warsaw ghetto told us that thousands of Warsaw Jews were being transported out of the ghetto each day to unknown destinations. Escapees from Treblinka reported that the Germans had built a camp near Malkinia Station, on the train line from Bialystok to Warsaw. Jews were being taken there to be gassed and burned.

ATTEMPTS TO BUILD UNDERGROUND HIDEOUTS.

These horrifying reports caused much anxiety among Bialystok's Jews. People started commenting that sooner or later it would be their turn to die. Hopes of work providing salvation were dimming by the day. Jews had to look for other solutions if they wanted to survive. In a frenzy of newly-found energy they started constructing secret hideouts, many of them underground. These hideouts required considerable planning and much hard work. Their entrances had to be well concealed and camouflaged.

THE JUDENRAT HELPS JEWISH REFUGEES ON THE RUN.

The Judenrat made every effort to absorb Jewish refugees on the run. They helped them blend into the populace by dressing them in local clothing and by co-opting them into the workforce. It was sometimes possible to obtain support for such people once they were in the workforce.

Former Senator Trokenheim of Wilna and his son were in this category. They were received with respect and finely outfitted. They spent several weeks in Bialystok before being smuggled out to Warsaw.

Another escapee from Wilna was Senator Leib Mintzberg, the former leader of Agudat Israel in Lodz. Because of his leadership skills, Mintzberg was asked to set up a new factory to produce marmalade and potato meal out of potato skins. Mintzberg remained in charge of this factory until the ghetto was liquidated on August 16th 1943. He was murdered at Majdanek Extermination Camp on November 3rd 1943 along with thousands of Bialystoker Jews.

ILLEGAL SMALL BUSINESSES IN THE GHETTO.

The summer of 1942 was a difficult time in the ghetto. To help combat hunger several hundred Jews resorted to their indomitable spirit and thought up new ways to eke out a living. They would ignore stringent Nazi prohibitions and establish illegal small businesses on the side. Inside their homes they ground wheat, corn and barley into meal by hand. They made soap, they cured leather, they washed knitwear, they made swaddle spools for thread. Theirs' was a most primitive form of cottage industry. Even one hundred years earlier it would have been behind the times. But it provided several hundred families with some extra income and slightly improved their quality of life.

If the Gestapo discovered the existence of one of these "small illegal factories," it would hold the Judenrat responsible for the crime. The Judenrat representatives would deny they ever knew of the factory. However once they were officially notified of its existence, they were obliged to close it down and confiscate its equipment.

LIQUIDATING TRAITORS INSIDE THE GHETTO.

Shortly after the Nazis captured Bialystok a traitor named Fenigstein rose to prominence. This shady fellow, a refugee from Warsaw, somehow managed to establish himself as a liaison officer between the Gestapo and the Jewish authorities. Fenigstein used his newly found power to terrorise fellow Jews and to extort large sums of money from them. Those who either refused or had nothing to pay were denounced to the Gestapo. They were then dragged off to the Gestapo's inquisition chambers to be tortured and killed. Finally some Jews, who had been rounded up at Fenigstein's request, managed to convince the Gestapo that Fenigstein was making fools of them too. This time it was Fenigstein who was arrested by the Gestapo and tortured and murdered in their lockup. This was a fitting end for a traitor, a criminal and a collaborator.

Another traitor, Zelikowicz, the son of the representative of the Nobel Company, was the Gestapo's stooge in the Law and Order Services Office. He was supposed to be a liaison officer mediating for the Judenrat against the Gestapo. Instead he used his position as a personal power base, dictating to the Judenrat against its own wishes on important issues. Barasz complained to his closest friends that Zelikowicz was a curse upon the ghetto, and that if this outrageous gangster was allowed to continue unabated, the current dangerous position of Bialystoker Jewry would worsen. Zelikowicz's official position within the Law and Order Services Office was not particularly significant, but because of his intimate relationship with the Gestapo, he regarded himself as more important than Commandant Markus himself. Zelikowicz would arrive at Jewish homes with thugs and stand-over men from the Law and Order Services Office. In the name of the Gestapo these villians would search the Jews and steal their money and valuables. Zelikowicz's arrogance grew by the day. It no longer mattered to him whether people allowed themselves to be robbed or whether they stood up to him. Either way he turned them over to the Gestapo and more often than not they were never seen again. Barasz continued to complain to both the German police and the Gestapo that Zelikowicz was playing both of them for fools. Finally they listened. In August 1942 German police, acting on orders from Police Chief Szymanski, invaded Zelikowicz's house and searched it extensively. They found much there; large sums of money; gold; jewellery; twenty chinchilla furs; numerous suits of clothing; material for many overcoats; large quantities of leather; et al. These stolen Jewish items were taken away on a truck and distributed to prominent Nazis. Zelikowicz, his face white like chalk, and his hands held high, was led away through a gauntlet of punches handed out by Jews lining the streets of the ghetto. Many of them wished Zelikowicz a difficult death and hoped that other traitors would be dealt with similarly.

The Judkowski brothers from Slonim were two blackguards who darkened the lives of those who lived in the ghetto. Jewish butchers would risk bringing a cow into the ghetto to slaughter it for food. To do so was a capital offence and fifteen butchers lost their lives because the Judkowski brothers informed on them. However one day the Judkowskis were caught performing an illegal act, and this time they and their families were arrested and placed in the Gestapo lock-up. From there they were transported to Nowosholke where they met a miserable end.

Another well-known traitor, Yankel of Lomza, proved just as troublesome. But by this time different arrangements were in place. Some young Bialystokers had organised a special fighting force. They tried Yankel in absentia and imposed a death sentence on him. On the specified night some members of the group led by Shepsel Borowski ambushed Yankel in Fabryczna Street and shot him dead.

For two shameful years these various Jewish traitors reaked bloody havoc on the suffering lives of the victims of the ghetto. All these traitors finally succumbed to an ugly end, after which the ghetto inhabitants started to breathe easier.

THE MARKET PLACE IN PRAGE'S YARD.

By the summer of 1942, most Bialystoker Jews had run out of clothes to sell to raise money for food. Some of them now turned their hand to black marketeering. Even though black marketeering was illegal, more people engaged in it every day. The desire not to starve was now stronger than the concern for Nazi illegalities.

The Judenrat agreed that the community needed a site where this sort of activity could be conducted. Prage's Yard was designated the ghetto's "unofficial business centre." By being part of the act itself, the Judenrat could charge participating merchants a small percentage fee in lieu of rent.

Whenever Nazi inspectors entered the ghetto, someone from the Law and Order Services Office would rush to Prage's Yard and warn the merchants to scatter. In their haste some of them left stock behind, which was lost. These were small items such as spools of thread or pieces of soap, not worth ten zlotys before the war. But in these times such losses were more than a poor merchant could bear. Fortunately richer marketeers would collect money among themselves, to help re-establish their less fortunate colleagues.

Wermacht (German Regular Army) officers and soldiers sometimes entered the ghetto in an unofficial capacity to privately photograph the Jewish black market.

A JEWISH WOMAN FROM BIALYSTOK GOES TO PALESTINE.

The great sensation of the summer of 1942 was the story of the Jewish woman from Bialystok who went to Palestine. The Judenrat asked Yente Lajzerson, Yechial the blacksmith's daughter, to pack her bags and to present with her children and luggage to Gestapo headquarters in 48 hours. The whole family was being sent to Palestine to be reunited with Yente's husband. Nobody in the ghetto could believe their ears. The Nazis were always lying. They continually fooled us with their broken promises! It made no sense to send a Jewish family to Palestine. Such a family could inform the entire world of the gruesome deeds being performed by Nazis on Jews. But on this occasion the Nazis were telling the truth. Yente Lajzerson and her children were treated humanely by the Germans and sent on unharmed to Palestine. It later transpired that Yente and her children were exchanged for a prominent German who was a prisoner in a camp in Palestine. Before Yente's departure many Bialystokers asked her to pass on their regards to relatives and friends in Palestine. We all hoped that one day we would be rescued in a similar manner, but this never happened.

DR. KERSHMAN AND HIS WIFE AND CHILD DISAPPEAR.

The second sensation that summer was the diappearance of the popular ophthalmologist Dr. Kershman and his wife and child. Rumour had it that high ranking Wehrmacht officers had helped the family escape to Switzerland. But this was not true. Dr. Kershman managed to acquire Aryan papers and the family slipped away to Warsaw to live on the Aryan side. It is not known to what extent Kershman participated in the Warsaw uprising of 1944, but his wife and child definitely survived the war.

A GESTAPO MAN IS POISONED IN A GHETTO RESTAURANT.

In August 1942 a death occurred, which could have had dire consequences for Bialystoker Jewry. A Gestapo operative working inside the ghetto visited an illegal restaurant, run by a woman named Kawarska, to get a whisky. Soon afterwards, on reaching home, the man died. When Mrs. Kawarska heard the news she went straight into hiding. Later that same day Gestapo entered the ghetto to look for Kawarska but she was nowhere to be found. The Gestapo ordered the Judenrat to produce her post-haste and arrested ten of its members and held them hostage. These ten captives were to be shot the next day should the Judenrat fail to deliver Kawarska to the Gestapo. The Judenrat used all available means at its disposal and by morning Kawarska was located in the nearby village of Borosht. She was brought straight back to Gestapo headquarters in Bialystok. Once again, to everyone's surprise, the Gestapo kept its word. Kawarska was arrested and the hostages were released a few hours later. The mood in the ghetto improved once the hostages were released, but people remained concerned as to what the findings of the ensuing enquiry would be. Kawarska was so frightened and stressed, she found it difficult to stand when being led into the hearing. She underwent a rigorous interrogation. She repeatedly pleaded that others had drunk of the same whisky and none of them had been poisoned. Once the hearing was over an autopsy was performed and it confirmed that the Nazi had died of natural causes. Mrs. Kawarska was released a few days later amid much relief and excitement. However her presence in Bialystok was short lived. She disappeared again a few weeks later.

THE PEOPLE SMUGGLERS OF THE GHETTO.

The one hundred or so Jewish horse and cart operators (wagoners and coachmen) held permits allowing them to exit and enter the ghetto. Some of them worked for German manufacturers. They would deliver raw materials to the factories and collect finished products from them. Some brought in official foodstuffs, which the Judenrat distributed to the populace. Others took out garbage and human excrement. These drivers also had an additional and equally important role. They were people smugglers.

Jews who escaped murderous marauding mobs in neighbouring towns and villages and made it to Bialystok were denied entry into the ghetto. They would have to wander the surrounding streets, waiting for an opportunity to sneak in. The warm hearted horse and cart operators welcomed these people with open arms and hundreds of them were driven into the ghetto as driver's assistants. Gangs of forced labourers returning to the ghetto at night also managed to camouflage roaming Jews in among their numbers.

TWO YOUNG MEN FROM GRODNO SHOOT A GESTAPO MAN.

Towards the end of the summer of 1942, a wagoner, who was taking garbage out of the ghetto, came across two young Jewish men on the road. This pair had escaped from Grodno ghetto and were now seeking to enter the Bialystoker ghetto. The wagoner greeted them warmly and offered them help. He placed their knapsacks in his wagon. One of the young men was told to hop on the wagon beside him. The other was asked to follow close behind. At the ghetto gate the Gestapo guards ordered the two young men into a booth. They walked the driver back to his wagon and commenced their inspection. When the Gestapo saw the knapsacks they opened them and found two fully loaded revolvers inside. Meanwhile the two young men had slipped away and vanished. The wagoner was taken into custody. He told the Gestapo he had met the two young men on the road, had brought them back with him and didn't know who they were. He had no idea they were carrying guns in their knapsacks.

The entire Gestapo was put on alert. The situation was very grave. Jews were trying to smuggle arms into the ghetto.

In order to fool the escapees, two Gestapo men changed into civilian clothes bearing yellow Stars of David. The wagoner was ordered to return to the spot where he had picked up the two young men. En route the two young men from Grodno, now in hiding, noticed the wagoner and his two suspicious looking companions. For some unknown reason their first impulse was to fire at them. One of the Gestapo was killed instantly. But his companion was immediately joined by more Gestapo passing by. Together they chased after the young Jews. The two heroes from Grodno continued to fire at their pursuers as best they could, but before long one of them had run out of ammunition and, not wishing to be captured alive, fired his last bullet into his own head. His companion managed to disappear, but not for long. Within minutes the whole area was infested by searching Nazis. They eventually spotted the second young man hiding in a peasant's stall. He continued firing at them for as long as he could, but then his gun jammed and he was captured. The Nazis tortured him for two days. They wanted to know where his ammunition came from and to which partisan group he belonged. This heroic young man maintained his silence until his interrogators murdered him.

This tragic news spread through the ghetto like wildfire. It affected every Jew. The next day the Gestapo allowed the

Judenrat to bury the first young man, the one who had shot himself. He was laid to rest in the ghetto cemetery and the tombstone erected to his memory contained the epitaph, *"Fell like a hero for the honour of the Jewish people."*

After these tragic events were over, the Judenrat announced to the populace that it had patched up matters with the Nazis. Bialystok's Jews breathed easier again.

THE GERMANS DEMAND MORE JEWISH SLAVES.

There was never a dull day in the ghetto. The Outside Workers' Office was now informed that more male slave labourers were required for the German firm of Kirchof and also for Markowczyna, a work camp five kilometres from Bialystok. More women were needed for heavy duties at Wolkowysk. In reality there was no way these demands could be met. Those who were fit enough for hard labour were already engaged in such activities, and only the very fittest could survive at it for more than a few months. People who had behaved immorally were the first ones chosen for the new jobs. The head of the Outside Workers' Office called for volunteers to make up the numbers by offering them an extra kilogram and a half of bread a day, but still only half the positions were filled. It was not long before he received a second directive in the form of a warning. The full number of men must be supplied for Kirchof's and for Markowczyna and the full number of women must be supplied for Wolkowysk.

Unable to fill the new quotas the Outside Workers' Office asked the Judenrat to help them with this difficult problem. The consensus reached was that all ghetto factories and institutions must supply the Outside Workers' Office with 10% of their staff at any one time. This 10% would be alternated with workmates on a fortnightly basis, so that after 20 weeks every worker would have contributed. This type of apportioning insured that the Judenrat always had a supply to draw from. This was essential because forced slave labour personnel needed to be changed frequently in order to survive. No-one was spared this fate, not even the several hundred boys and girls who were studying handcrafts.

This far-reaching decision was not to the liking of ghetto inside workers. No-one with an easier job inside wanted to slave labour outside. They made their dissatisfaction well known; so much so that the Judenrat leadership worried whether the workers rostered for hard labour would actually turn up to do it. To stamp its authority the Judenrat decreed that all factories and work places were to be patrolled by security guards from the Law and Order Services' Office. When the names of the workers rostered for hard labour were called out, the security guards were to collect them and escort them back to the Outside Workers' Office.

Parents became particularly concerned when security guards started patrolling the school building. More than 50 schoolgirls had been listed for slave labour at Wolkowysk. Most of these girls were very young, less than 15 years old, and many of them came from well to do homes. There was no need for such children to be dragged away from school and to be made to engage in hard slave labour.

When the mothers of these young girls discovered what was happening, they ran to the school building to protect their daughters. The security guards did not allow them to approach the girls. A scuffle developed. There was much shouting and infighting, but to no avail. The more than 50 girls were loaded onto trucks, driven to the train station, and sent by rail to Wolkowysk.

A few weeks later some of these brave young girls managed to escape back to Bialystok. The news that they brought with them was most disturbing. They were sleeping in lice infested caves, had been given very little to eat, and they were forced to labour from before dawn until after dusk. They pleaded for mercy for their companions, arguing that if they were not returned soon they would die.

When the girls' mothers were made privy to this information they complained vehemently to the School's Director, the Outside Workers' Office and the Judenrat. Their daughters had been suffering in Wolkowysk for nearly a month. It was time for the Judenrat to honour its original promise that the girls would be returned to Bialystok after one month's hard labour.

However neither the Outside Workers' Office nor the Judenrat had any jurisdiction over this matter. The German Work Committee had originally made the one month promise. Now it reneged on the grounds that there was still more work to be done in Wolkowysk. Only after this work was complete would the girls be allowed to return to Bialystok. The mothers refused to be deterred by such replies and continued pounding on the doors of everyone they held responsible.

LIQUIDATION OF JEWS IN THE BIALYSTOKER PROVINCES.

In 1942, at Sukkot, rumours started spreading through the ghetto that the Nazis were about to commence liquidation of all Jews in the Bialystoker provinces. Nobody doubted that these rumours were true. People only asked, *"Which of the many Jewish settlements in the region would be first and when?"*

Judanrat representatives stated they believed the rumours to be true, but they thought the first victims would be taken from small provincial villages, and not Bialystok itself!

The atmosphere in the ghetto was now like inside a pressure cooker. People clutched at their last straw of hope. They started working feverishly day and night building new hideouts.

The mood grew tenser still when Jewish outside workers reported that the streets of surrounding Bialystok were full of German Police, Gestapo and Lithuanian commandos, who specialised in Jew-killing.

This nerve-racking situation continued for more than a fortnight. Hundreds of Jews crowded Jurowiecka Street each day, waiting to hear some news from Engineer Barasz. Barasz was in discussions with Gestapo responsible for the fate of Bialystok's Jews. Then the gates of the ghetto opened and the Judenrat droshky drove in with Barasz inside it. All eyes were focused on him. People were trying to deduce their fate from the expression on his face. Barasz did not look worried, but he seemed not to like so many faces looking up at him. He left the droshky and addressed the crowd from the ground. "Bialystok remains for now!"

He then climbed back on the droshky and drove to the courtyard of the Judenrat building. Another large crowd awaited him there. He talked to the crowd again, but in more detail. ***"For the time being the danger of liquidation has by-passed Bialystok. But the Nazi murderers are about to commence the mass destruction of all other Jews in the Bialystoker district."***

Three weeks after Sukkot the genocide of Jews in the Bialystoker provinces began. Prior to the war more than 200,000 Jews had lived in the provinces. Now German police seized wagons from the local Christians and drove them into the smaller Jewish villages. Jews were ordered to pack their bedding and place it on the wagons. The old and infirm were ordered onto the wagons; the fitter ones had to follow behind on foot.

The Jews were lied to. They were told they were being taken to labour camps. They were even encouraged to bring their sewing machines along. Those who listened to the Nazis took their sewing machines to Treblinka Death Camp.

The Jews living in these smaller villages were not confined in walled ghettos. This made escape easier. They could run away and hide, perhaps with partisans, in the surrounding woods. Very few of them did this. They wanted to survive and they thought their best chance lay in cooperating with the Nazis. They refused to believe the Nazis were evil enough to gas them to death.

There were two tiny villages where events took a different course.

One of these villages was Sokoly, near Lapy. The Commandant of Sokoly was a decent man. One Saturday he informed local Jews that extermination squads were expected tomorrow, and warned them to leave straightaway! By dusk nearly every Jew had left for the nearby forests. The next morning there were no Jews in Sokoly except for the very old and the very sick. But the Jews of Sokoly did not survive long in the forests. Polish neighbours, who had already ransacked their homes, betrayed their whereabouts to the Nazis. They made sure the

Jews could not return home to reclaim property. Large numbers of German police were sent into the forests and they captured most of the Jews. Some were shot then and there. The rest were sent to the Bialystoker ghetto to make it harder for them to escape.

The other village was Jesionowka. Jews worked in leather factories there. Because these leather goods were considered important produce, it was suggested that Jesionowka be excluded from the action. But this was part of a cunning Nazi plan. The Nazis knew that Jews were hiding in the surrounding forests. By excluding Jesionowka from the action, Jews who couldn't cope with forest life were encouraged to drift there. Several hundred Jews took the bait. Then one night, the Nazi murderers pounced. They drove their trucks into Jesionowka and arrested every single Jew there, the leather workers included. These victims were loaded onto sealed railway cars at Knyszyn Station, and transported to the Treblinka Death Camp.

The Jews from the larger townships in the provinces, such as Suprasl, Wasilkow, Zabludow, Michalowa, Grodek and Sokolka, were taken to Bialystok and imprisoned in the Tenth Regiment Barracks. Conditions in the barracks were dreadful. The prisoners were only meant to stay a week, but many died of disease and starvation before the week was up. Those who made it through the week were packed tight into overcrowded railway cars, 150 per wagon, and freighted out to Treblinka. Many suffocated in transit because of the cramped conditions. Those who didn't were gassed at Treblinka later the same day.

Many village Jews, whilst in the barracks, wrote notes to relatives and friends in the ghetto. These heartbreaking letters begged the Bialystokers to take pity on them and to rescue them from their hell-hole, before it was too late. To their misfortune the hapless Bialystokers were in no position to render them aid.

THE BIALYSTOKER GIRLS FROM WOLKOWYSK AND THE LAST SURVIVING JEWS FROM GRODNO AND BIELSK PODLASKIE ARE BROUGHT TO BIALYSTOK.

When the Nazis began the liquidation of the Wolkowysk ghetto, the Bialystoker girls working there were inadvertently dispensed privileged treatment. This occurred because the Nazis adhered firmly to the letter of their own laws. The girls were classified as Bialystokers. As such they were not yet listed for immediate extermination. They were placed into their own separate railway carriage and not into one of the fifteen densely packed wagons of Wolkowysker Jews. The train stopped at Bialystok Station to let the girls off before proceeding to its final destination, the gas chambers of Treblinka or Auschwitz.

This return of the girls helped calm the mood of the populace. People saw it as a sign that the ghetto was still listed for survival, at least for the time being!

After a few weeks the liquidation of Jews from the Bialystoker provinces was virtually complete. At this time the last 300 surviving Jews from Bielsk Podlaskie were brought to Bialystok. They were shoemakers and it was only their craft that saved them.

Another 800 Jewish shoemakers were spared when the Grodno ghetto was liquidated. At first they continued to work in Grodno. Then they were ordered to pack up their machines and raw materials and move to Bialystok. In

Bialystok they were once again privileged to remain alive to work in shoe factories.

Bialystok was now the sole Jewish enclave in the region. This situation made life in the ghetto very tense. Every person was a bundle of nerves. The situation could only go from bad to worse. We would soon be murdered. We had to prepare ourselves to meet the same fate as most of the rest of European Jewry.

PREPARING FOR AN UPRISING.

In anticipation of the approaching horror, a small group of ghetto Jews called a meeting to help organise a self-defence fighting unit. Its leaders were Yoshke, a communist; Farber, a woman from Krynki and also a communist; Yitzhak, a young Zionist from Wilna; and Yudith Nowogrodzky, a socialist.

Yudith Nowogrodzky argued that every man and woman capable of bearing arms should escape to the forest and fight on as partisans. This was the best way to revenge themselves on their Nazi murderers. Yudith stressed that the forest was no guarantee of survival, but that it offered more hope and possibilities than the ghetto. Those who wished to remain in the ghetto should do their best to try to kill as many Nazis as they could. This will not save them, but will grant them a heroic death. They could not count on armed men and women from the forests coming to their rescue, even if they existed in their thousands. Yudith announced that she was too sick and frail to survive in the forest herself, but that she would fight on for the partisan cause as long as a single surviving fibre remained in her body.

When friends asked, ***"How is someone as sick and weak as you able to perform such serious work?"*** she replied. ***"My body might be broken, but my spirit is young, fresh and healthy. It is important that we taste revenge. We must revenge those near and dear to us!"***

Most of Yudith's colleagues opposed her. They wanted to defend the ghetto with an inside force, and remain in contact with the partisans rather than join them. Yudith was adamant that she would continue to agitate for her own point of view.

The setting up of the "Self-defence Fighting Unit" was a haphazard process. Serious and important work had to be done, if best guerilla tactics were to be established. This required open-mindedness and consensus, not different operatives, different secret agendas, and disagreement, as was the case!

MERSIK.

Mersik, a young idealist, and some of his fellow gardeners were among the first to heed the call to defend the ghetto. Mersik had been a member of He-Halutz, a Zionist youth group which promoted the ideals of the Jewish pioneer spirit; ***that is how to till the soil and how to engage in self-defence.*** He became the founder-chairman of the "illegal" branch of He-Halutz which existed inside the ghetto. He worked tirelessly for this group. He gave of his entire heart and soul for it. It is impossible to heap enough praise on him. He founded a special He-Halutz kitchen and he was one of the chief organisers of its self-defence arm. He was always on the lookout for new members. His special interest was the manufacture of ammunition and he was totally oblivious to any danger involved in it. His position and status in the community continued to rise and he willingly accepted all additional responsibilities which were accompaniments of this. Then all of a sudden he contracted typhus and died and a young and creative worker was taken away from us.

The Jews in the ghetto learnt of Mersik's death from several sources. The Judenrat, the He-Halutz Organisation, and the Provisional Council where he had served as secretary, all issued obituary notices. A huge crowd attended his funeral, virtually the entire Judenrat, the friends of He-Halutz, and the members of the Self-defence Unit.

YUDITH NOWOGRODZKY.

In December 1942 the "Committee to Defend the Ghetto" held a second meeting. The major differences between Yudith Nowogrodzky and the other committee members were once again highlighted. Yudith continued to defend her point of view. Once again the majority of the others continued to refuse to give her any credence. This time the committee went as far as labelling her traitorous. They called her "a servant of the Gestapo" and asked her to resign.

Yudith refused to be defeated. She continued to campaign relentlessly for her own point of view and won over a fair number of supporters. She organised some of these people into a group and sent them into the forest. Most of them perished as a result of heavy frosts during the last days of December.

Soon afterwards the leaders of the "Committee to Defend the Ghetto" acknowledged they had been too hard on the idealistic Yudith and withdrew their accusations against her.

They called for mutual co-operation between groups of differing viewpoints, but regretfully this did not occur.

Yudith was a woman possessed of great talent and much energy. Her role as the founder and sole organiser of the ghetto partisan movement affords her a special place in ghetto history. She came to Bialystok in 1939, together with her mother, as part of an influx of Warsaw refugees. Yudith was tall with curly black hair and her eyes seemed intense, almost on fire! She worked as a nurse in the Hospital for Chronic Diseases. She had a weak heart and bad lungs and was often ordered to bed. But a strong personality, characterised by tireless nervous energy, soon saw her back at work. She did everything she could to bring about acceptance of a ghetto partisan movement. She continually implored those who wished to stay in the ghetto not to surrender their lives without putting up a good fight.

DR. REIGRODSKY DIES.

During the winter of 1942, Dr. Alexander Reigrodsky, the well-known eye, ear and throat specialist, died after a long and severe illness. He was much liked by many people and the news of his death was a sorrowful occasion. Large numbers of Bialystoker Jews attended his funeral to pay him their last respects.

Reigrodsky, who was very active in communal affairs, was a legend in his own lifetime. When Russian soldiers started the Bialystoker pogrom of Thursday June 1st 1906 Reigrodsky, on his own initiative, risked life and limb and headed to the post office to telegraph the bloody details to Jewish and liberal members of the Russian Duma in St. Petersberg.

Two days later, on Saturday June 3rd 1906, three members of the Duma arrived in Bialystok. This delegation was led by the Jewish deputy Jacobson. It wasted no time in appealing to the Military Commander to call a halt to the pogrom. Needless to say the pogrom ended that very same day.

The Jews of Bialystok had no doubts that Reigrodsky was the hero of the moment. His initiative, energy and determination had set in motion a series of events, which had led to the cessation of the slaughter.

Dr. Reigrodsky was also well known throughout the community for his special commitment to humanitarian causes. For many years he had served as the local treasurer for the New York Bialystoker Centre Appeal, which raised large sums of American money for charitable institutions in Bialystok. Reigrodsky's special strength was the skilful manner in which he distributed the funds, a successful blend of consideration and restraint.

Dr. Reigrodsky was also Chairman of the charitable organisation "Toz." He dedicated most of his spare time to it. He even went as far as visiting the Trilling family in France to raise money for it. Reigrodsky convinced Mrs. Fannie Trilling that Toz needed to centralise its scattered departments into a single building. Mrs. Trilling responded by giving him $30,000. He used this money to re-develop Mrs. Trilling's former palace on Fabryczna Street into the Toz Sanitorium. This magnificent building, set in beautiful gardens, became a source of pride to all Bialystokers. Thanks to Dr. Reigrodsky's hard work the Trilling family continued to support the Toz Sanitorium.

When Dr. Reigrodsky died the Bialystoker Jewish Community lost an important personality and one of its finest sons.

FRESH DEMANDS ON BIALYSTOKER JEWS.

One could feel Nazi attitudes to Jews in the ghetto hardening every day. One day the Jews were ordered to hand over fur collars and coats, the next day copper pots and brass utensils, the day after that electric cookers and other valuables.

WE RAN OUT OF FIREWOOD IN THE GHETTO.

Winter was half over and most people had used their quota of firewood. More fuel was needed for heating. The 5000 Jewish outside workers were asked to start carting wood back from their work places. This was no easy task. First they had to steal the wood. Then they had to use tired, broken bodies to lug it the three to four kilometres home. Finally, after a gruelling day's work, they would reach the ghetto gates, only to have it confiscated by the Gestapo. No wonder they would eventually collapse into their narrow ghetto apartments angry, bitter, and in broken spirits.

A German agency was formed to sell former Jewish homes outside the ghetto to Poles, mainly peasants, for several hundred marks each. Jewish draymen, who travelled outside the ghetto, tried to buy some of these homes back to use the fixtures for fuel. Sometimes they were successful, but such deals proved very costly. There were even cases where a drayman bought back his former house. This was enough to make a grown man cry like a child.

And despite these difficulties, significant amounts of inflammable goods found their way into the ghetto. Wood was particularly expensive. Only the wealthy could afford it. If you had no money you simply froze.

The Judenrat was given some extra coal to distribute to the people, but it was only a few weeks worth. It did not alleviate the problem to any significant extent.

NAZI COMMISSIONS VISIT THE FACTORIES.

Nazi commissioners started inspecting the ghetto more regularly. Before they arrived Judenrat security guards would patrol the streets for several hours. They would round up unemployed Jews, clear them off streets, and hide them in courtyards. As far as the Nazis were concerned every Jew inside the ghetto was working and the Judenrat was happy to maintain this pretence. There were many instances where unemployed Jews spent their entire day hidden in a courtyard waiting for the Nazi commissioners to leave.

After the Nazi commissioners left, Jews ran to Engineer Barasz to question him as to what they had said. Barasz accompanied the Nazis during their inspections. 50,000 Jews knew well that life hung on a thread, dependent on a commissioner's whims and fancies. Life degenerated into a continual state of fear during these last days of 1942.

THREE JEWS ARE HANGED AFTER BEING ACCUSED OF HAVING SEEDS IN THEIR POCKETS.

On December 31st 1942, workers at the State Vegetable Oil Factory were searched after completing their shifts. The Gestapo were suspecting the factory's management of theft.

The management provided some luckless Jewish scapegoats to take the blame instead. Three Jewish workers were falsely accused of having stolen seeds in their pockets. They were handed over to the Gestapo.

This time the Gestapo decided to use the situation to depress downtrodden Bialystoker Jewry even further. They would not execute the innocent Jews themselves. They would get the Judenrat to do it for them. The Gestapo ordered the Judenrat to erect public gallows by the Biale Stream not far from its headquarters. When the ghetto populace realised what was happening all hell broke loose. An agitated crowd, protesting and shaking clenched fists in the air, converged on the execution site. The Gestapo stopped the Jews in their tracks. They warned the crowd to stay where it was for the moment, but that it was expected to come forward and watch, once the three men were being led to the gallows.

After a while the three men were dragged half-dead to the gallows. Thousands of Jews were ordered to assemble around them in deadly silence. A Gestapo officer delivered some words of warning. He seemed to relish the moment. ***"These three Jews are being hanged, because they stole from a State factory,"*** *he said.* ***"Everyone knows the punishment for stealing is execution. Never forget it!"*** He then issued the order to proceed and the three innocent men were hanged by their fellow Jews.

The crowd was stunned into sombre silence, watching the three innocents being hanged in this way. All gumption had left them. They stood still like statues, with hearts as heavy as stone. They had lost the ability to protest, to erupt!

When the three men were pronounced dead Engineer Barasz, in his capacity as Chairman of the Judenrat, approached the Gestapo and begged a final favour from them. He asked if the bodies could be cut down, not strung up on show for 24 hours as was originally planned. ***"Wouldn't it be better to bury them as soon as possible?"*** On this occasion the Gestapo decided to pander to him and granted his request. The bodies of the martyrs were cut down, placed in a wagon, and transported to the ghetto cemetery.

And while this was happening, the huge crowd remained passive and trance-like. It was as if they knew that 12,000 of their number were about to be earmarked for liquidation.

CHAPTER 6.

THE SLAUGHTER OF FEBRUARY 5th 1943.

RUMOURS ABOUND THAT THE JUDENRAT WAS ORDERED TO COMPILE A LIST OF 12,000 VICTIMS.

Towards the end of January 1943, rumours abounded that the Gestapo had ordered Engineer Barasz to draw up a list of 12,000 Jews to be transported away to work camps. These rumours added to the already melancholic mood of the ghetto. Everyone knew a terrible tragedy was close at hand and rapidly approaching.

THE SELF-DEFENCE UNIT PREPARES FOR BATTLE.

The newly formed Self-defence Unit, although small in numbers, began to prepare feverishly for future operations. It recruited new members. It sent its most trustworthy operatives out of the ghetto to try to round up ammunition. It distributed large quantities of caustic fluid to brave women fighters to throw into the faces of Nazis who came to take them. But in reality very little was achieved because the time available was so short.

THE PREPARATION OF HIDING PLACES RECOMMENCES AT A FEVERISH RATE.

Many Jews resorted to old habits and recommenced work on secret hideouts. Others, who had no hideouts, started building them feverishly day and night. They tried to make the hideouts as safe and comfortable as possible. Some were electrified. Others had systems for storing water. Some were very large, able to accommodate up to 100 people. Some had secret exits, which might one day help occupants to escape.

THE JUDENRAT PREPARES ITS LIST OF 12,000 JEWS.

Meanwhile there was a news leak that the Judenrat had already compiled a list of 12,000 victims. At the top of the list were the elderly, the sick and the insane. The unemployed were next. The third category remained a secret that only a few Judenrat officials were privy to. The ghetto mood was tense, on high alert! Everybody knew a terrible tragedy was close on their doorstep.

THE WELL-KNOWN BAKER AND LABOUR LEADER OF THE ARTISANS, ZVI WIDER, HANGS HIMSELF.

When it was confirmed that the Judenrat was about to hand a list of 12,000 victims' names to the Nazis, Zvi Wider, a well-known baker, artisan labour leader, and Judenrat member committed suicide. Wider wrote two last letters to his wife and to the Judenrat, and then hanged himself in his apartment. The people spoke of Wider's suicide with great respect, as if he was a hero. However realistically speaking his suicide was merely an expression of a sense of despair which was rife throughout the ghetto.

THE GESTAPO READIES ITSELF.

On February 3rd 1943, the Gestapo sent a commission to inspect the ghetto fence and its gates. The following day it revoked exit permits for Jews working outside the ghetto, and seized all Judenrat documents including the infamous list of 12,000 names.

There were cases where Germans, who managed factories outside the ghetto, warned Jewish slave labourers of the impending slaughter. These directors told their Jews not to return to the ghetto. They offered to accommodate them inside the factories until the slaughter was over. Most Jews refused these offers. They did not wish to desert their families in such stressful times. The few who accepted avoided the slaughter of February 5th.

The Jews were now fully cognisant that terrible events were imminent. The nights of February 4th and 5th were sleepless ones, as everyone awaited the fearful catastrophe.

THE FEBRUARY 5th SLAUGHTER BEGINS.

At 2 a.m. on Thursday February 5th 1943 everyone's worst fears were finally realised. The Gestapo executioner Fritz Gustav Friedel led a large contingent of Nazi vehicles, brim-full with killers, into the ghetto. The convoy stopped at the Judenrat building, where Law and Order Services' security guards were ordered to go fetch Judenrat Chairman Engineer Barasz. Barasz would be made to bear witness to Friedel's dirty deeds.

When Barasz arrived, the Nazis commenced their devilish work. Within minutes they had formed a cordon around Nowy Swiat, Polna and Bialystoczanska Streets and the small streets and lanes running at right angles to them. The killers were ready to pounce. They started firing machine guns to signal that the blood bath had begun.

Nazi killers started barging their way into houses in the cordoned off area. The 12,000 Jews on their lists, who were supposed to be resident there, had been expecting them and had fled. The Nazis were visibly enraged by this. Their response was to cease to be selective. They attacked every house, dragging out everyone they could find there. Those who resisted capture were shot dead.

Despite the lateness of the hour, news that the slaughter had begun spread through the ghetto like wildfire. Within minutes 50,000 Jews had rushed into their hideouts. Very few of them managed to gather essentials, not even water! The Nazis plundered their deserted apartments.

A HERO, ISAAC MALMED, THROWS CAUSTIC SOLUTION INTO A NAZI KILLER'S EYES.

At 4 a.m., with the slaughter in full swing, a detachment of Nazi killers entered Kupiecka Street. At 29 Kupiecka Street they came across the building's residents hiding in a small courtyard. One of these Jews, a brave young fellow by the name of Isaac Malmed, whipped a flask of caustic fluid out of one of his pockets and threw its contents into the eyes of a Nazi. The Nazi was instantly blinded, but still he tried to defend himself. He unleashed his revolver and fired several shots. Miraculously he accidentally shot and killed one of his fellow Nazis. In the ensuing confusion Malmed managed to escape.

Friedel the Nazi Commander retaliated by ordering that 100 men, women and children from the courtyard be herded straight to Prage's Yard, be lined up against the wall of the former Nowy Swiat Prayer House and School there, and be instantly machine-gunned.

When the massacre was over the Nazis brought more Jews to Prage's Yard and ordered them to dig a large ditch there and to dump the bodies of the victims in it. Some of these martyrs were probably buried alive, because the thin layer of earth, which was hastily thrown over them, appeared to undulate from underlying movements.

Those murdered included Malmed's wife and child; Mila Zabludowsky, a well-known ladies' seamstress; Naftali Feldman, a printer, and his wife; and the popular Bishka Zabludowsky who, in his role as first newsboy and best known newspaper seller in Bialystok, had disseminated Yiddish and Zionist culture for more than 40 years.

The corpse of the slain Nazi was carried by his fellow killers to the Judenrat Building and dumped on Engineer Barasz's desk. ***"See what your law-breaking Jews have done,"*** the Nazis taunted Barasz, ***"Now we will exact our revenge on you! Now you will see what we can really do!"***

Concurrently Friedel the Nazi Commander issued an order that Barasz be brought to him. ***"See what 'lovely' acts you ungrateful Jews commit,"*** he threatened him. ***"If you don't bring me the criminal within 24 hours I will not keep my promise to only take 12,000 Jews. I will destroy the entire ghetto instead!"***

Engineer Barasz had no doubt that Friedel's threat to murder every Jew in Bialystok was genuine. Barasz arranged for messages to be immediately sent to every Jew in hiding. In particular Barasz asked that Malmed be personally notified of Friedel's threat, and that he be asked to surrender himself and save tens of thousands of Bialystoker Jews being murdered instead.

As soon as Malmed heard of Friedel's threat he again displayed much courage and surrendered himself to the Nazis.

The next day Isaac Malmed was hanged from a tower in the same courtyard, where he had valiantly tried to defend himself. Malmed, who had been severely tortured by his

Nazi captors, still managed to denounce them in a fiery speech prior to his execution. After Malmed's corpse had swung for several minutes, the rope broke and his body fell to the ground. The Nazis riddled it with bullets. Then they strung Malmed up again and let him hang there for two more days.

OTHER JEWS FROM KUPIECKA STREET MOUNT A GRIM RESISTANCE.

When a Nazi detachment entered 10 Kupiecka Street, they once again met with heroic resistance. This time the residents attacked them with axes, knives and irons. Mendel Kuriansky's wife, a very brave woman, poured caustic liquid over them and was about to set the building on fire. The Nazis fell back at first, but they quickly returned with reinforcements and threw Mrs. Kuriansky and her child down two flights of stairs. And when this brave woman somehow managed to pull herself up and run away, they riddled her body with bullets. Her bloody corpse collapsed on top of the body of her dead child.

When Friedel was notified of these events he became savage like a wild animal. He ran into the courtyard at 10 Kupiecka Street and fired bullets into the heads of the Jewish prisoners there. Within minutes he had littered the courtyard with the bodies of Jewish martyrs.

At 8 a.m. the slaughter stopped so that the Nazis could breakfast.

At 10 a.m. the Nazis returned with more troops. Some were Ukrainian and Belarus, beastly collaborators who revelled in this bloody work with a festive fervour. Jewish security guards and firefighters accompanied these killers, lugging machinery and equipment for them.

The Nazis sent the Jewish security guards into areas where they feared armed Jews might be hiding. In many instances the security guards came across Jews and risked their lives, by reporting back to the Nazis there were no Jews there. This behaviour deserves special commendation. It was rare for Jewish security guards to betray Jews in hiding to the Nazis.

The Jewish firefighters were also made to search for hidden Jews. They were given axes and picks and told to break down double walls. They were ordered onto rooftops and made to open up disguised attics. Nobody in the ghetto blamed them when hidden Jews were discovered as a result of their activities.

A GESTAPO OFFICER FORCES THREE SECURITY GUARDS TO CLIMB DOWN A DEEP WELL TO SAVE A CHILD.

On the first day of the slaughter, the Nazis discovered a hideout on Ciepla Street. A woman led out of it was holding a small child. She started shaking badly, so much so that she accidentally dropped her infant down a deep well in the building's courtyard. A Gestapo officer who witnessed the terrible scene was still capable of showing a semblance of humanity. Tears welled up in his eyes, as he ordered three security guards to go try save the child. One of the guards was lowered into the well on an iron chain. He nearly died down there, but then the Gestapo officer and the other two guards gave a heave-ho and he was pulled up out of the well holding the half-drowned child. While this was happening an elderly woman crawled out of the hideout. The Gestapo officer tapped her on the shoulder and pointed her in the direction of the transports for Treblinka. One of the security guards appealed to the Gestapo officer's conscience. He mentioned that the child's natural mother had been sent away to Treblinka and pleaded that the older woman be allowed to be a surrogate mother to the child. The Gestapo officer listened and told the woman to take the child to the hospital. An act of compassion had allowed both woman and child to survive the first day of the slaughter.

THREE ORPHANS HANG THEMSELVES.

At the orphanage at 7 Czenstochowska Street, Abramczyk, an orphan, tried to convince his fellow inmates that they should all kill themselves. He told them this was preferable to dying in the gas chambers. There were about 100 orphans in the orphanage. Two decided to commit suicide with Abramczyk. The three children hanged themselves at the entrance to the orphanage. The orphanage was protected by a Red Cross sign, but this did not stop Nazis coming there. However, the sight of three dead children hanging there did soften some Nazi hearts for a short while. The killers turned around, bowed their heads, and walked away. Abramczyk and his two mates, by hanging themselves, had enabled 100 other orphans to survive the first day of the slaughter.

The slaughter of February 5th 1943 lasted fifteen hours, from 2 a.m. to 5 p.m. During that time the Nazis captured 3000 Jews and took them to Judenrat headquarters which had now become Nazi headquarters. These Jews were then moved in larger groups to the railway station and herded into box-cars. The doors of the box-cars were sealed with boards. That evening the trains left for Treblinka or Auschwitz.

Darkness fell and the shooting stopped. The bravest Jews saw this as a signal to venture out of their hideouts. It did not take them long to return and report on the horrors they had seen. Outside silence reigned. The Nazis had left the ghetto and bullet ridden corpses were strewn everywhere. More Jews now risked crawling out of their hiding places. This time they did it to stretch their legs and get some fresh air. They had just spent a most trying day in very cramped and stuffy conditions.

THE EXPERIENCES OF THOUSANDS OF JEWS IN THEIR HIDING PLACES.

75 people would hide out in a space designed for 20-25. They were crushed together, almost to the point of choking. Conditions were so bad that even the slightest movement was likely to elicit a violent response. People would bicker and the Nazis would hear them arguing. Heavy footsteps would close in and then the building would be attacked. In a matter of minutes the hideout would be broken into and the Jews would be discovered.

Small children could be troublesome when hiding out. Most of these children were sedated by their mothers, but if a child was suddenly awoken it might start to cry. The Nazis would hear the noise and the hiding place would be discovered.

There were instances where mothers put pillows over the faces of children about to cry, only to inadvertently smother them. It was not unusual for such mothers to then lose their minds.

People with coughs were a major concern. Most people didn't want to share hiding places with someone coughing.

The quietest cough could spell tragedy for dozens of people. Some people with coughs would lie that they were okay. Others would threaten to expose a hideout if they were refused entrance into it. One cougher, who was expelled from a hideout, turned its 60 occupants over to the Nazis. They were all sent to Treblinka. There were other instances where people with a cough were suffocated by their fellow Jews.

Tens of thousands of Jews had to live under these terrible conditions for more than a week. It was no surprise to learn that many perished in the hideouts during that time.

THE SELF-DEFENCE ORGANISATION WITHDRAWS FROM THE FIGHT.

The self-defence organisation was small in membership and poorly equipped. The Judenrat warned it that its feeble attempts at resistance could lead to total extermination. Not wishing to be responsible for such an outcome, the "Committee to Defend the Ghetto" decided to opt out of organised resistance. However individual members were still free to act as they wished.

WORKERS IN THE GHETTO ARE OFFERED PROTECTION.

On the first day of the slaughter, very few ghetto workers realised that the factories had been designated as safe houses. Those who stayed inside a factory were in no threat of danger. Even Judenrat officials were ignorant as to this fact. The Gestapo had failed to notify Engineer Barasz of this particular directive until after the slaughter had begun.

By evening news of this directive had permeated the hideouts. Knowing that the Nazis had left for the day, factory workers took their wives and children to their workplaces. Before long there were hundreds of Jews outside factory doors. Workers were desperate to save family members, but the security guards would only admit the workers themselves. Wives and children were turned away and told to go home.

Heart-rending scenes were now enacted. Wives and children pleaded to stay with husbands and fathers. Workers argued that family members should be allowed into the factories. Factory managers and security guards replied that such decisions were not their prerogative, but needed to be endorsed by the Gestapo. All they could do was comply with Nazi regulations.

Factory security guards had to use considerable force to clear away the hundreds of women and children. It was late at night before the last of them gave up and left to return to their cramped hiding places. There they could ponder how long it might be before they were likely to be discovered.

THE SECOND DAY OF THE SLAUGHTER.

On Saturday February 6th, the Nazis returned at 7 a.m. With their usual Teutonic efficiency, they managed to search each house several times in a few hours. Consecutive brigades would arrive, search and leave, each one hoping to find something the previous one had missed. But the Jews had learnt from the mistakes of the previous day. They were more brazen, less cooperative and harder to find. As a consequence the second day yielded only half the number of victims.

The Nazis conducted this horrible slaughter with an obsessive punctuality. At precisely midday they stopped for lunch. At precisely 5 p.m. they stopped for the day. Half an hour later there were no Nazis left in the ghetto.

Then after 6 o'clock Jewish silhouettes started appearing. They emerged through crevices that led out of hiding places. They slid cautiously along the walls of darkened ghetto streets. They moved as if they were frightened of their own shadows. Most of them were now aware that ghetto factories were functioning as safe houses. Under cover of darkness they headed there carrying bundles on their backs. Throngs crowded outside the factory gates but once again only the employees were let in. The mob now threw caution to the wind. It became more vocal. It expressed more rage. Men shouted and women screamed, *"Worker's wives, children and parents should be allowed in!"* The mood became savage. For a while it seemed that some security guards might be lynched. But in the end nothing happened. The crowd's bark was louder than its bite. Those who were not permitted entry left and made their way back to their hiding places.

Engineer Barasz begged the Gestapo to allow workers to take their wives and children into the factories. The Gestapo promised him that this would soon be the case.

A PAUSE IN WHICH TO BREATHE.

The sun rose peacefully on Sunday February 7th 1943. One hour passed, then two, and still nothing happened. No humming of automobile engines, no echos of heavy footsteps of Nazi jackboots, no fire-engine alarms, no sounds of gunfire! The boldest of the Jews crawled out of their hideouts. They gathered to talk. Then they returned to tell their companions that all was well today. People asked,

"Why is this so? Are the beasts resting on Sunday or is the slaughter over?"

By noon more pale and frightened looking Jewish faces could be seen creeping through ghetto courtyards and alleyways. They asked each other about family and friends. Women left their hideouts to prepare food for starving children. Their families had been cramped together for three days with little food or water.

This Sunday was ***a pause in which to breathe, a victimless day!***

THE THIRD DAY OF THE SLAUGHTER.

At 7 a.m. on Monday February 8th, the slaughter began anew. The Nazis surrounded every street and assaulted every house, every bit as aggressively as previously! Walls were broken. Floorboards were raised. Ceilings were pulled down. Yards and gardens were dug up. And despite this less Jews were found than on the previous two days. Then at 5 p.m. the ghetto became a ghost town again, and then two hours later there was movement. Women were walking to the factories carrying children on their arms. They had heard that Engineer Barasz had negotiated with the Gestapo for worker's wives and children to join them in the factories. These factories were overcrowded. A factory with 350 workers a shift, and three shifts a day, would have to accommodate over 1000 workers. Add wives and children to this and you have more than 2000 people. But somehow the factories found the room for them.

Some people who worked for the Judenrat were afforded special protection. Engineer Barasz issued working cards to the families of Moshe Wysocki; Asher Truszanowicz; Mr. S.

Rawet, the Registrar of Births; H. Goldberg, the author of a ghetto diary; and to some security guards and their families. These cards allowed these people entry into factories from this day onwards. Firefighters' wives and children were similarly granted refuge in the garage of the fire station.

Pesach Kaplan, the former Editor of 'Undzer Leben', received a room for his family on the third floor of Director Szloser's clothing factory on Kupiecka Street. My family and I (Rafael Rajzner) were also staying there. These rooms were previously part of the Trade High School. The windows offered a clear view of the street.

Pesach Kaplan was very sick when he arrived at the factory. He had contracted a severe cold during his several days of confinement in a crowded hideout. He was told to rest but, despite his weakened state, he couldn't lie still. He jumped out of bed every few minutes and ran to the window. This was strictly forbidden. People could be shot for looking out of windows, but Pesach couldn't help himself. He wanted to witness what was going on outside. Death was everywhere. The streets were full of it! People were continually being dragged out of hideouts and marched to the station. The trains took them straight to the gas chambers at Treblinka. Kaplan and I went up to the attic to watch the terrible tragedy. From up there it was possible to see into several streets. There were starving people walking everywhere, young and old, men and women, boys and girls. Someone who was too frail to walk suddenly staggered and was shot on the spot by the Nazis. The shooting was a cue for some of the younger people to scatter, to break into a run. More shooting followed. Hundreds were shot. A few managed to escape. The streets were littered with corpses. We watched it happen with our own eyes!

We saw another group of Jews being herded past Joseph Waksman's clothing factory. All of a sudden two women, with infants in their arms, ran out of the hordes of people towards a factory building. They were trying to save their babies. They threw them through open windows into the factory. The Nazis didn't allow the mothers to get away with this. They ordered the entire group to stop. Then some Nazis entered the factory, retrieved the infants, and handed them back to their mothers. While all this was happening a few youngsters managed to escape.

Pesach Kaplan watched all this unfold. He became very distressed. He ran backwards and forwards. ***"Revenge!"*** he stammered. He couldn't stop stammering. ***"Revenge! I can't take any more of this. I want to die."*** His wife Rivka and his daughter Sonia, who was a manager in the factory, did their best to calm him down, but to no avail.

Then suddenly the butcher Friedel arrived. This murderer was always on the prowl for "illicit" Jews in factories. Usually he would drag them out onto the street and shoot them. Sometimes he was lenient. He put them on a train to Treblinka instead!

THE FOURTH DAY OF THE SLAUGHTER.

A NEW DEVILISH PLAN.

For the Nazis the third day of the slaughter was a failure. They failed to capture enough Jews. So, on Tuesday February 9th 1943, the fourth day of the slaughter, they formulated a new devilish plan. If they came across a number of Jews in a hideout they would offer them their lives. All the quivering victims had to do was to tell where other Jews were hiding. There were dark instances where frightened Jews collaborated, and in the short term the Nazis usually kept their promise and spared the traitorous informers. But on some occasions they executed them on the spot declaring, ***"You are dying as Jewish traitors!"***

This new plan of persuading Jews dragged out of hideouts to reveal the whereabouts of other Jews was quite effective. The fourth day of the slaughter yielded many more victims than the third. And then it was 5 p.m. again and with classic German precision the killings stopped. As soon as darkness fell, Jews once again emerged from hiding places. They scurried to the factories to check out rumours that Engineer Barasz had negotiated successfully with the Gestapo for workers' parents to now be admitted. The workers' parents pushed and shoved while factory officials did their best to accommodate them in the attics. Through the attics' windows these new occupants watched suffering fellow Jews, family and friends among them, being herded by the Nazis towards the trains for Treblinka. Some of these people were so overcome by emotion that they ran downstairs onto the streets to offer help. Many were shot for their efforts. Others were made to join the columns for Treblinka.

That same evening the Gestapo ordered Engineer Barasz to bury the hundreds of corpses that littered the streets. Barasz directed the Chevra Kadisha (Jewish Burial Society) to put on more workers. Hundreds of Jews rushed to volunteer their services. These jobs were tickets for survival. Chevra Kadisha workers were a protected breed.

Every day Barasz would plead with the Gestapo, begging them to spare prominent people dragged out of hideouts. Three he tried particularly hard for were S. Herszberg, a writer; Abram Tyktin, a Judenrat member; and Dr. Beilin, his former neighbour. He failed dismally. They were sent to their deaths at Treblinka or Auschwitz.

THE FIFTH DAY OF THE SLAUGHTER.

On Wednesday February 10th 1943, the terrible slaughter continued. The new Nazi plan of Jew betraying Jew was working effectively. More victims were taken than on the previous day.

On this day there were cases of Jews committing suicide if their hideouts were discovered. At 26 Fabryczna Street, a father slit the veins of his wife and two daughters and then his own veins as well. His son who didn't want to die ran away and ended up a mental case.

The six thousand Jews in the factories were untouched.

After the Nazis left and darkness fell, Jews again emerged from hideouts, to witness the havoc the five murderous days had brought. Silence reigned. It was so quiet it was possible to hear the faintest whisper, but sounds were few and far between. One could see inside every house. The doors and windows were all open. Nothing of value remained. Anything that remained was covered in dirt. Many people were now gone. Some had been killed on the spot. Others had been dragged away to death camps. The streets were pitch-black. It was easy to trip over a corpse. There were some horses and cows walking around. They were hungry and thirsty. The cows had big udders. They needed milking, but their owners were dead. To witness this was to reel with pain, physical and mental pain, the pain of broken hearts and shattered souls. A breeze was blowing. It sounded like people wailing. The elements were mourning the tragedy of the Jews.

Women slipped out of hideouts to cook for their children. They never cooked inside their own buildings. They preferred the forsaken homes of people sent to Treblinka. *"When the Nazis return in the morning and see signs of activity, let them waste their time searching deserted buildings."*

MIRACLES OF THE KILLING DAYS.

While some Nazis were checking out a building, a startled child woke in a hideout and started to cry. The inhabitants of the bunker were very stressed by this. One of them tried to suffocate the child but this only made matters worse. The child's mother started to scream louder than the child. The situation became tense. Frightened Jews cramped together in a cold sweat. They all thought their end was near. But then a miracle happened. A second louder noise! Another Nazi brigade was demolishing a shed in the courtyard. The knocking and hammering was so loud that the sounds from the bunker were not heard. Finally the Nazis left the building and everyone wept, in part from fear, in part from the joy of having escaped certain death.

Another miracle occurred in a hideout so oppressively hot that its occupants opened the entrance to let in fresh air. At that precise moment some Nazis arrived to look over the building. The occupants of the hideout held their breaths. It would have been too noisy to replace the cover. So they left the entry open and to their surprise, the Nazis did not notice it. Every minute the Nazis spent in the building seemed like a year, and when they left some of the women fainted.

THE SIXTH DAY OF THE SLAUGHTER.

On Thursday February 11th 1943, the sixth day of the slaughter, more than 2000 Jews were captured. The Nazis were more brutal with captured Jews than previously and shamefully more of them submitted and informed on family and friends.

THE SEVENTH DAY OF THE SLAUGHTER.

Friday February 12th 1943 was the seventh and final day of the slaughter. Few Jews were captured that day. The quotas for the transports had already been achieved. Conditions inside most bunkers had become unbearable. Many died and their bodies just lay there. Others became so weak that they were ready to crawl out and surrender to the Nazis. Jewish security guards did their best to reassure them that this was the last day of the slaughter. The populace tended to be distrustful. They regarded the guards as agents of the devil. They hoped that what they said was true, but they could never bring themselves to believe them.

Everyone wanted to survive, to continue living. They hoped to wake up in the morning to a more secure future. But in reality few people slept that night. They expectantly awaited the new day.

At 7a.m. on Saturday February 13th 1943, everyone's ears were pricked up. This was the time the punctual murderers usually arrived. But like last Sunday there were no voices, no humming of automobile engines, no heavy steps of jackboots, no fire-engine alarms, no crackles of gunfire, not even a rustle. Shadows slowly started appearing out of the cracks concealing hideouts; human shadows. Two little girls edged out of a building and sneaked along the edge of a ghetto street. These two little doves evoked images of Noah's Ark after the flood. Some older Jews seized some courage and followed them. They became bolder and stayed out a little while, before reporting back to their hideouts with the news. ***"The Nazi bandits are not in the ghetto, but at present it seems prudent to remain in hiding."***

By midday more people were coming out of hideouts. This movement generated hope. Some stayed out for more than an hour, and when they returned they brought good news. They had been to Judenrat headquarters. Officials there declared that the slaughter was over. It was okay for people to leave their hideouts.

The joy that this news generated defies description. People kissed, they cried on each other's shoulders. At the same time they were grief-stricken. They wanted to run around and check on family and friends.

The ghetto was in a dreadful state. Buildings were plundered, walls were broken, roofs were torn apart. Hundreds of families had disappeared. The ground was littered with corpses. Inside buildings Jewish bodies were still hanging. Inside hideouts there were bodies of parents who had self-administered poison after choking their children. The survivors emitted heart-rending shreiks. They couldn't look each other in the eye. Everyone felt guilty. Phlegm stuck in their throats as they cursed the informers. They blamed the traitors for all this carnage, for the many beautiful Jewish lives that had been so brutally and tragically lost.

The security guards knew who the informers were. Three were arrested and tried that first day, no matter that it was the Sabbath. They were found guilty and one was sentenced to hang. But the vigilant crowd attacked and beat up all three of them, and then hanged the lot on a vacant block on

Kupiecka Street, near the bridge over the Biale Stream. They left the vile informers swinging for three days and during that time nearly every Jew went to look at them. This proved very painful, because the villain's disgrace was an addition to our own misfortune. Nevertheless it taught people that it is immoral to save oneself in exchange for hundreds of one's bretheren.

That night many Jews started restoring their shattered homes, but most only stuck at it for a little while. They were worn out by starvation, sleep deprivation and melancholia and needed to rest.

On Sunday the local Nazi newspaper, "The Bialystoker Times," published a cynical report of the events of the last nine days. It wrote that 10,000 Jews had been sent to work in Germany. Another 2,000 had rebelled against this and had been shot inside the ghetto.

The Jewish populace spent Sunday scurrying around the ghetto looking for relatives. Those who were told that absent relatives had been sent to gas chambers showed little emotion. They were somehow detached, as if this was to be expected, inevitable! This response, a state of induced shock, was said to be brought about by the absence of bodies. In contrast those who identified relatives at the ghetto cemetery, where hundreds of corpses were piled up like logs, wept cascades of tears and shrieked freely.

The one hundred martyrs executed at Prage's Yard were dug up by the Judenrat Chevra Kadisha and other Jewish helpers. Their bodies were covered by a layer of dirt so thin that hands and feet protruded. They were transferred to the Zabia Street Cemetery to be buried with all the other victims in three mass graves, one for men, one for women and one for children.

In the years immediately prior to the war Jews in Bialystok were buried at the Bagnowke Cemetery. It was usually Cantor Chudin, of the Nowy Swiat Street Synagogue, who conducted these services. Chubin would joke to friends that he wanted to be buried elsewhere. He got his wish. He died from a heart attack during the days of the slaughter and was buried in the Zabia Street Cemetery.

As a result of the seven days of slaughter from February 5th - 12th 1943:
(1) 2000 were shot inside the ghetto,
(2) 6000 were deported by six trains to Treblinka,
and
(3) 4000 were deported by four trains to Auschwitz.

Virtually nobody who was deported to Treblinka survived. A few of those deported to Auschwitz survived, but only after living through hell.

THE SLAUGHTER AT PRUZHANY.

At the same time a similar slaughter took place at nearby Pruzhany. Most of the 1000 Bialystoker deportees still living there were transported along with their fellow Pruzhaners to Auschwitz. About 15-20 managed to escape and survived to see the liberation.

CHAPTER 7.

BETWEEN SLAUGHTER AND DEATH.

JUDENRAT OFFICIALS COLLECT THE POSSESSIONS OF MISSING JEWS.

Now that the slaughter was over, Judenrat officials collected the victims' possessions.

Livestock, such as cows and horses, were given to the Jewish Hospital or to the Provisions Office. Furniture tended to be stored in storehouses. Bedding and soft furnishings were distributed among those most needy.

The Judenrat published a list of secret informers. These people were labelled as ***'Traitors and Betrayers of the Jewish People.'***

For the first three weekdays after the slaughter (Monday February 15th - Wednesday February 17th 1943) the ghetto gates were closed to Jews. Only Engineer Barasz was allowed in and out. On Thursday February 18th Yaacov Goldberg, the Head of the Provisions Office, was granted permission to bring a container of flour into the ghetto. For a few days there was some fresh bread to eat.

On Friday February 19th some Jewish tradesmen were given new documents, which allowed them to work outside the ghetto again.

THREE THOUSAND JEWS ARE EVENTUALLY GRANTED PERMISSION TO WORK OUTSIDE THE GHETTO.

On Monday February 22nd the Gestapo granted permission to some German firms to re-employ former Jewish slave labourers. Later this was extended to all German firms that had previously employed Jewish slave labourers. A month after the slaughter 3000 Jewish slave labourers were working outside the ghetto.

TWENTY ESCAPEES FROM THE DEATH TRAINS RETURN TO BIALYSTOK.

20 Jewish children, some as young as ten years of age, jumped off the death trains and sneaked their way back and into the ghetto. In all 100 children had risked life and limb by leaping off trains destined for Treblinka and Auschwitz. Many were crushed under the wagon's wheels. Others were shot dead by Ukrainian guards manning machine guns on the wagons' roofs. The return of the children was greeted with much joy, but their grizzly tales were hard to bear. These children had been to hell and back. They had been dragged off to the transport trains. They had been so tightly packed into wagons it was almost impossible to breathe. Their adult companions sawed bars off windows and tore planks off walls to give them openings large enough to jump through.

THE SECRET INFORMERS MEET THEIR MISERABLE END.

The re-appearance of these children on the streets of Bialystok terrified the secret informers. The children could identify them. The traitors suddenly disappeared. They hid away in secret hideouts. The Bialystokers looked for them. When they found them, they were merciless. They dragged them out of their holes and started killing them like dogs.

They used any implements they could find, axes, knives, irons and sticks.

Ciepla Street suddenly came to life. Five youths were chasing an informer. It was a terrible scene. They caught him. They surrounded him and went in for the kill. They tore him to pieces. He was already dead, but they didn't stop. His execution continued relentlessly.

The Judenrat supported such actions. It declared publicly that informers should be harshly dealt with. There was no place for leniency. ***"Those who squealed to the Nazis so as to survive at the expense of fellow Jews, deserve swift and brutal retribution!"***

Nevertheless to have to witness such punishment tore one's heart with grief. The Nazis, by their murderous deeds, had degraded our state of mind to the extent that we too had become like wild animals. The hunt for informers lasted more than a month. Most of them died a cruel death.

THE JUDENRAT RESUMES A DEGREE OF NORMALITY.

The Judenrat began to resume normal activities. It conducted a probe into the slaughter, to determine who and how many had been killed? It soon became clear that most of the victims were outside workers. They were not eligible to receive refuge in ghetto factories. They had spent less time in the ghetto and were less able to secure their hideouts. After these findings were released people no longer wished to work outside the ghetto.

This placed the Judenrat leadership in a difficult position. Outside workers wanted new jobs inside the ghetto. The elderly did too. And 10-12 year old children lied that they were 15 and entitled to a job. Everyone thought that work in the ghetto factories offered them the best chance of survival.

The Judenrat had no wish to favour certain groups. Instead it looked for solutions to help make peoples' insecure lives a little more certain.

Engineer Barasz's tried to get the ghetto factories incorporated under Wehrmacht (Regular Army) jurisdiction, rather than under the S.S. or the Gestapo. After much effort he finally succeeded. And before long most ghetto factories bore signs to the effect that they were now Wermacht property.

But the Judenrat still had to cater to those who worked outside the ghetto. Workers who returned to previous outside work places were issued with certificates stating they were ghetto factory workers. These certificates would gain them entry into ghetto factories in the event of a second slaughter.

HARD WORK REBUILDS THE GHETTO FACTORIES.

Within a few days the Judenrat started rebuilding ghetto industries. People worked hard, slaved at it feverishly, day and night. Once again the Judenrat urged the populace to surrender hidden machinery in its possession. Everyone who brought in a machine or machine parts was guaranteed an immediate job. People wanted to believe that work offered them salvation. So they took machines and machine parts out of hiding places and gave them to the Industry Office. People who didn't own machines or machine parts spent their last groshen purchasing equipment outside the ghetto. Everyone wanted something to give.

Once construction work was completed the inside workers' Employment Office started allocating jobs. People who had brought in machines and machine parts were employed first. Skilled workers were next. Hundreds more, the unskilled and those without machinery, remained in the ranks of the unemployed. These people saw lack of employment as a death sentence. They regarded the Judenrat as a bitter enemy.

Work conditions were now less sanitary. Workers were becoming more noticeably blackened by their labours. Their faces looked like they had been painted.

THE JUDENRAT DECIDES TO EXPAND HORTICULTURE.

The Judenrat decided to free more land for horticulture in the ghetto. This provided a dual benefit, more jobs and more vegetables.

Agronomy Engineer Shalit had resigned as Director of Horticulture. His place was taken by Agronomy Engineer Trop-Krynski, originally from Grodno. Trop-Krynski had prior experience as the director of an agricultural farm at Grochow near Warsaw. He laboured hard, day and night. No job was too much for him. He was tilling gardens or instructing young students as early as 4 a.m. In a very short time he raised the standard of horticulture as practiced inside the ghetto to an extraordinarily high level. Even older, more experienced agriculturists stood in awe of his achievements.

KITCHEN CONDITIONS ARE IMPROVED.

Bunim Farbsztejn also improved his kitchen. It had always been hospitable and clean, but now it offered more and better food.

BUNIM FARBSZTEJN ORGANISES A COMMUNITY SEDER IN CYTRON'S PRAYER HOUSE.

Bunim Farbsztejn celebrated Pesach (Passover) 1943 by organising a community seder (Passover dinner) in the women's section of Samuel Cytron's Prayer House. The price was very reasonable, but people who couldn't afford it were welcomed free of charge. Several hundred Jews came. In those dark days it was not possible to hold a seder in a private home. Many rabbis participated in the seder, but its true leader was Bunim himself. He delivered a long and moving speech which brought everyone to tears.

THE GHETTO SHRINKS AGAIN.

Immediately after Passover the Nazis decreed that the ghetto should be made smaller again. New walls were built that removed Zydowska Street and some of Kupiecka, Czenstochowa, Polna and Rosenberg streets.

Bialystoker Jewry held its breath once again.

TWO ENVOYS FROM THE WARSAW GHETTO RESISTANCE ORGANISATION ARRIVE.

At this same time two envoys from the Warsaw Ghetto Resistance Organisation came to Bialystok to hold secret meetings with leaders of the Resistance Group. They decided that the Resistance Group should recruit more members. Most horticultural workers were members, but factory workers had tended to form their own resistance organisations.

Yudith Nowogrodzky, the leader of the partisans, was against forming a coalition with the Bialystoker Resistance Group. In April 1943, Yudith's group dispatched a second band of partisans into the forest. This band was led by Dr. Simon Datner and it remained in contact with colleagues in Bialystok.

As the Resistance Group increased in size its leaders were confronted with new problems. ***"Where do we get the money from to buy arms? Once we have the money, how do we get the arms into the ghetto?"*** A favourable solution was required!

There were Bialystoker Jews working in German arms warehouses, who volunteered to steal weapons from their workplace and smuggle them into the ghetto. One can't overemphasise the danger involved in this. A young man named Galant was one of their leaders. He took incredible risks in order to supply the Resistance Group with arms. He even bribed a Wermacht soldier, who later betrayed him to the Gestapo. The Gestapo tortured Galant mercilessly, but at no time did he betray his companions. He refused to confess to anything or name anyone to whom he had supplied weapons. He died as a result of brutal torture in the Gestapo cellars. The brutality was reminiscent of the Spanish inquisition. He deserves to be honoured as a heroic son of the Jewish people!

A DECISION IS MADE TO BUILD AN ARMS FACTORY INSIDE THE GHETTO.

The quantity of arms smuggled into the ghetto was not sufficient. More needed to be done. The leaders of the Resistance Group organised a meeting and invited Heniek Farber, an energetic and talented chemical engineer, and some other young Jewish chemists to attend. Farber and his colleagues were asked to set up a secret arms factory inside the ghetto. They built it at 3 Czysta Street and produced explosives and hand grenades there. Farber was to die a hero's death in February 1944 fighting the Nazis in the Suprasl Forest.

THE RESISTANCE GROUP ROBS THE JUDENRAT'S MAIN FOOD STOREHOUSE.

Late one night, towards the end of April 1943, the Resistance Group enacted a plan to raise money to buy arms. Fighters broke into the Judenrat's main food storehouse at 5 Novy Swiat Street. They overpowered the nightwatchmen and made off with several wagonloads of food.

When these events took place, rumours abounded that this was just a straight-out robbery. Some however expressed the opinion that the crime had been committed by the Resistance Group with Engineer Barasz's approval. The latter version was correct. Barasz had changed his mind, and now secretly supported the Resistance Group. In accordance with his change of heart, he had sacked one of his less sympathetic adjutants and replaced him with a He-Halutz leader, who was an active and highly respected member of the Resistance. This administrative change made it easier for the Resistance movement to raise money. Barasz also approached partisan leaders at this time and asked if he could join them in the forests. The partisans rejected his overtures. ***"They did not want a betrayer of the Jewish people in their midst."*** The partisans were also always on the lookout to purchase weapons and were not beyond extorting money from wealthier Jews in order to do so.

A SECRET RADIO AT 15 CIEPLA STREET.

If the Nazis found a radio, they shot its owner and his neighbours. Yet despite this, there were brave people inside the ghetto, who were not prepared to cut themselves off from the rest of the world.

Aron Gelczynski, a graduate of the orphanage at 7 Jurowiecka Street, operated a shoe repairs business in a small shop at 15 Ciepla Street. Members of the Resistance used the shop as a meeting point. Gelczynski established a secret radio listening post there. He had obtained his wireless from Chanan Efros, a well-known community activist and social worker. Gelczynski and Meyer Muchnik, a student, risked their lives listening to two broadcasts from abroad every day. Muchnik made notes of these broadcasts and secretly distributed them to all factory workers. Their closest co-workers inside the Resistance were Lazer Wysocki; Leibel Shewin, the son of Shaike Shewin from Czchow; and Abraham Nayman, also known as Memke Nayman.

THE TRAGIC DEATHS OF WYSOCKI AND SHEWIN.

Two resistance fighters, Lazer Wysocki and Leibel Shewin, were sent on a secret mission to make contact with partisans. They were dressed in German military uniforms. The partisans spotted them in the forest, mistook them for real Germans, and shot them dead. The error was discovered several days later to the consternation of those involved.

YUDITH NOWOGRODZKY DISPATCHES A THIRD BAND OF PARTISANS.

In May 1943, Yudith Nowogrodzky's group dispatched a third band of partisans into the forests. This band was led by Chaim Chalef, a wood carver by profession, who had lived near the Great Synagogue prior to the war. In the early days of the war, Chalef had been sent to a German prisoner of war camp in Lublin where he witnessed Germans slaughtering local Jews. In 1942 he escaped and made his way back to Bialystok. Back in Bialystok he immediately started agitating for Jews to leave the ghetto. He argued that to stay put was to accept the same fate as the Jews of Lublin. Chalef's ideas made him a natural to join Yudith Nowogrodzky's partisan organization. He soon became one of its most active and capable members, an important cog in its planning activities. Because of his previous military experience he was made Deputy-Commandant to Dr. Simon Datner, together with whom he worked and survived in the woods. They remained in contact with colleagues back in the ghetto.

THE GERMANS DEMAND MORE JEWISH SLAVE LABOURERS.

Summer arrived and many German construction firms found themselves short of slave labourers. Many perished during the February slaughters and those who survived no longer wished to work outside the ghetto. These firms complained to German officials that Jews inside the ghetto should be made to work for them.

As a result a German workforce commissioner issued a directive which ordered the Jewish Workers' Employment Office to supply these firms with required numbers of slave labourers. The Jewish official responsible found himself in a most difficult situation. He knew that nearly every Jew was now employed in a ghetto factory and the few who weren't refused to work outside the ghetto. His only option was to offer substantial privileges to those who volunteered for outside work. 500 new workers volunteered and temporarily satisfied the Nazi craving for more slave labourers.

LIFE IN THE GHETTO DURING THE SUMMER OF 1943.

Despite recent horrific events, life in the ghetto normalised during the summer of 1943; if one dare use the word "normal" in relation to such a life. The Provisions Office opened several new stores which operated on a similar basis to the one in the Judenrat building. These stores provided ghetto dwellers with breadcards and divided home-grown vegetables equitably among them. Dozens of smaller private shops sprung up. These were crude wooden constructions made of boards. For a few groshen, people could purchase merchandise from them, which enabled their owners to eke out a living. There were also a few 'unofficial restaurants' which served the best food. These meals were expensive and only the very rich could afford them.

Nevertheless despite this hapless misery, on Lag Ba-Omer 1943, 30 Jewish couples decided to marry. *(There is a 33 day gap between the festivals of Passover and Lag Ba-Omer, when Jewish couples cannot marry.)*

Bialystokers tried their best to deny they were starving to death or waiting for the Nazis to exterminate them. To some extent they succeeded.

EDITOR PESACH KAPLAN DIES.

A few weeks before Shavuot 1943, Pesach Kaplan died. (Shavuot or Pentecost is the festival celebrating the commencement of the harvest, and starts 50 days after the first day of Passover). The news of Kaplan's death spread through the ghetto like wildfire. Kaplan had been a man of many talents in Bialystok - a fine journalist, the Editor of 'Undzer Leben' the city's premier Yiddish daily newspaper – a multi-lingual educator who promoted Yiddish and taught Hebrew – a cultural leader who was, at the same time, a gifted author, an art critic, a theatre reviewer, a musicologist and the Director of the Jewish Arts Association's choir - a long-term City Councillor, who was both a founding member and leader of the People's Party in Bialystok – and the Chairman of the committee of the Dr. Josef Chazanowicz Library.

Immediately after the February slaughter Kaplan fell ill, became weak, and was confined to bed. After several weeks his condition improved and he got up again, but only for a few days. A severe lung infection soon put him back in bed for a final time. He died despite the best efforts of his wife, his daughters and his sons-in-law.

The Judenrat helped organise Kaplan's funeral. Engineer Barasz headed a special delegation of its members. Most ghetto dwellers came to pay Kaplan their last respects, making his funeral the largest turnout of mourners ever seen in the ghetto. Kaplan's pall bearers included fellow former editors Moshe Wysocki and Asher Trushanowicz, and his old friend Aaron Albeck, the former publisher of 'Dos Naye Leben.'

Engineer Barasz, Moshe Wysocki and Aaron Albeck all wanted to speak at Kaplan's funeral. But at the actual moment a large detachment of Gestapo troops arrived at the section of the cemetery fence, which was also part of the ghetto fence. These killers had a reputation of being trigger happy whenever they saw a Jew addressing a crowd. It was therefore decided no eulogies would be given.

Many Bialystoker Jews envied Kaplan. He died in his own bed and he was buried in a Jewish cemetery.

A few weeks later Joseph Waksman, Kaplan's son-in-law, died suddenly. Waksman was the manager of the largest clothing factory in the ghetto. As a young man he worked for ten years in the administrative offices of 'Dos Naye Leben,' and then, from 1934-39, he managed the Bata Shoe Store. Under the Soviets he again managed a large footwear business. Many mourners attended his funeral.

MORE ENVOYS FROM THE WARSAW GHETTO RESISTANCE ORGANISATION ARRIVE IN BIALYSTOK.

Special envoys who were also experienced ghetto fighters came to Bialystok. One of them, Chajke Grossman, was an energetic woman. She played a major role in helping to organise the Bialystok Resistance Group. A self-defence cell was established in every factory. It was there to defend workers in the event of another slaughter. If the situation became indefensible, the self-defence cell was trained to burn the factory down and continue fighting in the streets. Its members were shown how to fill glass lamp fittings with inflammable liquids. These little cocktails were prepared in advance. It was hoped they would provide the Germans with a warm reception.

THE GERMAN EMPLOYMENT OFFICER DEMANDS EVEN MORE SLAVE LABOURERS AND THREATENS SANCTIONS.

Towards the end of May 1943, the German employment officer demanded more outside slave labourers. If they were not supplied heavy sanctions would be imposed.

The Jewish employment officer found himself in a most precarious position. He had no unemployed Jews to mobilise and could not comply with the German demands. He called a combined meeting of the Jewish Workers' Employment Office and the Judenrat leadership in order to obtain a ruling. The meeting resurrected a previous decision. Ten per cent of ghetto factory workers would be sent to work outside for two weeks at a time. This would enable quotas to be met.

The decision was a fair one, but Jews who were rostered to work it were not pleased. They constantly looked for ways to get out of it. Nevertheless the administration prevailed and the quotas were met. Then a new demand was made for several dozen tailors and shoe makers to be sent to Konigsberg. This order was similarly met with.

On June 15th 1943, the Gestapo directed the Judenrat to supply six graphic artists for work at Sachsenhausen Concentration Camp, 30 kilometres from Berlin. There was a German secret service printshop there, which forged documents and counterfeited English pounds.

Every few days the Gestapo would drive into the ghetto and round up dozens of Jews. These Jews were trucked to Nowosholke, where they were made to dig large pits. The Germans would then bring local prisoners to the pits, shoot them, and force the Bialystokers to bury them. Later that same evening these grave diggers would return, totally exhausted and broken in spirit.

Other Bialystoker Jews were rounded up for the dreaded transgressors' labour camp at Markowczyzna. These unforunates were kept there for several weeks at a time. They were given minimal amounts of food and received frequent beatings. By the time they returned to Bialystok they were usually very sick.

A SECRET WEAPONS WORKSHOP EXPLODES.

In July 1943, the ghetto was rocked by an explosion. This occurred in the secret weapons workshop at 3 Czysta Street. Three members of the resistance, Siomke Kucharewski, the son of well-known accountant Sholem Kucharewski; Lifszyc, an eighteen year old; and Lewin, a sixteen year old, were blown up and killed. Lewin looked typically Aryan and on missions would don a cross on a chain. He often sneaked out of the ghetto to deliver messages to the partisans. These three martyrs sacrificed themselves for the honour of the Jewish people and their memory deserves to be hallowed.

A Gestapo commission was quick on the scene to survey the premises. All they found was the blown apart remnants of the martyrs.

Everyone in the ghetto felt tense. Severe reprisals were expected. But three days passed and nothing happened. The Judenrat spread a rumour that it had managed to hush up the incident, but this was not true. The German's reprisal was that the destruction of the ghetto was hurried up a few months.

This explosion was an unfortunate setback for the members of the Resistance Group. If the Gestapo had managed to trace the explosion back to them, large quantities of explosives might have been found.

THE GHETTO IS NOW FREQUENTLY SUBJECTED TO NAZI INSPECTIONS.

After the explosion the ghetto was inspected daily, by either the Gestapo or the Wehrmacht. These commissions were important in determining the ghetto's future. Engineer Barasz accompanied the commissioners on their rounds and was privy to their disturbing thoughts. When he informed others of them, the mood in the ghetto became progressively gloomier.

Once again people looked for ways to save themselves. A few, who had procured false documents, managed to escape from the ghetto. Most started building new hideouts or tried to improve old ones. People worried that neighbours might eventually denounce them, as had happened during the February slaughters. After all everyone knew everyone else's business.

THE LUBLIN COMMISSION SEALS THE FATE OF BIALYSTOKER JEWRY.

In the middle of July 1943, an important Nazi commission from Lublin visited Bialystok. **"It had come to inspect the Bialystoker ghetto."** Its arrival generated much fear. People were frightened to venture out on the streets. This was the **"Commission on Life or Death."** There were only two large ghettos left, Lodz with 80,000 Jews and Bialystok with 40,000 Jews. One would survive, the other would be liquidated.

After the commission left, Engineer Barasz confided pessimism to his closest associates. ***"Lodz is destined to remain. Bialystok is about to be liquidated."*** All one could do was hope that the disaster might be delayed.

THE RESISTANCE GROUP MAKES ITS FINAL PREPARATIONS.

Realising that genocide was fast approaching, the Resistance Group met to re-confirm policy. ***"The fighting cells inside factories must pull together with their workers. The Nazi killers must be denied access to the factories at all costs. Once the situation is hopeless the factories must be burnt down and the battle continued in the streets."*** Final plans were now cemented. The ominous day was near at hand.

CHAPTER 8.

THE LIQUIDATION OF THE GHETTO.

THE LAST TWO DAYS OF THE BIALYSTOK GHETTO.

Daily life in the ghetto became more tense, more nerve rattling!

On Saturday August 14th 1943, the Gestapo inspected the ghetto fence and gates. Jewish outside workers returning to the ghetto started reporting new developments, which they had seen in town. Many empty carriages were parked at the railway station. The place was seething with Ukrainian collaborators. Some of these killers were walking the streets but most had been ordered into the many courtyards to help conceal their presence. German soldiers started coming into the ghetto to reclaim watches, which they had left with Jewish repairers. The soldiers told the watchmakers that their brigades were leaving Bialystok, but we Jews knew better.

Events started to follow a similar course to that of the February slaughter. Judenrat officials tried to reassure the populace. ***"The Wermacht has recently ordered large quantities of fabrics, fabrics that will take months to produce. Nothing sinister will happen in the meantime."*** The Wermacht officers who ordered the fabrics, had always feigned friendship with the factory managers. Now they told them the terrible rumours had no substance.

Ominous news alternated with optimistic reassurances. Saturday August 14th and Sunday August 15th passed and all was quiet. People hoped for a reprieve, hoped a disaster might be postponed.

THE COMPLETE DESTRUCTION OF THE 40,000 SURVIVING JEWS BEGINS.

At 2 a.m. on Monday August 16th 1943, Jews living by the ghetto fence awoke to the frightening sound of large numbers of hobnailed boots marching towards them. It took only minutes for news of this to spread through the ghetto. A terrible panic gripped. Close to 40,000 Jews ran through the dark streets in a state of confusion. ***"Was this definitely the end? Was there no longer any hope? Would the ghetto be totally liquidated or only partially destroyed?"*** Nobody had the answers!

At 3 a.m. several hundred fully armed Nazi killers entered the ghetto. They were led by two mass-murdering criminals, Obersturmfuhrer Tuman, the Lublin Camp Commander, and Fritz Gustav Friedel, the leader of the Bialystok Gestapo. It took them no time to occupy the factories and the Judenrat building.

At 5 a.m. more news spread through the ghetto. Engineer Barasz had been told, that the Bialystokers and their machinery would be moved to Lublin. They would continue working there. Jews from Polna, Nowy Swiat, Czenstochowska, Bialystoczanska, Okrongla, Szlachecka, Linas Hatzedek, Czysta, Zytnia, Zamenhof, Kupiecka and Gieldowa Streets and adjacent alleyways were ordered to assemble at 9 a.m. in the morning. Assembly points were on Jurowiecka, Fabryczna, Ciepla, Nowogrodzka and Chmielna Streets and in the yard of the Judenrat building. From these checkpoints everyone would be marched to the railway station. Anyone who stayed behind in the prohibited areas would be shot dead on sight. The situation was now clear. The ghetto was to be liquidated. And at 7 a.m., despite this knowledge, the streets designated as assembly points were full of men, women and children carrying miserable bundles. They were so crowded people couldn't pass through them.

THE RESISTANCE GROUP IS CAUGHT BY SURPRISE.

The Nazi assault caught the Resistance Group by surprise. They realised that their plan to defend the factories and then set them on fire would never eventuate. But these fighters would not be deterred. They met and decided against waiting until 9 a.m. They went straight into the streets. At 3 Chmielna Street, one of the resistance fighters addressed the crowd. ***"Be warned! You are not being sent to Lublin to work. You are being sent to Treblinka to be gassed! If you allow this to happen, you will share the same bitter and disastrous fate as the rest of European Jewry. Our only chance is to set fire to our houses and all our possessions. Leave nothing behind for the enemy. Grab your weapons and try to break out of the ghetto. Try to join our partisan brothers in the woods."***

The Resistance Group hoped that fires would burn down the fence surrounding the ghetto. This could enable some Jews to escape. Inspired by the resistance fighters' words, many young people seized weapons.

THE GHETTO IN FLAMES.

By 8 a.m., Ciepla, Fabryczna, Nowogrodzka, Chmielna and Gorna Streets were all ablaze. Large haystacks were burning in the Judenrat garden. Jews from the other side of the ghetto ran to these streets to see what was happening, but were driven back by the heat. Many more ran towards the Judenrat garden. There were perhaps twenty thousand Jews there and they soon found themselves face-to-face with a new disaster. The Nazis didn't wait until 9 a.m. Once they realised the ghetto was being set alight they commenced their bloody slaughter. They opened up machine-gun fire, firing down into the Judenrat garden, from balconies and windows outside the ghetto. Terror and chaos reigned. There was no escape. Bullets flew in from one side, flames charged in from the other. Hundreds of people fell to the ground, dead or wounded. Others threw themselves onto the ground. Others still were trampled in the panic and confusion. Screams could be heard kilometres away. The scene was so horrific it defies description.

A thousand Jews fled into the yard of the former 'Toz' building, which was now the Jewish Hospital. These people hoped the hospital would be spared. It was during the February slaughter. Not this time! The Nazis shot into the yard from all sides and most of the Jews were murdered. The well-known paediatrician Dr. Segal was killed at this time.

SOME YOUNG RESISTANCE FIGHTERS STAGE A HEROIC STAND.

The machine-gun fire served as a signal. 700 fully armed Nazis marched into the ghetto through the Jurowiecka Street gate. Tanks followed them. This time most of the killers were not even German. They were Ukrainian and Belarus. Some young Jewish resistance fighters decided to stand up to them. Despite overwhelming odds, these brave young heroes managed to get some shots at the Nazis and to throw a few hand grenades onto their tanks. Tadek, (a nick-name), was one of the leaders of this group. He managed to kill a few Nazis before being shot dead himself. Chava Chalef, the 16 year old sister of well-known wood carver, partisan leader and survivor, Chaim Chalef, was shot dead in a hail of bullets, while throwing a hand grenade. Jews were firing down on these Nazis from windows and lofts, but despite this it did not take the Nazis long to reach the Judenrat building. There were still fifteen thousand Jews inside the Judenrat garden, but many of them were lying dead or wounded on the ground.

THE GHETTO BECOMES A BATTLEFIELD.

This bloody slaughter of Bialystoker Jews was carried out with military precision. At 3 a.m. the Nazis set up a Central Command inside the Judenrat building. Contact with their groups of killers was maintained with portable telephone lines and an elaborate system of messengers. The messengers were armed to the teeth. They carried machine-guns and hand grenades. Some ran along the streets. Others sped through them on motorbikes.

A NAZI ARMY THREE THOUSAND STRONG CONDUCTS THE LIQUIDATION.

The Nazis used nearly 3000 heavily armed killers to conduct their atrocious and barbaric liquidation of Bialystoker Jewry. 700 Ukrainian and Belarus collaborators were inside the ghetto. 1000 more were waiting outside its fence as possible reinforcements. Another 1000 were close at hand, waiting to receive victims and transport them to the gas chambers.

AN ARMY OF SEVEN HUNDRED TROOPS ARRIVES AT THE JUDENRAT BUILDING AND PREPARES FOR AN ASSAULT ON ITS GARDEN.

Suddenly the gunfire from outside the ghetto stopped. This was the cue the 700 killers who had arrived at the Judenrat building were waiting for. They began their assault on the Jews in the Judenrat garden.

The Resistance Group fought heroically, but the Nazis were armed to the teeth. Jewish fighters fell and were immediately replaced by others. Young Jewish girls, oblivious to mortality, continued supplying the fighters with bullets and hand grenades. Many were killed before even reaching fighters, but others replaced them and the struggle continued.

Abrasha Gelter, the son of Gelter the master spinner, was one of the most ferocious fighters in the ghetto. When he saw his badly wounded sister lying in agony on the ground, he shot her in the head to protect her falling into the hands of the Nazis. Abrasha Gelter was one of a select few, who escaped from the ghetto. He joined the partisans and continued fighting. He died in the woods one day, when a large battalion of Nazis surrounded his small group of partisans. The fighters in the Judenrat garden mounted a heroic struggle. It lasted nearly half a day. The Nazis suffered 30-40 dead and about 50 wounded. Many more ghetto fighters lost their lives, but their effort was superhuman. It is impossible to imagine a more uneven contest. People armed with the most primitive of weapons confronting a powerful fully equipped military machine.

By 4 p.m. the fighting was over. A few Jewish fighters managed to escape and fight another day.

THE SURVIVORS ARE HERDED TO THE PIETRASZE FIELD.

More than 15,000 Jews survived the battle. The Nazis rounded them up and herded them down Jurowiecka Street towards the Pietrasze Field. The Jews were hurried along by gun butt blows to their heads and backs. Bialystoker Jewry had celebrated the Soviet October Festival on the Pietrasze Field in 1939. Now they would be humiliated there and shipped to their deaths from there.

THE JUDENRAT GARDEN RESEMBLES THE WORST OF BATTLEFIELDS.

I could see the Judenrat garden from the window of our attic at 1 Chmielna Street. Bullet-ridden bodies were strewn everywhere, the dead, the near dead, men, women, children! The near dead emitted weak cries. "Help!" A plea for water! Begging to be put out of misery! Begging to be shot in the head! These thousands of bodies were not alone. The belongings of 20,000 Jews, assembled there a few hours earlier, were lying in-between them. The scene of it all wrenched my heart. The bloodiest battlefield of the Great War would not have looked worse. In among the dead lay Welwel Wolkowiski, a heroic fighter who served as a liaison officer between the Resistance Group and the partisans. His home at 13 Ciepla Street had served as a frequent meeting place for members of the resistance.

THE NAZI MURDERERS TRY TO EXTINGUISH GHETTO FIRES.

While the battle for the Judenrat garden was still in full force, another brigade of Nazis followed a fire engine into Ciepla Street. The engine was trying to extinguish a fire next to the ghetto fence. Resistance fighters shot at the Nazis from overlying windows.

TWO FIFTEEN YEAR OLD HEROES.

My son Samuel Rajzner and his best friend Nahum Kozak, the son of Herschel Kozak who is now in the United States, were hiding together in an attic at 12 Ciepla Street. From the attic's window these two daring fifteen year olds took aim at the Nazis following the fire engine. Their well placed shots killed two of them. The boys then fled the attic to continue fighting elsewhere.

RESISTANCE FIGHTERS DIE AT THE CORNER OF CIEPLA AND NOWOGRODZKA STREETS.

Baran, the son of Joseph Baran the shoe manufacturer, led the resistance fighters who defended the entrance of one side of Nowogrodzka Street from Ciepla Street. They were shot down in a hail of bullets. At the height of this battle I saw Nahum Manischewitz, a delivery man by trade, running out of Nowogrodzka Street. Ukrainian devils chased him, caught him, and tore him to pieces. Manischewitz was a dedicated, energetic member of the Resistance Group, one of its greatest contributors. He was extraordinarily heroic. He risked his life several times, smuggling stolen weapons into the ghetto. Yudith Nowogrodzky, the partisan leader, also died in this action.

THE RESISTANCE GROUP TRIES TO PUSH THROUGH THE FENCE.

All day Jewish resistance fighters, armed with handguns, tried to penetrate the ghetto fence. They were repeatedly forced back and suffered heavy casualties.

THE HORRIFIC FIRST DAY OF THE LIQUIDATION.

Many young Jewish families thought that hiding out in the ghetto was not synonymous with survival. So they assembled when the Nazis ordered them to.

In all there were less than 40,000 Jews in the ghetto. 5,000 died in the Judenrat garden. 25,000 were herded to the Pietrasze Field. The last 10,000 were in no hurry to go to Treblinka. They retreated into hideouts. These people believed that hiding out was the best option. Fighting in the open was akin to committing suicide. A few resistance fighters joined them. At nightime some of the resistance fighters armed themselves, emerged from hideouts, and tried to escape from the ghetto.

ENGINEER BARASZ, ISAAC MARKUS, SOME FACTORY DIRECTORS, SOME JEWISH SECURITY GUARDS, AND SEVERAL VOLUNTEER FIREMEN REMAIN IN THE GHETTO.

Engineer Barasz, Isaac Markus, some factory directors, some Jewish security guards, and several volunteer firemen sought refuge in a garage on Polna Street. Several hundred other Jews, who had worked for high ranking Nazi officials and the S.S., moved into the former carton box factory on Kupiecka Street.

NAZI PRECISION AND EXACTITUDE.

At 5.50 p.m. two tanks drove down Ciepla, Nowogrodzka and Chmielna Streets. From these tanks hand grenades were thrown into many houses. Ten minutes passed and the tanks left. The ghetto had suddenly emptied and there were no Nazis to be seen. The first day of the liquidation had ended precisely at six o'clock. Shortly afterwards a cannonade started and the ghetto was showered with bullets all night.

A thousand Ukrainians were shooting into it from the other side of the fence. The Nazis had created an overnight battlefield, to discourage Jews from leaving their hideouts. They didn't want Jews to look for food or to try to escape through the ghetto fence.

NIGHTIME IN THE JUDENRAT GARDEN.

I belonged to a group who strived to stay alive. We would not assemble at checkpoints. We would hide in the ghetto instead.

At our apartment house at 1 Chmielna Street, we made a hideout for several families. My beloved son Samuel and his best friend Nahum Kozak were supposed to be with us. But these 15 year olds were easily influenced by a resistance fighter from 3 Chmielna Street. They went to get guns and didn't come back.

"We didn't see or hear from them all day. We were so worried. Our hearts wrenched with heartache. As soon as it was dark, I slipped out of our hideout and disregarding the danger, crawled on my belly into a neighbouring building. I called out to the boys, but nobody answered. I saw or heard nothing, so I crawled on into the Judenrat garden. I kept low because bullets were flying over my head. I suddenly found myself crawling over bodies. Some were dead. Others were near death, sniffling, moaning and groaning with a close to last breath. To my horror I found some babies still living alongside the corpses of their mothers. These tiny tots had been left there, ignored or unnoticed by the murderous Nazis. Their muted whimpering was tragic, impossible to bear. Suddenly two older men called to me. They asked me if I knew of a house nearby, where they could hide away. I pointed to our house and bade them follow me. Suddenly it

began to rain. It didn't just rain. It started to pour. The rain started to douse the fires that were still burning and light faded into dark. I felt that nature was weeping for us. The last glare from the fires highlighted the Judenrat garden. I could now see thousands of dead and wounded lying on the ground. The cries they must have uttered might have moved rocks! And in among the bodies were a sea of packages and suitcases, all drenched by the pouring rain. What a horrible sight! How could I have stood it? My heart must have been made of iron or stone. And throughout it all I failed to find a scent of my son. Together with the two living men I shuffled back to our hideout and my family. I told my family everything I had seen, and that our beloved son and his best friend were no longer in the land of the living."

TWO O'CLOCK IN THE MORNING AND MY SON AND HIS BEST FRIEND RETURN TO THE HIDEOUT.

At 2 a.m. we heard a noise in our house. It sounded like soft steps and then the steps were upon us. Next there was a scratch on the hideout door and a soft murmur, ***"Papa - Papa - we are here - can you hear us - Nahum and I - open up - don't be afraid."***

Our hands and feet had been shaking with fear. Now they started to tremble with joy. Our fingers shook so much it seemed to be forever before we managed to open the door. And then overcome by joy and happiness, we welcomed the two boys back into the safety of our bunker. Samuel talked about their horrible day and how they managed to survive it. They were hiding in an attic at 12 Ciepla Street. From the window they looked down onto the roadway and saw several Nazis following a fire engine. They took aim and fired and with pin-point accuracy managed to kill two of the beasts. To avoid capture they ran off. They shot a third Nazi in the Judenrat garden, but it was not safe to continue fighting there. They were sitting ducks. Quick as a flash they dropped their guns and threaded their way into a crowd, which was being herded to the Pietrasze Field. Along the way they were always on the lookout, waiting for the moment to make a run for it. Shots whistled by but they were not hit. They ran into other Jews, who had similarly escaped the Pietrasze field. These Jews painted a grim picture. All the way from Jurowiecka Street to the Pietrasze field, the roadway was littered with bullet-ridden bodies of men, women and children. Some were runaways who had been intercepted by Polish hooligans and handed to the Nazis. The Nazis shot them on the spot in front of their Polish captors. Then everyone laughed out aloud, as if at a party!

THE JEWS IN THE HIDEOUTS SCAVENGE FOR FOOD.

Jews hiding out in shelters had to scavenge for food. They had to creep out at night and search for it in dark abandoned buildings. They had to ignore a continual barrage of gunfire when stepping outside. They had to accept tripping over body parts of hand grenade victims when searching inside.

On such an occasion some of us left our hideout to search for food, only to confront a young married couple and an older woman, the man's mother, hiding nearby. The three of them had been out scavenging for food when they heard tanks approaching. To avoid detection they ran inside our building. When the tanks rolled by a hand grenade was thrown into the building and the young woman sustained serious injuries to the abdomen. We gave them refuge in our hideout, where regretfully the young woman, who was suffering severe pain, died in my bed.

RESISTANCE FIGHTERS ONCE AGAIN FAIL TO ESCAPE FROM THE GHETTO.

Later that night resistance fighters made several more attempts to breach the ghetto fence. Each one failed. In the end the fighters retreated, leaving their dead behind.

THE MASSACRE AT PIETRASZE FIELD.

The hideous manner in which Jews were murdered at the Pietrasze field defies description. 25,000 Jews, men and women of all ages and children, were crowded together in a confined space. The heat generated by the overcrowding caused many to choke. The Jews were surrounded by three cordons of Nazi murderers armed to the teeth. Ukrainian devils stood in front of them. Latvian and Belarus monsters stood behind them. The third and outer cordon consisted of smaller numbers of highly trained machine gunners. These were placed peripherally in the field, so as to command a view of the Jews and all the roads; the main roads to Bialystok and Wasilkow and surrounding side roads. The Nazis forced the Jews to run up and down the centre of the field as fast as they could. There wasn't enough room to do so. Many Jews fell over during the stampede and were trampled to death by the hundreds following. They were told that if they stopped running they would be shot. When they were finally ordered to stop Nazis shot into the crowd. The Jews became thirsty and many pleaded to exchange their last possessions for a drop of water. The Nazis were quick to take the possessions, but seldom gave water in return. If perchance a kinder Nazi returned with water, it was usually spilt in the crush. The Ukrainians beat the women with sticks and pulled rings off their fingers. And then the skies opened and it started to pour. The downpour was torrential and all the Jews were drenched. Many of them had no strength left. They couldn't even lift themselves off the ground. Those who were still standing could see the fires in the ghetto petering out. And as the flames extinguished themselves, they realised their lives were doomed for a similar fate.

THE SECOND DAY OF THE LIQUIDATION.

At 6.40 a.m. on Tuesday August 17th 1943, more than 800 Nazis rode into the ghetto. They started this day as they had the day before. A Central Command was set up inside the Judenrat building. Reconnaisance groups were sent out laying down telephone lines. At 7 a.m. those still at the Judenrat building organised themselves into killer squads of ten men, each one with its own leader. The squads went out, but this time there were no Jews waiting for them on the streets. The Jews had stayed in their hideouts.

The killer squads marched up and down the streets. Their orders were continually updated by officers manning field telephones. The manhunt was now on. One squad was usually considered sufficient to plunder a building, but two squads were sometimes provided for larger buildings. The squads pillaged anything they thought valuable. While tearing empty apartments apart, many an object was snatched up and placed inside a Nazi pocket. If Nazis suspected Jews were hiding in a building, they started to yell. They warned the Jews that the building was about to be blown up and they better come out. No Jew ever answered. The Jews knew what was in store for them if they did. Hand grenades would be thrown into rooms of the building and the body parts of hidden Jews might be seen flying through the air. A building might be searched in this manner up to ten times a day. Consecutive searches were usually performed by different killer squads.

THE LIVING HELL THAT BIALYSTOKER JEWS ENDURED IN THEIR HIDEOUTS.

Only the 10,000 Jews who hid away can understand the living hell they endured. Different killer squads searched every building, every hour, every day. Hideouts built for 20 people often contained 60. One could suffocate from overcrowding alone. Such circumstances caused adults to argue, and small children, not realising the gravity of the situation, could suddenly start to cry. Any noise could lead to a hideout being discovered. People's nerves were continually on edge, on tenterhooks. One wonders how any of us managed to endure such tension. Many couldn't. It became simply too much. In our hideout the Cukier family, father, mother, son and daughter-in-law, all poisoned themselves.

The Nazis had technology on their side. They had listening devices and sniffer dogs. On this second day they used them to extract 2000 Jews from hideouts. Some such as Yaacov Goldberg, the Director of the Judenrat's Provisions Office, were shot on the spot. Others were taken to an assembly point on Linas Hatzedek Street. Later that evening all the Jews collected there were herded to the Pietrasze field.

Several hundred Jews who had worked for high ranking Nazi officials and the S.S., and had temporarily sought refuge in the former carton box factory on Kupiecka Street, were transported from Bialystok to Grodno on the second day. From Grodno they were sent on to Lomza Prison in hermetically sealed vans. Some suffocated along the way. At Lomza a special contingent of seventy skilled tailors was chosen for Stutthof Concentration Camp. At Stutthof these tailors received warmer working conditions and more food. About 20 of them survived the war.

THE NAZIS ORDER A SMALL GROUP OF JEWS TO REPAIR THE SCORCHED FENCE AND TO BURY THOUSANDS OF MARTYRS.

There was a small group of Jewish slave labourers who continued to work for the Nazis. That second evening they were ordered to report to work the following morning. Some were made to repair burnt down sections of the ghetto fence. Others, who were horse and cart wagoners, were made to collect thousands of corpses from the city's streets and gardens and take them for burial.

THE NIGHT AFTER THE SECOND DAY OF SLAUGHTER.

At 6 p.m. the Nazis left the ghetto. When they left the continuous cannonade from outside the walls began again. Later that night, under cover of darkness, shadows started emerging from hideouts. They slithered along the ground to other buildings, looking for food, kerosene and matches. When entering neighbouring buildings, they often encountered or frightened other Jews who lived there or were there on similar missions. These Jews identified themselves and calmed each other down. They discussed Nazi activities of the day. They analysed why so many hideouts had been discovered. The Nazis had turned off the water and disconnected the electricity. Jews who needed water had to go to wells, and those who needed to cook had to use smoky stoves. Such stoves were recipes for capture. Countermeasures needed to be instituted. Jews collected water at night and they were told if possible to stop cooking. People who continued cooking did so in abandoned houses far removed from their own. During the second night surviving resistance fighters tried repeatedly to escape. They lost more colleagues and returned disheartened. Some other fighters tried to dig a tunnel under the ghetto fence. They were also unsuccessful.

THE SECOND DAY AT THE PIETRASZE FIELD.

At 2 p.m. on the second day mass murderer Friedel arrived at the Pietrasze field together with some S.S. officers. *"Get into rows,"* he yelled. The Jews started to panic. Nobody wanted to be in the front row. Some Nazis started shooting and the panic worsened until a ceasefire was called. The Jews were warned to calm down and line up in rows. If they didn't, they would all be shot. The Jews obeyed.

Some of the S.S. officers started inspecting the rows of Jews. Using the crooks of their sticks, they pulled younger, fitter ones out of the lines by the scruffs of their necks. These Jews were told they had been selected as slave labourers, and slave labourers they shall remain until their last drop of blood is spent. Those who begged to stay and die with their families were beaten black and blue and then forcefully taken as slave labourers anyway.

The selection continued until 6 p.m. 3000 young people, a few hundred women among them, were herded to one side of the field.

At the same time the other S.S. officers were loading the frail and elderly onto wagons. They were being taken to the cemetery. Jewish volunteer firemen had been forced to dig large pits there. The pits were two metres wide, ten metres long and three metres deep. When the first 200 Jews were delivered to the cemetery, mass murderer Friedel arrived in a car. He ordered that the Jews be lined up along the edges of the pits. He set the example by firing the first shot, and then his Nazi henchmen followed him with a hail of bullets. The dead fell into the pits. The wounded were pushed in after them. The bodies were then covered up with soil. Yaacov Lifszyc, the well-known former Chairman of the Merchant's Guild, was murdered in this way. Rafael Gutman and his wife saved themselves from this ordeal by swallowing poison before being taken to the cemetery. Gutman had been Engineer Barasz's secretary and was also a well-known author of Hebrew text books.

ISAAC MARKUS MANAGES TO RESCUE RABBI DR. ROZENMAN FROM THE PIETRASZE FIELD.

Rabbi Dr. Gedalja Rozenman was standing in the Pietrasze field at this time together with his wife and two daughters. The daughters had shaved off his beard to make him look younger and hopefully improve his chances of survival. They had been there for about two hours when Isaac Markus, the Commandant of the Judenrat's Law and Order Services Office, arrived with an S.S. officer. Markus still wielded some influence and he asked for the Rabbi and his family to be spared. Others implored Markus to help them and he managed to get some more reprieves. These people were taken back to the Judenrat building, where more than 50 Jews, still of use to the Nazis, were housed.

1200 CHILDREN ARE BROUGHT BACK TO THE GHETTO FROM THE PIETRASZE FIELD.

The same S.S. officers, who had selected the slave labourers, now ordered that all children aged ten years or less be sent back to the ghetto for care. This caused the parents of the children much anguish. They didn't want to entrust their children to murderers, but they were powerless to prevent it.

The 1200 children were taken to a building in Fabryczna Street opposite the Toz Hospital. They received good care there. Several dozen women were reprieved to look after them. These women, who did their best to care for the children, were sarcastically warned they better see the children miss out on nothing.

LIBERMAN, THE MANAGER OF THE GHETTO SHOE FACTORY, RESCUES 30 SHOEMAKERS FROM THE PIETRASZE FIELD.

On this second day Liberman, the Manager of the Ghetto Shoe Factory, came to the Pietrasze field with a Gestapo operative. He was looking for shoemakers to help pack the factory's plant and stock for transport. Hundreds begged to be given one of the 30 jobs. Anything to escape from this hell hole! From the men selected a few survived.

THE FIRST TRANSPORTEES FOR TREBLINKA ARE DISPATCHED FROM THE PIETRASZE FIELD.

Those who remained on the Petrasze field were now classified as 'unemployables.' They were taken to the railway station and packed into freight cars. Doors were boarded up and nailed shut behind them. They were gassed and cremated at Treblinka the following day.

THE THIRD DAY OF THE LIQUIDATION.

Once again, on the third morning, 800 Nazi killers arrived at the ghetto punctually. This time they brought axes, picks, saws and crowbars with them. They used these tools to tear down partitions where they thought Jews were hiding. Jews found were slaughtered instantly with the axes and picks.

300 Jews without water, electricity or hope simply surrendered. They were transported to Treblinka.

EIGHTY GHETTO FIGHTERS STAGED A HEROIC RESISTANCE.

80 ghetto fighters were hiding out in Jurowiecka Street near the fence. They were planning an armed breakout but before they could attempt it they were discovered. At 2 p.m. 100 S.S. killers surrounded their hideout. An intense battle ensued, a fight to the finish. The Jews fought valiantly, fiercely! They managed to resist for three hours and to kill several Nazis. But by then 70 fighters had been killed and the S.S. had overun their position. The last ten fighters succumbed to a hail of bullets and hand grenades. When the Nazis finally entered the bunker, they hacked at their victims' corpses with axes and picks. The memory of these brave fighters deserves to be hallowed.

On the third day more than 1000 Jews were discovered. Some were killed on the spot. The others were sent to Treblinka.

THE HORSE AND CART WAGONERS COLLECT MARTYR'S BODIES FROM THE GHETTO AND FROM PIETRASZE FIELD.

On the third day, the remaining Jewish wagoners started collecting bodies from the ghetto and Pietrasze field. These bodies were carted to the ghetto cemetery. Ukrainians were supervising this and insisted that unconscious Jews be treated as dead Jews. All the Jewish bodies should be carted and buried together. Some of the Jews regained consciousness on the carts and begged to be spared. The Ukrainians showed them no mercy and buried them alive.

FRIEDEL SHOOTS A JEW FOR NOT DIGGING A PIT NEATLY AND SYMMETRICALLY.

Friedel issued an order to employ more pit diggers. He wanted his pits dug neatly and symmetrically and returned every hour to see if this was being done to his satisfaction. On one occasion Friedel thought a digger's work was not sufficiently neat, so he pulled out a gun and shot the man dead. He then warned the other diggers that if their work was similar, their fate would be similar too.

THE GESTAPO ORDERS THE CREATION OF A NEW MINI GHETTO.

The Gestapo's next duty was to empty ghetto factories of their plant and stock as soon as possible. To do this some Jewish slave labourers had been spared. They would start work tomorrow, Thursday, August 19th 1943. Their first task was to build a fence around the Toz building and some adjoining houses. They would sleep in the mini ghetto while they were emptying out the factories.

THE THIRD NIGHT INSIDE THE GHETTO.

At 6 p.m. the Nazis left the ghetto and the customary cannonade began. Under cloak of darkness, Jews started emerging from hideouts and scurried about looking for food and water. When they met they talked about the terrifying events of the day. They praised the heroism of the resistance fighters. They lamented that more people had died. The situation in the hideouts was becoming progressively more desperate. Some Jews spent the night digging new hideouts, because they thought their current ones were no longer safe.

They felt a need to strive to survive, to expend blood, sweat and tears!

THE JEWS IN HIDING ESTABLISH A PASSWORD.

Can you imagine the fear felt by a ghetto Jew crawling down a dark broken street, or creeping through a dark abandoned building, searching for food and water? Such a Jew rebounds in horror at the slightest sound, in case his enemy has heard it. His first reaction when he stumbles across someone is ***'friend or foe - Jew, Nazi or Pole?'*** The Jews formulated the password "Tsk" to help them identify one another. If it was not forthcoming, better run for your life! A Polish looter would hand a Jew over to the Nazis. A Nazi would simply shoot him.

26 JEWS ARE BURNT TO DEATH IN A HIDING PLACE.

On the third night a fire broke out not far from the Judenrat building. It occurred in a two-storey building on Kupiecka Street near the Biala Stream. 26 Jews hiding in the building were incinerated. Nobody knew how the fire started. Jews wondered whether the Nazis lit it and whether they were planning to set fire to every building in the ghetto.

THE EMPTYING OF THE PIETRASZE FIELD.

By Wednesday August 18th 1943, the Pietrasze field was emptied of its Jews. Most were transported to Treblinka, the rest to Poniatowa and Majdanek near Lublin.

Earlier that morning, while 3000 Jews were still assembled there, an S.S. General from Markowczyna arrived at the field with some Gestapo officers. From the 3000 Jews he chose 100 able-bodied ones as slave labourers. At 12 noon the Jews were lined up in rows of five and herded to the railway station. The 100 slave labourers were forced with cattle prods into the front wagons of the train. The 2900 chosen to die were crowded like sardines into the 20 rear wagons. The wagons were then locked and sealed. Ukrainian guards sat on the roof of each wagon. They were armed with machine-guns. Their job was to shoot any Jew who tried to escape. Many Jews realised that to enter a wagon spelt certain death. Some of them made a last desperate effort to escape. They tried to disarm Nazi soldiers of their weapons. This diversion encouraged other Jews to jump off the train. But in a matter of seconds the bestial Ukrainians had opened fire and scores of Jews were wounded and killed. The remaining open wagon doors were quickly shut and sealed and the train left Bialystok in the direction of Warsaw.

THE UNBEARABLE CONDITIONS EXPERIENCED BY JEWS INSIDE THE WAGONS.

The Jews were jam-packed into the carriages. It was impossible to stand up freely or to breathe properly. To fall was to risk being trampled to death. The living had to walk on a carpet of the dead. Those who screamed added to their own asphyxia. The Ukrainians on the wagons' roofs were annoyed by the screaming. Their solution was to shoot down into the wagons and wound and kill more Jews. This led to more screaming, which led to more shooting, and the cycle repeated itself. Some daring young Jews tried to jump off the moving train. This evoked more machine-gun fire which claimed many victims. The few who survived the jump and the bullets still had obstacles to face. The Nazis had placed armed guards along the whole length of the railway line from Bialystok to Treblinka. The train came to a halt at Malkinia Station. From there a new railway line had been constructed to Treblinka. The last 20 wagons were uncoupled from the rest of the train and re-connected to the locomotive for Treblinka. The Jews selected for slave labour were in the front wagons, which remained attached to the original locomotive. At first they could hear the deafening cries and screams of their detached bretheren in the rear wagons. These faded out once the train for Treblinka headed off into dense forest.

The Nazi guards then turned their attention to the front carriages. Some had sections of walls missing where boards were damaged by Jews trying to escape. The Nazis decided to teach these Jews a lesson. Ten Jews were pulled off the train and shot dead. The rest were warned that if more boards were damaged they would be treated in the same way.

More guards were brought to the train to increase surveillance. New locks were fitted to the wagon doors. Once the train was deemed secure it was allowed to recommence the last 48 hours of its grisly journey. The Ukrainians re-mounted the wagons' roofs. They continued firing down into them, killing and wounding more Jews. Others died from lack of food and water. The living and dead were so crowded together, it was impossible to move without stepping on or over a dead body. It was impossible to sit without sitting down on one. Bladders and bowels were emptied inside the wagons. There was no other choice. The stench was ghastly. By the time the train arrived at its final destination, Poniatowa Concentration Camp near Lublin, many more prisoners had died. Motel Rubinstein and his eldest son were two of them. Rubinstein had been Principal of the Mendele School in Bialystok. His wife, the sister of well-known Bundist Jacob Pat, had been a popular teacher there. Mrs. Rubinstein had trouble coping emotionally with the Nazi occupation. She would have committed suicide on several occasions, if not for the efforts of close friends and admirers. Nobody knows what became of her. She was last seen alive alive inside the ghetto on Monday August 16th 1943.

When these Jews were off loaded at Poniatowa, they were inspected by Camp Commandant Obersturmfuhrer Tuman astride a white horse. This was the same Tuman, who had come to Bialystok on August 16th 1943 to help commence the liquidation of the ghetto. Tuman rode in and amongst his new charges. Those not to his liking he ordered shot.

THE FOURTH DAY OF THE LIQUIDATION.

On the fourth day the Nazis devised a new plan to help them capture hidden Jews. S.S. troops would enter a building for 30-60 minutes and conduct a thoroughly noisy search. Then they would create the impression they were all leaving, whereas in reality several silent spies stayed behind. If the spies heard a sound; a movement, a cough, or a voice; one of them would sneak out to gather reinforcements. In no time the building would be surrounded and re-invaded by S.S. troops. A loud call was made stating that it was known Jews were there. If the Jews failed to surrender, they would be dealt with on the spot. These tactics frightened many Jews and confused them into thinking they were lost no matter what. If they laid low the Nazis would throw hand grenades into various sections of the house. If the Nazis found the entrance to a bunker they would throw hand grenades into it. Many men, women and children were blown to pieces in this manner and those who survived were brutally beaten or shot on the spot. Those still alive were hustled off to Linas Hatzedek Street, loaded onto trucks, and taken straight to the railway station. There they were crammed into cattle trucks destined for Treblinka that night. More than 2000

Jews were processed this way on the fourth day, including a group of resistance fighters. A few resistance fighters managed to escape later that night by digging under the ghetto fence, but most who tried were shot dead during the attempt.

THE MURDERED HEROES OF CHMIELNA STREET.

At 12 noon on the fourth day, the Nazis attacked a Resistance Group cell hidden in an underground bunker on Chmielna Street. How the Nazis managed to discover this bunker remains a mystery, as its entrance was well camouflaged down a deep well. This bunker was extremely well stocked. Its occupants had plenty of food, water and ammunition. They had no need to go out at night. They could have hidden there for a long while. One theory was that Nazis had seen smoke emanating from the well at night, but others suggested the fighters had been denounced by an informer. The Germans attacked the bunker ferociously indicating they must have known the occupants were well armed.

First there was a sound of hobnailed boots. Then out of nowhere, a large number of heavily armed Nazi troops appeared. They all had rifles and plenty of hand grenades. Behind them were machine-gunners, the guns mounted up on motor vehicles. The young Jewish fighters were totally taken by surprise. Surrounded and beseiged, they didn't even have a few minutes in which to think. Powerless to defend themselves, their hearts seemed to stop from the fearful realisation that this was their end. The Nazis in contrast exploded into action with battlefield precision. There was a continuous hail of rifle fire, rapid bursts of machine-gun fire, and hand grenades going off all over the place. The battle was over as soon as it had begun. Young pale-faced Jewish boys and girls, with their hands held high, were marched away by Nazi troopers, but not before breaking out into a rendering chorus of revolutionary songs. At the corner of Jurowiecka and Kupiecka Streets, a high ranking Nazi officer recognised the popular shoemaker Berel Schatzman and pulled him away from the rest. Because of this Schatzman survived. Shortly afterwards a second Nazi officer picked out four more of the fighters and ordered them to accompany him. The young men decided to act out a farce. They started to mimic Nazis, but shouted out anti-Hitler slogans. They were gunned down in a crossfire of bullets. The disturbance acted as a cue for their colleagues. They started bolting in all directions. But the Nazis had machine-gunners strategically placed on elevated platforms. Within a few seconds the entire group was wiped out. The Nazis brought some horse-drawn carts and started throwing the bodies into them. One fighter Kucharewski, a seventeen year old, miraculously survived. He was the younger brother of Siomke Kucharewski, the resistance fighter who blew himself up in the secret weapons workshop at 3 Czysta Street. Kucharewski pleaded with the Nazis that he was still young and wanted to live. The Nazis replied by shooting several bullets into his head. Then his corpse was dumped into one of the carts along with the others.

AN UNDERGROUND HIDEOUT AT THE GHETTO CEMETERY.

Jewish gravediggers and firefighters, who were burying the corpses at the cemetery, thought up an amazing idea. They would dig a hideout in the cemetery. They took great care to conceal its entrance. It was big enough to shelter 30-40 people.

When Jewish wagoners collected corpses at the Pietrasze field they often recognised them. In some cases they recognised parents, siblings or children. The same was true for the grave diggers. Unimaginably grievous scenes took place. There were even cases of workers committing suicide.

THE FOURTH NIGHT OF THE LIQUIDATION.

By the end of the fourth day there were probably less than 2000 Jews left in the ghetto. They were distressed, in an absolute state of agony, hopelessness and despair. That night even the most daring were reluctant to leave hideouts. The few who did, and then only after midnight, realised that they had lost many of their remaining colleagues that day.

The few Jews, from Nowogrodzka and Jurowiecka Streets, who surfaced that night, met in the Judenrat garden. They exchanged the news of the day and advised each other how to prevent being caught. They also foraged for vegetables such as cucumbers and tomatoes. The Nazis had removed wagonloads of vegetables from the garden, but there were still some to be found.

It was decided that the best course of action was to sleep during the day and to cook and eat at night. In reality such measures were not very helpful. At best they only slowed down a little the Nazis' efforts to liquidate the ghetto.

TWO MORE MAJOR FIRES OCCUR INSIDE THE GHETTO.

At 2 a.m. that night two more major fires blazed inside the ghetto. Nobody could explain why they erupted. It was suggested that Nazis had lit them to smoke Jews out of hideouts.

THE FIFTH DAY OF THE LIQUIDATION.

On Friday August 20th 1943, the Nazis attacked the Jewish Hospital. They murdered the 200 patients and some doctors and nurses. Dr. Zvi Lukaczewski, the well-known Chief of the Linas Hatzedek Ambulance Service, was among the murdered.

The 200 in-patients were classified as either 'seriously ill' or 'fit to walk.' The 'seriously ill' ones were loaded onto wagons. The 'fit to walk' ones were made to march between the wagons. Gestapo Commandant Fritz Gustav Friedel insisted that this configuration be maintained all the way to the Zabia Street Cemetery. The patients knew well that they were embarking on their final journey. Their cries and screams, manifestations of their sufferings, were heart-wrenching. As was Friedel's usual manner, he insisted that all patients should stand upright beside the pits. He set the example for his men by picking up an automatic rifle and firing the first shot. His Ukrainian lackeys quickly followed suit. In a matter of minutes 200 fresh corpses were lying in the pits. One of these martyrs was Raya Leah Lew, the wife of Zionist activist Hersz Lew and the mother of Fishel Lew, the Chief Accountant of the Jewish Kehilla or Jewish Community Services in Bialystok.

After performing this dastardly deed the Nazi killers rested a while. Then it was time to reform into their killer groups of 10 men, and to recommence their normal duties throughout the ghetto. They entered houses. They conducted detailed searches for up to an hour. They departed but several silent spies lingered behind. On the fifth day only 200 Jews were dragged out of hideouts. Jews who were captured were taken to the cemetery where Friedel personally ordered their execution. Some were members of the Resistance Group, one of whom tried to personally attack Friedel, but was gunned down in the process. In all the fifth day yielded 400 victims, 200 from the hospital and 200 dragged out of hiding places.

THE FENCE AROUND THE MINI GHETTO.

The new mini ghetto was centred around the Toz building. Its fence was completed during the fifth day. Jews living in the mini ghetto enjoyed a degree of protection from the Gestapo. A bakery operated within its walls and food was freely available courtesy the Judenrat's Provisions Office. These 'lucky' Jews hoped to be able to retain these conditions, but their hopes were short-lived.

THE 1200 CHILDREN.

The 1200 children spared at the Pietrasze field were housed in reasonable conditions in Fabryczna Street opposite the Toz building. The Judenrat's Provisions Office ensured the children were well fed. And the Nazis granted reprieves to 20 women and a few physicians so that the children could be well cared for.

THE FIFTH NIGHT OF THE LIQUIDATION.

On the fifth night Jews from remaining hideouts met again in the Judenrat garden. They exchanged the day's news. They decided that yesterday's tactic of sleeping during the day had been the correct one. Thanks to it less Jews had been captured during the previous 24 hours. However, there was a new problem. Polish hooligans, who plundered the ghetto at night, had discovered the Jewish password. This struck fear in everyone's heart. ***"Were these Poles really looters or were they Nazi spies sent in to help flush us out?"*** Despite our fears, it is fair to say in most instances the Poles caused us no problems. But conditions in hiding continued to deteriorate.

THE SIXTH DAY OF THE LIQUIDATION.

On the sixth day, Saturday August 21st 1943, there were still more than 1000 Jews hiding out. These were hardened survivors with few children in among them. They were difficult to find. This enraged the Nazis and made them more brutal. Their anger was probably compounded by the fact that they thought there were even more Jews hidden away. They seemed to have forgotten that 5000 Jews had died in the ghetto. Now if Nazis suspected Jews were hiding in a building, they would demolish it completely. And after they were finished with the house, they dug up the yard and the vegetable garden. There were still 700 Jews in the mini ghetto. Many were slave labourers, who were helping to liquidate the ghetto's factories.

Close to 70 Jews were dragged out of hiding places on the sixth day. None were shown any mercy. They were killed on the spot. By 2 p.m. the Nazis had left the ghetto for the day.

THE SIXTH NIGHT OF THE LIQUIDATION.

The Nazis had left the ghetto four hours earlier than expected, but no Jew came out of a hideout while daylight persisted. After darkness fell, the braver ones came out. They met with fellow Jews and discussed the day's events. They learnt about the Jews in the mini ghetto. The most daring ones edged their way towards the mini ghetto. Noticing that the fence was not well guarded, they snuck in. Their fellow Jews were pleased to see them and supplied them with loaves of bread. This was much appreciated, because their only other food supply was vegetables from the Judenrat garden.

The few surviving members of the Resistance Group saw little point in its continued existence and disbanded it. Some became so dejected they committed suicide. Others decided to continue the fight and unsuccessfully attempted to escape on several more occasions.

THE REST DAY.

The Nazis declared Sunday August 22nd 1943 a rest day. The Jews were not lulled into any false sense of security. They remained in their hideouts all day. Again, under cloak of darkness, the most daring ones ventured out to the Judenrat garden. The news of the day was that a number of women and children were granted access to factories, where Jewish slave labourers were packing machines into shipping cartons. The men told the Gestapo that these were their wives and children. The Gestapo didn't believe them but granted the new arrivals protection anyway. The Gestapo now had these women and children in their clutches and knew they were doomed.

THE SECOND WEEK OF THE LIQUIDATION - THE SEVENTH DAY.

On Monday August 23rd 1943 400 Nazis entered the ghetto. They divided themselves into 80 brigades of five men. Each brigade was dispatched to another part of the ghetto. This change of tactics was because of the poor results of the prior two days. The brigades looked in rubbish tins for fresh garbage. They looked at kitchen stoves to see if they had been recently lit. They marked objects in a special way to help them ascertain whether they might be used or moved in the future

On the seventh day the Nazis captured 100 Jews. But Jews were quick to learn and adapt to the new tactics. They limited cooking to abandoned houses at nightime. They took great care to ensure that no smoke could be seen emanating from buildings. They set up a system of guards in case the Nazis changed tactics and decided to enter the ghetto at night.

TWO THOUSAND MORE JEWS ARE SENT TO PONIATOWA AND TREBLINKA.

While machines and merchandise were being packed for shipment in the factories, the Nazis used many more slave labourers than just the 700 who had passes to live in the mini ghetto. Seven days later the job was over and the extra workers were no longer needed. They were made to assemble on Kupiecka Street, together with the hundreds of other Jews, who had been living in the firemen's garage on Polna Street. These two groups, 2000 people in all, spent the night in the mini ghetto. At noon the next day they were led away to the station. There the Nazis divided them into two new groups, strong able-bodied men in one, and weak men, elderly men and women and children in the other. They were then loaded onto the train, the stronger men in the front wagons. The wagon doors were closed and sealed and the heavily guarded train set off in the direction of Warsaw. This train, like those before it, stopped at Malkinia Station. The rear wagons were detached and hooked onto a second locomotive, the train for Treblinka.

When these wagons arrived at Treblinka, the disorientated victims were quickly unloaded and forced, under duress, towards 'bath installations.' Those who were slow to respond were beaten to hurry them up. Once the Jews were inside the bath installations, which in reality were gas chambers, there was no longer any hope.

The wagons attached to the front of the train, carrying the able-bodied men, continued on to Poniatowa near Lublin. This leg of the journey took a couple of days, and a significant number of the men died along the way. Some were asphyxiated by the overcrowding, some died of dehydration. Others were shot by the Ukrainian guards sitting on the wagons' roofs.

At Poniatowa skilled tradesmen, mostly tailors and shoemakers were separated from the rest. The remaining 1000 were shipped to a work camp at Blizyn a few days later. Blizyn was no picnic. It was every bit as hard as a concentration camp. During the ensuing winter months, hundreds died there from malnutrition and other illnesses.

THE EIGHTH DAY OF THE LIQUIDATION.

On the eighth day, Tuesday August 24th 1943, the Nazis continued their search for hidden Jews. They were always trying out new tactics, but this day even the newest of tactics failed. Not one Jew was found.

On this day the Gestapo shot Samuel Finkel's son, the manager of the large Oskar Steffen Factory. When Steffen was told of Finkel's death, he expressed his profoundest regrets. He thought it must have been a terrible mistake. Finkel's murder disturbed the hundreds of Jews living inside the mini ghetto. They all thought the Gestapo would never touch Finkel.

During the last week the horse and cart wagoners had been busily collecting the thousands of murdered corpses lying everywhere. They took them to the ghetto cemetery for burial. But no matter how quickly they took them, more always seemed to replace them. The number of dead bodies seemed to multiply with each passing day.

INSIDE THE MINI GHETTO.

The 700 Jews living in the mini ghetto led a harrowing existence. They were continually harassed. German patrols would check their passes every few hours. The Nazis had warned Engineer Barasz ad nauseam that if a Jew was found without a pass, it would spell immediate death for all of them. And despite such warnings, there were still Jews who could no longer bear to be in hiding. They sneaked out of their hideouts and entered the mini ghetto.

The horse and cart wagoners, who delivered factory machines and merchandise to the station, reported they were loaded onto carriages marked 'Lublin - Poniatowa.' Everyone in the mini ghetto dreamed of being sent to Poniatowa. They knew it was a work camp. To be sent there might be to survive a little longer, perhaps until liberation! In these dark hopeless times, when every day spelt doomsday, people only wanted to survive a few more months. A few months might be enough to survive the war. All hopes and aspirations were based on the fact that the Soviets had launched a massive offensive. This took place between the 5th and the 10th July 1943. It was successful and Orel, Belgorod, Kharkov and Bryansk were rapidly recaptured. But for the Jews of Bialystok this was all too late. Their thinking had been wishful and their wishes would never materialise. The mini ghetto was liquidated soon after, and Jews, who thought themselves lucky to be transported to Poniatowa, met a similar end.

Notables still living in the mini ghetto included Rabbi Dr. Gedalja Rozenman and his wife and two daughters; Engineer Barasz and his wife and son; Isaac Markus and his wife and children; Mr. H. Liman and his wife and son; Dov Subotnik; and nearly all the other factory directors, their assistants, some foremen, and their families.

THE NINTH DAY OF THE LIQUIDATION.

On the ninth day, Wednesday August 25th 1943, only 200 Nazis entered the ghetto. There were probably 500-600 Jews hiding there, but the Nazis thought there were more. Every day the Nazis tried new tactics to flush Jews out. They started measuring internal dimensions of rooms and attics to see if they corresponded with external dimensions. If they thought there was a discrepancy, they looked for partitions or double walls. Their success was very limited. They found less than 50 Jews, who were mainly shot on the spot. The fact that fewer hunters were used offered the Jews no respite. Frustrated by their lack of success, the Nazis would sit and rest in a building for hours. Dozens of Jews might be hiding immediately beneath them. It is not hard to imagine how such Jews felt. Soon after one Nazi brigade left it was not uncommon for another to arrive and also stay several hours. Jews in hiding, who survived such stresses, felt they had died a thousand deaths.

TWELVE HUNDRED CHILDREN ARE REMOVED FROM THE GHETTO.

The 1200 children were taken from the ghetto at this time. They were farewelled by Dr. M. Katzenelson and more than

20 Jewish women carers. The wives of Engineer Barasz and Dr. Beilin were two of these carers. S.S. officers escorted the children to the train. They were locked in cattle trucks and railed to Theresienstadt in Czechoslovakia. On arrival there, they were placed in separate barracks. Other inmates were denied access to them. To attempt to contact them was to risk death.

A Jewish lady from Czechoslovakia, Pauline Fabian, worked as a hygienist with the children after they arrived at Theresienstadt. Fabian was liberated after the war, and it is from her that we have this account of the children.

When the children arrived at Theresienstadt, their hair was badly infested with lice. Fabian wanted to shave their heads, but the children argued against this. They told her if she was really Jewish, she would know that Jews have their heads shaved before being gassed. Pauline Fabian knew nothing about gas chambers. She had been a long term resident at Theresienstadt and had never heard of them. She couldn't follow what the children were saying, and repeatedly tried to reassure them that they were worrying over nothing. Later on Fabian learnt the truth and realised that the children's worst fears had been well founded.

In the end it mattered little what the children wanted. Their heads were forcibly shaved. The children remained in Theresienstadt for three months. The Nazis used Theresienstadt as an advertising model for their concentration camps. The children certainly had a better life there than they would have had elsewhere. There was even some talk of exchanging them for captured German civilians. But this was short-lived and the children and their adult carers were deported to Auschwitz instead. On arriving at Auschwitz, the children and their carers were made to form five columns and were then herded straight to the gas chambers.

A hideous incident occurred after the children were gassed. A Jewish slave labourer was about to place the gassed body of a ten-year-old girl into a crematorium oven, when the child begged him not to do so. She was still alive. The Jew failed to heed her plea. He threw her into the oven alive. The whole camp was ablaze with this story for several days. The Jew, who performed the heinous act, was driven insane by the gossip. In a fit of madness he was murdered by S.S. guards and his body cremated.

It is important to realise that this tragic episode was not unique. There were other reported instances of gassed children, who showed signs of life when about to be cremated.

THE DIFFICULT CONDITIONS EXPERIENCED BY THE REMAINING JEWS IN HIDING.

Very few Jews were discovered during the second week. Nevertheless there was no respite in the grimness of everyone's mind. We were all convinced that the Nazis would stay until the last one of us was captured.

Our situation, with respect to food and nourishment, worsened every day. We were able to prepare flour at night, but it was risky to bake it into bread. There were daredevils who risked everything. These Jews would sneak out to a deserted building at night and bake bread. To return the next night would be to pay for it with your life. The Nazis could detect an aroma where bread had been baked at night. They would leave spies there until the bakers returned.

Two weeks in hiding stretched everyone's limits with respect to exhaustion and despair. Conditions were filthy and many of us started contracting lice and disease. For such reasons some Jews left hideouts and entered the mini ghetto. In the short term their living conditions would be better.

By the end of the second week there were probably 500 Jews still in hiding.

The third week arrived. Rumour now had it that the mini ghetto would be liquidated any day. The Jews there had made themselves redundant. All machinery and merchandise had been shipped out of factories. All corpses had been cleared off streets. There was nothing else to do.

THE MINI GHETTO IS LIQUIDATED.

At the end of the third week, the mini ghetto was liquidated. Its 1200 occupants were ordered to assemble to be transported to Lublin-Poniatowa. The number 1200 represented the original 700 inhabitants and 500 extra who had sneaked into the mini ghetto from hideouts.

When these Bialystoker Jews arrived in Poniatowa, they were put to work in factories. Conditions were not too bad, and for a short while they fared better than Jews in other camps. However, on November 3rd 1943, the 15,000 Jews at Poniatowa, with thousands of Bialystokers among them, were marched out of the camp to a large field, where Camp Commandant Obersturmfuhrer Tuman ordered them shot dead. The camp orchestra played Strauss waltzes to camouflage the gunfire. Virtually every surviving leader of Bialystok's Jewish Community perished at this time.

THE FOURTH WEEK OF THE LIQUIDATION.

During the fourth week, the search for the several hundred Jews in hiding continued unabated. We all experienced sorrow, resignation and despair, following the liquidation of the mini ghetto. There was no longer a place to sneak into for a piece of bread and a gossip. We were now totally on our own. Some of us became apathetic, lethargic, indifferent about discovery, but others remained strong and determined to continue the struggle. The strong ones encouraged us and strengthened our resolve. They argued that we needed to search for food at night with a renewed sense of energy so that we could store enough food for a prolonged period of hiding. New stoves were built in hidden places where smoke could be concealed. This was no easy task. But the will to survive can sometimes overcome seemingly impossible obstacles. In a short while the stoves were constructed and people started baking rolls and cooking meals to help sustain their families.

THE LIQUIDATION IS OFFICIALLY ENDED.

On September 16th 1943, the liquidation ended. That night no shots were fired into the ghetto. At daybreak a new contingent of Nazi guards arrived to commence duty. These 40 men were much older than their predecessors. They set up headquarters in Jurowiecka Street, in the building that had housed the Jewish Workers' Employment Offices. These new guards patrolled the streets in pairs. If they heard a sound emanating from a building, one of them would run back to headquarters to fetch reinforcements. The larger group would come back to hunt for hidden Jews. More often than not they found some Jews, but because these guards were older and sometimes infirm, the Jews had a better chance to escape.

CHAPTER 9.

FROM HIDING OUT IN THE GHETTO TO SACHSENHAUSEN.

JEWISH GOODS AND PROPERTY ARE REMOVED FROM THE GHETTO.

After September 16th 1943, the ghetto was divided into two distinct parts. A large gate was built across the end of Kupiecka Street at Jurowiecka Street. Along Jurowiecka Street windows were boarded up, and high fences were built across Smolna, Ciepla and Fabryczna Streets on the north-east side, and across Zamenhowa Street on the south-west side. Streets to the north-east of Jurowiecka Street, like Ciepla and Fabryczna, were now cut off from streets to the south-west, such as Bialystoczanska, Polna and Nowy Swiat. This was done to prevent Jews hiding on one side of Jurowiecka Street from contacting bretheren on the other side. It was also hoped that if they tried to do so the barrier would make them easier to catch.

Next the Germans started removing Jewish property from the ghetto. This task was outsourced to a private German firm. It employed a Polish foreman who supervised slave labourers from Russia, Ukraine and Belarus. Work began in the smaller north-east section of the ghetto, in Fabryczna and Ciepla Streets.

This theft of Jewish possessions was performed with German planning and precision. During the first week soft goods were taken. During the second week furniture was loaded onto trucks and taken to warehouses. The better items were sent back to Germany, the others were sold to Poles.

A month later, on October 16th 1943, the whole of the north-eastern part of the ghetto had been emptied of Jewish property. Nothing had been left behind. Even old clothes hidden in attics for years were removed. Stables no longer contained as much as a piece of firewood. All books, photographs and documents were incinerated in the backyards. The empty dwellings were squeaky clean. They gave the impression of having been specially prepared so that new occupants could move in.

LIFE IN THE HIDEOUTS BECOMES EVEN MORE DIFFICULT.

The few hundred Jews still in hiding had a most difficult month. Workers were on site the whole day and they could hear the slightest sound. These workers had no sympathy for the Jews. Indeed they relished helping the Nazis capture the last remnants of them. Whenever they discovered Jews they handed them straight over to the Nazis. For the Jews such discovery was usually synonymous with death.

At nightime the Nazi patrols took to wearing soft soled shoes. This made them harder to hear in the dark and helped them sneak up on Jews. One night some Jews went to the Judenrat garden to collect water from the pond. They failed to realise that Nazis were there until they were shot at. Three of the Jews were seriously wounded. Others no longer wished to venture out at night, not even to collect water!

In the month from September 16th - October 16th 1943, the Soviet slave labourers helped the Nazis find 200 Jews. Initially Jews were imprisoned locally, but when groups of 50 or more were gathered together they were transported to

Nowosholke. Those sent to Nowosholke were never seen or heard of again.

From September 16th less Nazis guarded and patrolled the ghetto wall. The few remaining resistance fighters exploited this situation. Under cover of darkness they escaped over the ghetto wall. A number even managed to survive the war.

Some of the furniture had been used to disguise the entrances to hideouts. Removal of this furniture constituted a serious threat. The Jews were forced to fashion new entrances to existing hideouts or to move to new hideouts. Some Jews would remain sealed in their hideouts for a week at a time. The Soviet slave labourers had Sundays off. This gave the Jews a small window of opportunity to empty out last week's rubbish and refuse and to prepare food and water for the coming week.

When the problem of removed furniture was solved, a new one arose. Winter arrived earlier than normal and it snowed every night. Jews who ventured out looking for food and water would now leave footprints in the snow. The conditions for survival were continually deteriorating, and people started hoping and praying for miracles.

POLES BETRAY THEIR JEWISH FRIENDS.

Eight weeks after the liquidation began there were still a few hundred Jews hiding in the ghetto. As conditions deteriorated some of them sneaked out to make contact with Polish Christian "friends." There were instances where Poles agreed to hide Jews in their homes provided they bring valuables with them. But when the Jews arrived with their families, the Gestapo was waiting for them there. Many Poles turned against old Jewish friends in this way.

THE JEWS BEGIN TO DAMAGE THEIR OWN BUILDINGS.

Now that the buildings around Fabryczna and Ciepla Street were clean and empty a new problem presented itself. What if the Nazis settled new enemies into these houses? Such people would present as great a danger as the Nazis themselves. We decided on a plan to make the buildings cold and uninhabitable. We ripped out our own window frames and damaged the ovens. Other Jews did likewise. It was important to duplicate this damage in adjacent buildings, ones that didn't contain hideouts. This work was time consuming and dangerous, because it created noise. It had to be done at night, when hopefully no-one would see or hear it.

WE ARE DISCOVERED.

On the morning of Hoshana Rabba, the seventh day of Sukkot (the Feast of Tabernacles), we lay fatigued and sleepy, silently hidden away in our shelter. Suddenly there were heavy footsteps on the double floor above us. There was no time to think, no time to figure things out. Above us hammers and hatchets were pulling up floor boards, quickly, effortlessly, as easy as plucking feathers from a chicken. We were underneath it, half naked in a basement bunker. Nine of us, my family of four, my brother-in-law Joshua Binder with his wife and two children, and my son's best friend Nahum Kozak. We had worked hard for nights before. We had built ourselves a reserve bunker. Fearing the worst we now shoved ourselves into it, but we were too late. There was no time to close the opening behind us and disappear completely.

After the double floor above us was ripped up, an older Gestapo officer lowered himself down towards the entrance of our reserve bunker. He was shouting and shooting as he edged his way towards us. He demanded that we surrender and come out. Even here we had our ounce of luck. We had dug the opening into the reserve bunker in a zigzag fashion. It shielded us from the Gestapo killer's bullets. The shells lodged themselves in the bunker's walls.

Another Nazi murderer stood on guard on the street outside our house. The rest of the house was surrounded by Soviet slave labourers. These Christian workers had been searching our house for Jewish treasures and they must have heard something, perhaps a rustle, perhaps a cough! They went straight to the Nazis to report that Jews were hiding out in the building.

Disregarding the fact that our house was completely surrounded my son Samuel; my twenty-three year old daughter Nehama; my brother-in-law Joshua Binder and his ten year old son Israel; and my son's friend Nahum Kozak; made a dash for it. They broke out through a disguised exit and ran down the street. The Nazis shot at them and the Soviet slave labourers chased after them. My son Samuel and his friend Nahum Kozak were very nimble and knew every nook and cranny in the neighbourhood. This helped them escape. My brother-in-law Joshua Binder was not so lucky. He collected a bullet while he was wrenching himself out of our concealed shelter and he started to haemorrhage. He ran a short distance to the burnt out house of a local locksmith, then fell down in a pool of blood. Nehama and Israel hid themselves in some burnt out houses. Only four of us remained in the bunker, me; my wife Chaika; my wife's sister Hannah Binder; and my niece Hadassah Binder.

The Nazi killers were outraged by the boldness shown by the escapees. They shouted at us to get out of the bunker or they would throw hand grenades into it. My wife, my sister-in-law, and my niece crawled out of the bunker. I decided to remain behind, hidden by some of its contents.

Two Nazis delivered my wife, her sister, and our niece to a detention centre on Jurowiecka Street, where all three were interrogated as to who was hiding in our bunker. From the information gleaned and the number of known escapees, it was concluded that I might still be hiding there.

After the Nazi killers left I thought about trying to escape, but it seemed futile because our house was completely surrounded by Soviet slave labourers. Shortly afterwards the two Nazis, who had detained my wife, her sister, and our niece, returned to look for me. One of them lowered himself into the basement; the other stayed on guard outside. The one in the basement had a revolver in his right hand and a torch in his left one. He put the flashlight down and started rummaging through our stores. Finding something he liked, he yelled to his companion, *"These Jewish vermin had good stuff here."* He then threw something, I know not what, up to his friend.

I was only a few steps away from this killer, and could see and hear everything. My heart was pounding and I was drenched in cold sweat. I envisaged my future as a matter of seconds. Then the Nazi saw me. He seemed as shocked as I was. The items, which he had intended to plunder, dropped out of his hands. He was quick, however, to regain his composure. He called up to his companion that he had captured a Jew.

I left the bunker with my captor still behind me. His companion ordered me to lie face down on the ground. Once I obliged he started to interrogate me. He wanted to know why I had continued to hide when I knew that to do so was a capital offence. He chattered continuously. He told me he had never shot anyone - that Bialystoker Jews sent to Lublin to work were very happy there - that it was a terrible mistake to hide out - that it would not hold me in good stead - and that now I would not be sent to Lublin. Then he played the complete naive fool, insulting my intelligence by telling me how much I might have earned working in Lublin the past nine weeks.

I told him I had always been a working man. *"What you see in front of you is everything I have accumulated after many years of hard labour and economy. I could not bring myself to leave it all behind."* He looked at me noddingly. Then he enquired whether I had money or a gold watch. *"If you do you should give it to me,"* he said, *"because if you don't the Gestapo will confiscate it anyway."*

All this happened while I was still in a prone position on the ground. I was like that for more than an hour. Meanwhile the Nazi who had found me was emptying out our bunker. He went back and forth, emerging each time with arms laden with goods. Eventually he told his companion that the bunker had been cleaned out. The Nazis then ordered me to stand up. They informed me I was under arrest and warned me if I tried to escape they would shoot me. They marched me from my bunker to the detention centre in Jurowiecka Street. The scene was straight out of a horror story, deserted, desolate, desperate! Bialystok was a giant cemetery. I imagined I could hear hordes of Jewish souls wailing. They were lamenting the unimaginable degree of Jewish destruction.

At the detention centre, I was thrown into an empty cell. Its emptiness tore at my heart. I took it to mean my nearest and dearest ones were already dead. I stayed there for several hours before a Nazi threw me a morsel of bread. I asked him if he knew what became of the women from our hiding place. He told me they had been taken to the prison.

That night in the detention cell was a nightmare. My mind was a racetrack of thoughts. My whole life flashed by in front of me. On the wall of my cell there were hundreds of inscribed Jewish names with dates, presumably being when these poor souls spent their final hours here.

All these names are now forgotten save for one, that of Gershoni, the son-in-law of Chaikil Olian, who sold textiles in Ciepla Street. Gershoni was a popular leader of the services in our synagogue.

At 10 o'clock the next morning I was taken to Gestapo Headquarters at Ostrowski's Hotel on Sienkiewicza Street. We passed some German civilians on the way. They looked at my escorts and asked, *"Who is this murderer?"* The guards remarked that I was a recently captured Jew from the ghetto. The civilians offered some 'friendly' advice. *"You should finish him off here and now,"* they said.

IN THE GESTAPO PRISON.

At Gestapo Headquarters I was taken into a courtyard where, for 2 hours, I was made to stand facing a wall. Then I was thrown into an empty basement dungeon. I saw some of my sister-in-law's belongings strewn over the floor. There was also a pair of socks and in a corner, a ten dollar bill. My head started pounding. I convinced myself that my family had been led away from here to be shot. The Belarus Gestapo, who had followed me into the cell, picked up everything off the floor.

A few hours later the door opened again and two Polish prisoners were shoved in. They were farmers. One was about 50. The other one, a particularly sturdy fellow, looked 35. I asked them what they were doing here. The older man had been accused of using a plank to smuggle people and horses, partisans included, onto a ferry. He told the Gestapo the plank didn't belong to him. It was there for everyone to use. The Nazis were not impressed by his explanation. He told me he had been a wealthy farmer, who loathed Bolsheviks and collectivism. When the Germans came, he was pleased to see them. He welcomed them with open arms containing flowers and had never been disloyal to them. The younger Pole had a different story. He was in dispute with some neighbours over the ownership of a piece of land. They decided to have their revenge on him. They told the Gestapo he had murdered two German gendarmes during the Nazi handover of Bialystok to the Soviets in 1939. The Germans had detained him in Knyszyn for a week, and tortured him mercilessly. Then they brought him here. *"These accusations are not true,"* he said. *"I am the victim of cruel and malicious lies."*

The two Poles were nervous and fidgety. They paced up and down the cell. They saw some red stains on the cement floor. It drove them crazy. They knelt down and studied it more closely. *"Its human blood,"* they said. This discovery was a cue to pray. *"Oh good Lord please do not allow us to be brutally murdered here. If we have to die please show us some mercy. Allow us to be shot so that we can die quickly without suffering."*

During this performance the door opened, and a young blond fellow, about 25 years of age, was shoved into the room. This chap started cursing loudly. He protested that there were too many Jews here. He began to scream he hates Jews. He didn't want to look at them, let alone be in the same room as them. He begged the Gestapo officer, an obese lump in civilian clothes, to put him into another cell. The Gestapo man calmed him down. He told him I was the only Jew in the room. The young man complained that he had been accused of being a Jew travelling on false Aryan documents, and that he had even been checked to see if he was circumcised. He looked Jewish, and I thought he might have been a Jewish collaborator who had been planted in our cell to spy on us.

A JOURNEY THROUGH THE RUINED STREETS OF BIALYSTOK.

At dusk, all four of us were handcuffed and dragged out of our basement dungeon. We were ordered by our guards onto a truck already containing ten Belarus peasants, who were alleged partisans. The truck started moving down Suraska Street towards the open plaza. I was certain this journey would be my last.

The streets were still and empty. Dead like a cemetery! There was no Jew to be seen, only destruction; as far as the eye could see. My thoughts drifted back in time. I thought of streets teeming with Jewish life. I thought about happy little Jewish children, a comfort to their parents, standing on corners, playing in yards, singing Jewish songs. They were our future - future students and professionals - future workers, builders and merchants. Our Jews were hard working, honest and diligent! They made homes, grew families, built businesses, created workplaces. I remembered the workers - the locksmiths - the carpenters - the shoemakers - the tinsmiths - the hairdressers - the weavers - the lady cloth inspectors - the shopkeepers. I remembered the thinkers - the religious ones - the Hebrew scholars - the Yiddishists - the graduates - the free thinkers - the dreamers - the crusaders - the right wingers - the left wingers. I warmed inwardly as I thought about the players who loved to entertain us - the actors - the singers - the sports people. Together they made a nation - the living organism of a worldly people!

I remembered how I always used to watch them, all the time - daytime, nightime, weekdays, Sabbaths, holidays, Holy Days! I watched them all bustling - the happy and the dejected - the toiling and the weary - the wealthy ones and the domestics - the Hassidim and the Mitnagdim - the men and the women - the young and the old. They would rush to and disappear into prayer houses - the Great Synagogue - the smaller Hassidic Synagogues - the houses of study - the minyans (the quorums of ten men). I was reminded how, in these ravaged houses on these empty streets, our dear mothers and grandmothers celebrated the Sabbath and the Holy Days. At these times homes were spotless and fragrant. Tables were beautifully prepared. Lit candles cast a divine glow.

I was in a trance, a daydream! My eyes were looking for those wondrously honest Jews from the Piaskower Synagogue; Reb Simon Zelig Charnowski; Reb Samuel Elkes; Rabbi Eckstein; Reb Israel Meir Rubinstein; Reb Mordechai Levinson; Reb Isaac Jajchmenik; Reb Zelig Tartatzki; and the Makowski and Najdus brothers; to mention just a few. Then suddenly I returned back to the present. I had been looking for them, but of course they were gone. They were dead and gone. The city was a cemetery. The prayer says **"Hear O**

Israel," but there was no Israel. Everywhere was void. Everyone was dead!

The Nazi criminal from Belarus next to me in the truck interrupted my train of thought. He fired a series of anti-semitic questions at me. *"Jew, why did you hide for such a long time? Jew, why do you all like to hide gold? Jew, why are you all Bolsheviks?"* I failed to reply; so he thumped my head and shoulders with his rifle butt. These wounds troubled me for nearly two months.

The truck stopped. I found myself in a yard surrounded by a high walled fence. The Nazi criminals spoke to each other. From their conversation I made out we had arrived at our destination, the inside of the Bialystok Prison. A spark of hope reignited itself. Perhaps we won't be shot just yet? I felt happier for a moment.

INSIDE THE BIALYSTOK PRISON.

We were unloaded off the truck and searched by Polish guards. I was then sent to spend the night alone in a cell. The next morning I was moved into a larger cell with five other Jews. One was Nahum Karp, a former merchant who I knew well. Karp told me that my wife, her sister, and my niece, had all been brought to the prison yesterday evening. I was encouraged. They might be still alive. Karp mentioned that 100 Bialystoker Jews had been brought here from the Pietrasze field during the first days of the liquidation. *"These Jews have been here for nine weeks,"* he added, *"but Jews brought after them have not been so lucky!"* The Jews brought later were held prisoner until 40-50 had been collected. Then they were loaded, lightly clothed, onto a black truck at dawn. The truck returned half an hour later with the prisoners' clothing. The prisoners had been forced to remove all garments before being shot. I felt discouraged again. For a moment I wished my suffering would end. But then I thought of my children again and drew hope from the fact that we might all survive.

One day ran into the next. Each morning, after 5 a.m., keys would rattle in the locks of our doors. It was a signal. The criminals were coming to collect a few more Jews. To be taken was a death sentence. We did our best to calm each other down. We cuddled, we kissed, and we cried. That was our way of saying good-bye.

Our daily rations were minimal, 130 grams of bread and four cups of watered-down soup. And despite this, longer standing inmates gave away part of their rations to more recent arrivals. This was because the arrivals were more poorly nourished and their comrades didn't want them to starve to death in the prison. A number of the longer serving inmates worked as slave labourers in the town during the day. They were provided with extra rations. Sometimes they brought some of the extra food back to the prison, but even if they got it past the Polish guards, there was no guarantee they could get it to us. They would have to beg the Polish guards a favour and these leeches would only ever deliver a fraction of what they were given. Guards would offer to buy the last shirt off a prisoner's back for some bread. There were cases where inmates lost their shirts, but the promised piece of bread never eventuated.

Some of the longer standing prisoners were well-known to me. There was Bunim Farbsztejn, the leader of the Agudat Israel Religious Party; Hersz Sofer, a well-known shoe merchant, and his son, and son-in-law Elkes; Mottel Weinstein, a popular Fire Chief; Granowich a tailor and his fifteen year old son; the editor Yudel Gurewich; and one of the Chwat brothers, an iron merchant.

Every day more Jews were caught and brought to the prison. Some were hiding inside the ghetto. Others were living on Aryan papers outside the ghetto, and had been denounced by Poles. Once the Gestapo interrogated them and checked they were circumcised, they were gone. Such Jews tended to be tortured prior to imprisonment. Engineer Sztupler, the son of Michael Sztupler, was one of them. He married a Christian woman, who had hidden him. A trusted Pole then turned them over to the Gestapo. Sztupler was taken prisoner together with his wife and their one year old child.

Ten days passed and 80 more Jews arrived. I wondered whether the Nazis would come for us in the morning. They had more than enough Jews to fill up two death trucks.

After two weeks the number of Jews captured rose to 120. We were very nervous and restless. Each dawn we expected to be taken out and shot. There was the occasional optimist among us, who suggested the Nazis had stopped murdering Jews. *"They are taking such a terrible beating on the Russian front they need extra workers!"*

INFORMATION ABOUT MY CHILDREN.

I asked newly captured Jews whether they had seen my children. I struck gold with Moshe Zubowski. Zubowski had been captured in a burnt-out house on the corner of Ciepla and Nowogrodzka Streets. On the night of our capture the children went to his hideout and searched for its entrance. At first Zubowski thought they were Nazis and everyone kept still and quiet. Then they heard Yiddish spoken above them. They opened the entrance, saw our children, and invited them into the bunker. They discussed the news of the day. The children were hungry and lightly dressed and asked for food and clothes. *"We fed them and gave them some shoes,"* Zubowski told me. *"They stayed with us till midnight. Then they decided to leave."* This pepped me up. It gave me extra courage with which to endure the expectation of death each dawn.

By the end of October 1943 the number of Jews captured had risen to more than 250. The most recent arrivals included choir director Samuel Portnoy's brother and his wife and daughter; Fainsod, a glass and mirror merchant; Aliahu Czechocki, the shoe merchant, his wife, two daughters and his elderly mother; Karp the grocer's wife and her only son; and Lew, the furrier, and his son.

I SEE MY CHILDREN.

On the fifth Sabbath of my incarceration, I was standing by my cell window, looking at the prison gates. The gates opened and my son Samuel, my daughter Nehama, and my son's best friend, Nahum Kozak, were all brought in. I was overcome by nerves. I became agitated. It was difficult for me to speak. But somehow I drew on inner strength and my senses came back to me. I started to yell. I called out their names. My daughter heard and noticed me first. She was trembling from emotion. Then my son broke down and started crying convulsively. I watched them shoved into an office where they were thoroughly searched. Then they were led away to solitary cells.

I begged the prison guards to put my daughter in a cell with her mother and to bring the boys to us. When my son Samuel entered our cell and saw me, he collapsed into my arms and wept incessantly. It was difficult to calm him down. After some time he composed himself and told us how he had spent the last month.

Samuel ran from our hideout, with a gang of Belarus workers in hot pursuit. Because he knew every nook and cranny in the ghetto, he was successful in losing them. He hid himself in a large garbage can until darkness fell. Then he cautiously made his way back to our hideout. Fortune favoured him and both his sister and his best friend were waiting for him there. There had been no time to specify a particular meeting place, but fate had dragged all three of them back to our former hideout. The hideout had been well-stocked with food and clothing, but now it was empty. The situation was hopeless. They needed food and water. The ghetto had been liquidated for nine weeks and all houses in our section had been emptied of their entire contents. The children were forced to try to access the other side of the ghetto. There the clean-up was still incomplete. There was a chance of finding food. All three of them were fired upon, while hopping the three metre high fence, but fortunately nobody was hit. On the other side they looked for Zubowski's hideout, found it, and got a meal. After leaving Zubowski's they came across a deserted hideout at 3 Chmielna Street and managed to conceal its entrance, better than it had been before. Perhaps they could hide out there until liberation. If it were not for mean-spirited Polish criminals, they might well have succeeded and been alive today. Some Poles were looting the building and one of them discovered the hideout. The Pole was startled at first, but recovered his composure quickly. He told them he was a friend of the Jews and would return soon with some bread. The children believed the brigand. He returned fifteen minutes later, but together with the Gestapo. The three children were cornered, tragic victims of yet another example of Polish collaboration.

I SAY GOODBYE TO MY SON.

On Sunday October 31st 1943, we were advised that Jews who were captured during the previous five weeks would be shipped out tomorrow. A sombre gloom spread over us. Some people began to weep, the believers started to pray. They recited psalms and confessional prayers for the dying. People embraced and begged each other forgiveness for past offences. I held my son tightly and he did likewise. I told him not to worry about us. He should only try to save himself. *"If an opportunity to escape arises, grab it! Only survivors will be in a position to avenge this tragedy which has befallen our people."*

THE SELECTION.

That night none of us slept. When dawn finally broke, guards started patrolling the corridors. They told us the 100 Jews who had spent 11 weeks here were lucky today. They had been given the day off work. This news only served to increase our anxiety.

At noon all Jewish men were ordered outside. This included the 100, who had been brought here from the Petrasze field 11 weeks earlier. We were ordered to stand in the cold for a couple of hours, in rows of five. Our teeth began to chatter, partly from the bitter cold, partly from the icy fear enveloping us. The prison gates opened and an elegant car drove in. It stopped, and five tall and robust men stepped out of it. They were dressed in civilian clothes. They wandered up and down all the rows staring at us. They stopped at individuals and addressed them. They seemed interested in younger men; men who looked less than 35 years of age. They questioned them as to their trades. Most said they were carpenters. From 200, 80 were selected. My son was one of them. This group was set aside from the others.

The inspectors left the prison yard. Warden Rode, the governor of the prison, addressed us. He told us all was well, we were going to be employed. Some of us would be sent to Germany to work, together with our wives and children. The rest would remain and join the prison workforce. Those who were chosen for the prison workforce were sent upstairs, to the third floor, where the 100 men from the Petrasze field had been held. The rest of us were directed back to our own cells, wherefrom prisoners were taken to be shot. My beloved son ran into our cell to say good-bye to me. But before I could embrace him, the prison guards had dragged him away from my outstretched arms. This time we were separated forever.

FRIEDEL COMES TO SEE US OFF.

Despite the fact we had spent a sleepless night and were suffering total exhaustion, none of us slept the next night either. We were too much on edge. The rattle of prison keys, or keys being placed in a lock, was enough to make us shudder and develop a cold sweat. We lived every minute as if it was our last.

At dawn the prison guards returned and told us not to be afraid. We were being shipped out today, but bread and marmalade had been prepared for us. They would not have done this if we were going to be shot. We were being sent away to work.

At 10 a.m. the war criminal Friedel arrived. He ordered us out of our cells into a corridor. We were counted there. Then we were made to assemble in the prison courtyard. Here 25 children, all of them less than 15 years of age, were forcefully separated from their mothers. Pleading or weeping didn't help. The criminals merely replied that mothers were unable to work with their children hanging about. We were 'reassured' that the children would remain in the prison and be well cared for.

We were forced from the first prison yard into a corridor, where everyone received half a loaf of bread and some marmalade. We then continued along the corridor to a second yard, where Ukrainian and Belarus devils awaited us with two empty wagons. The men were made to stand on one side of the wagons and the women on the other. Those deemed old and feeble were ordered onto the wagons.

Before we were marched off, Friedel addressed us. He told us how lucky we were. The prisoners who had preceded us were all shot. We were being sent to Lublin to work for Engineer Barasz. If we tried to escape, we would be shot on the spot. Then he noticed some women nibbling at their bread and marmalade. He interrupted himself. He warned them they were in for a long journey and they should not be too quick to eat all their food. He then turned to his criminal subordinates. They were ordered not to hesitate to shoot anyone who showed an inclination to escape. He also warned them not to accidentally shoot one another. They would be severely punished if they did.

THE END OF A BIALYSTOKER PARTISAN GROUP.

During the nine weeks following the commencement of the liquidation of the ghetto, more than 1000 Jews were taken from the Bialystok prison and shot. This number included 100 young Bialystoker partisans. These valiant fighters had been surprised in the woods. Heavily armed Ukrainian and

Belarus Nazis surrounded and captured them before they had time to defend themselves.

PLANS FOR AN ESCAPE.

After we received our final instructions, heavily armed guards marched us through a series of tunnels. We emerged at a deserted railway siding, well away from the centre of the city. There were three cattle trucks waiting there. We were forced into them and the doors were closed and locked behind us.

That evening the train started to move. The failing light and the speed of the train made it impossible to assess in which direction we were moving.

There were nearly 100 Jews in our cattle truck. Ten were metal workers, who had smuggled tools on board, small files and other implements. As soon as the train started to move they set to work. They planned to cut a hole in the wagon's wall large enough for a man to escape through.

Bunim Farbsztejn called for a vote. He pointed out we didn't know where we were being taken to, and that if one man escaped the rest might pay for it with their lives. *"If most people agree, let the walls be cut,"* Bunim argued, *"but if only a small number agree, it is not fair to risk everyone on the whim of a few."*

A vote was taken and only seven wanted the walls cut. Bunin pleaded with the seven men not to risk everyone else's life. The seven decided to ignore him and they set to work.

The train slowed down and we soon realised that we were travelling in the direction of Grajewo. This offered us hope. The seven metal workers stopped cutting their hole, but it was already sizeable and no longer maskable. The Ukrainians perched on the roof noticed it and fired three shots into the wagon. Three people were wounded. One, Mordechai Wrobel a master craftsman, was later tortured to death at Stutthof Concentration Camp. Another, Engineer Sztupler, suffered severe leg wounds. The wounded were in agony but there was nothing we could do to help them.

At the next station two Ukrainian killers climbed down from the wagon roof, holding torches in their hands. They inspected the hole and opened the doors to see the damage their shots had caused. Engineer Sztupler protested he had been shot. The Ukrainians weren't perturbed by this. They calmly replied it was wrong to cut a hole in the wagon wall. Then they locked the door and climbed on the roof again. Back up they fired three more shots into the wagon and wounded three more Jews. Chaos ensued! Panicking Jews crushed one another as they tried to avoid the shots. The wounded were the prime victims. They were climbed over and trampled on despite protestations of pain.

When dawn broke it became obvious that Engineer Sztupler's right leg had been almost severed. Dr. Wainer, the former Bialystok Prison Medical Officer, was also in the wagon and he bandaged Sztupler's leg with a towel, but to no avail! Sztupler realised he was dying and asked that his wife and child, who were still in the Bialystok prison, be notified of his death. He asked that his wife bring up his young son in the best Communist tradition of human fraternity, but at the same time teach him to want to revenge the spillage of innocent Jewish blood. Sztupler's body convulsed for nearly 36 hours. He died in the middle of the next night.

Sztupler's father owned a sewing mill in Bialystok. He brought up his children in accordance with his own capitalistic beliefs, but young Sztupler was a dedicated rebel, who embraced Communism as mankind's only hope of salvation. On a more personal level Sztupler was honest and decent, happy to give someone less fortunate the shirt off his back or his last morsel of food. He deserves to be remembered!

ON EAST PRUSSIAN SOIL.

Two days passed. We were travelling on East Prussian soil and getting thirstier by the hour. Everybody wanted a glass of water. We tried to bribe the Ukrainians to give us a bucket of water. They accepted but only threw a bottle into the wagon. Many of us made a grab for it. Tempers flared and most of the water was spilt. In the second wagon the Ukrainian devils reaped a higher price for water. When they opened the wagon door they spotted a woman from Grodno wearing a nice overcoat. They demanded she take it off. The woman refused. She had no idea with whom she was dealing. The Ukrainians shot her on the spot and when her husband came to her help they shot him also. When the occupants of the third wagon heard what happened, they decided against asking for water.

At stations, we pleaded with some German women to throw snow through the air vents of our carriages. When the Ukrainians went to the rest rooms, some of these women obliged us. Our thirst was so severe that many of us were prepared to fight for the tiniest bit of snow. Arguments erupted and tempers took a long time to settle down.

DANZIG.

We arrived at Danzig Station four days later, at midday on Friday November 5th 1943. The cattle cars were opened and we were herded out. Five wounded Jews and three dead ones were taken away in a truck. The rest of us were ordered into lines and marched through the streets. We were very weak and every few minutes one of us fell. The others were ordered to lift these people up, to continue supporting them on their own feet, and to walk holding on to them for the rest of the march. So Jews started walking in pairs, and every few minutes two Jews fell to the ground together. We observed the many German women on the streets. They were a sad lot. They seemed to be genuinely moved by our plight. Empathy was etched on their faces, radiated from their eyes. Even the Gestapo officer in charge of our transport noticed it and responded in kind. He commandeered a car and helped the weakest of us into it. We marched for two hours to the other side of the city, where we saw some cattle trucks on a narrow gauge railway line. They were waiting for us and we were loaded onto them. We were packed tight. The doors were slid and locked behind us. We rode on this train for another hour. Then it stopped suddenly and we were ordered off. A broad river flowed in front of us. My first thought was, *"The Nazis are going to chase us into it and drown us."* My mind became a cavalcade of thoughts. It was as if a movie of my whole life was unfurling itself before me. Scenes were flashing past. Then suddenly, I was being chased onto and across a pontoon bridge. Before I realised it, we were on the opposite side of the Wisla (Vistula). And then another railway line! More cattle cars! Packed into cattle trucks again! And then another journey for another hour and we reached another railway station! This time it was a solitary building in the depths of a forest. It was Stutthof Station.

STUTTHOF CONCENTRATION CAMP.

It was nightime when our train pulled into Stutthof station. A reception committee was awaiting us there. It included the camp Commandant and a platoon of heavily armed troops. Motor vehicles fitted with blinding giant reflectors illuminated the scene. We were ordered to form two distinct lines, one for men, the other for women, and then made to run all the way to the Concentration Camp. To speed things up Nazis threatened and hit us with rifle butts. At the camp we were handed over to Polish office clerks. These Poles were no kinder than the Nazis.

THE DEATH OF DR. WAINER.

We were in a wretched state following our harrowing journey. For four days we had been hungry, thirsty, sleep-deprived and cold. It was a major effort to even stand up. But the Nazis showed us no mercy. They made us stand out in the cold for three more hours, while the formalities associated with our arrival were dealt with.

Dr. Wainer recognised one of the Polish clerks. He knew him from Warsaw, thought him a decent fellow, and questioned him as to our chances of survival. The Pole pointed to a tall chimney and said we would all pass through it in a few days. He then suggested that Wainer give him his valuables. It was better that he have them rather than a Nazi. Dr. Wainer took the man at his word and immediately placed something in his hand. After we entered the barracks Wainer swallowed some poison, which he had smuggled out of the Bialystok Prison. He did not die quickly. We watched him convulse all night. The Germans took him to the camp hospital in the morning but made no effort to save him. Instead they gave him an injection to hasten his death.

Dr. Wainer was originally from Warsaw. In Bialystok he served as the Corrective Services Medical Officer in the prison. His professionalism was held in high esteem by the prison's administration, staff, and inmates alike. Some staff members used him as their personal physician. During the German occupation he lived in the ghetto with his wife and son, but left every morning to go to work in the prison hospital. His Nazi employers told him they were so impressed with his work they would rescue him if need be. When rumours began to circulate that the ghetto was being liquidated, Wainer pleaded with his employers to be allowed to bring his family to the prison. His request was denied. His employers lied to him that the rumours were false. When the fateful day of Monday August 16th 1943 arrived, Wainer found it impossible to go to work. Instead he hid out with his family for more than a week, before being discovered and taken to the prison. In the prison Wainer was scolded for not having turned up for work. There was no-one to replace him, so he was offered his old job back. Once more he asked if his wife and child might join him, and again he was refused. His wife begged him to save himself, but Wainer refused to desert his family and stayed with them. The Nazis responded by taking him from his family and moving him to the third floor of the prison. The next morning, from his prison window, he watched a group of near naked Jews, his wife and son among them, being forced into a black truck in the prison yard. Half an hour later the truck returned empty, except for its victims' garments. These tragic events broke Wainer's spirit and he contemplated suicide. His friends did their best to dissuade him. They urged him that he had to continue living in hope.

For a while they succeeded, but at Stutthof he took his young life at the first opportunity.

THE BARRACKS AT STUTTHOF.

The barracks, where we were accommodated, were in a gross state of disrepair. Every window had a broken pane. When a severe snow storm raged outside, icy winds blew in over us. A Pole was in charge of our block. He returned every few minutes to issue orders under threat of death. ***"Do not leave your block! Do not look out of the windows! Do not smoke! If you do any of these things you will be shot!"*** He then approached some of us and spoke in whispers. He told us we would be taken to the Karantin Baths tomorrow, where we would be relieved of all our possessions. He suggested if we had any gold or diamonds we give them to him now. This would enable him to provide us with extra rations.

When our 'new benefactor' took leave of us, we discussed our situation. Many thought tomorrow's journey to the Karantin Baths might be our last, but some optimists were keen to convince us that we would out-survive our enemies.

Our four days of hunger had added to our exhaustion. In comparison to our hunger and fatigue, the events of tomorrow suddenly seemed irrelevant. Those who had bread left shared it with others. The rest of us fell like flies. Within minutes, the wooden floor was strewn with bodies in deepest sleep.

At dawn, the barracks' doors opened and our Polish 'benefactor' returned. He gave us a repeat dose of yesterday's advice. When no-one responded he turned around and left. He returned in less than an hour. He ordered us out of the barracks into the yard in queues. Then some SS men arrived. These cold-blooded killers looked us over from head to foot. They told us that if we possessed valuables we better hand them over now. Anyone found to be in possession of valuables at the Karantin Baths would be shot.

THE KARANTIN BATHS.

Before we left for the Karantin Baths, an SS officer pulled one of the two Krawcow brothers from Bialystok out of a line. He asked Krawcow where his diamonds were. Krawcow said he didn't have any. The SS man was not satisfied with the answer. He beat Krawcow relentlessly and sent him to the camp hospital to have his stomach pumped. When Krawcow returned, he looked haggard.

Before we entered the baths, we were taken into a changing room. Three Polish guards were seated there. Once again they asked whether we had money or diamonds. ***"There is no point leaving anything in clothing. All clothing is to be searched. Those who deposit their valuables at the office now will reap benefits when they shop at the camp canteen. Those who fail to comply will be shot when they are found out."***

After delivering this advice the Poles ordered us to undress. They searched our clothing thoroughly. They looked inside our mouths and felt up our back passages. They removed bandages and looked underneath them. Then Polish barbers started cutting our hair and shaving us.

Clipped and shorn we were forced into the showers. They were boiling hot one second, icy cold the next. After we finished showering, a fat Polish beast sprayed disinfectant on us. This thug did not limit himself to his job. He punched every one of us in the ribs, felling us to the concrete floor. Then he sprayed us. If we stayed on our hands and knees for any length of time, he kicked us. If we tried to get up quickly, he punched us in the face.

Next we were pushed naked into a freezing room. It was so cold that our teeth started chattering. We stood there for a long while, before being issued with regulation barracks' clothing. The uniform consisted of a pair of underpants, a short shirt, short trousers, a torn sweater, a jacket, a short coat, and a pair of wooden clogs. It seemed to be camp policy to supply small people with large items of clothing and vice versa. This was particularly true of clogs and most disconcerting. Most of us felt our clogs would be the end of us. It was impossible to move freely in them.

Once we were dressed it was hard to recognise us. We looked like beggars, the lowest of the low. Next we were taken out into the frost, and made stand there for more than half a day. Our legs would give way under us, particularly when nature called. Late that afternoon a middle-aged Pole from Torun approached us. He announced he was in charge of our block. He ordered us to arrange ourselves into rows and then he started marching us. Our frozen legs seemed reluctant to move, but somehow we managed to force them. While we walked snow fell into our clogs and hardened into ice. This made walking more difficult and if someone stopped to clean out a clog, he was either threatened or beaten. We were back in hell on earth. After more than an hour of it, we saw the barracks.

WE MEET UP WITH FELLOW BIALYSTOKERS.

As we approached our block, we looked through the windows and recognised some fellow Bialystokers. This brightened us up. We entered the building and embraced them. We all started weeping, uncontrollably! There were close to 70 of them. When the ghetto was liquidated, they were sent to Lomza gaol to work for the S.S. They stayed there till last Tuesday, the day we were shipped out of Bialystok. Like us they arrived yesterday.

The Block Master brought the reunion to an end. He climbed onto a bench and addressed us. He was keen to deflate and depress. ***"I have been appointed your Block Master,"*** he roared, ***"and I can do with you whatever I like. I was an inmate here and I suffered a lot. If you Jews think you are going to get it easy you are mistaken. I can kill twenty-five of you with my bare hands and nothing will happen to me. It might take me a few days to do it, but then you will believe me. For the next three weeks you will be subjected to special exercises. I warn you, they are particularly harsh! While inside the block you must maintain total silence. I want to be able to hear a fly. You must keep the block spotlessly clean. I want them cleaner than the Aryan blocks. I have appointed your Dr. Sonabend as my unofficial deputy. In my absence his word carries the same authority as mine."***

He left us in no doubt that our slightest transgressions would be dealt with harshly. A veil of sadness descended over our barely expressive faces.

TORMENTED.

The next two days were the weekend and we were left to ourselves. At 8 a.m. on Monday the torture began.

We were marched outside to a large snow-covered square. Here we were forced for hours on end to slide on our bellies, to run from one end of the square to the other on a single breath, and to exercise our hips and knees through torturous excursions. If these manoeuvres were not performed to the Block Master or Room Master's satisfaction, two Poles would stand over and stamp on the victim, and pummel him mercilessly with a rubber truncheon. Almost instantly a broken Jewish body could be seen lying half-dead in the snow. During these sessions, the SS officer who supervised us, would often carry out an inspection. While he was there we experienced real hell on earth. At first he stood on the steps leading up to the block. From there he enjoyed watching his two Polish minions subject Jews to extreme brutalities. A Jew was ordered to lie prone on the ground. The two Poles stamped on him, kicked in his testicles and beat him on the head with a truncheon. Then suddenly the SS thug was no longer satisfied just watching. Tall and broad and displaying the coarse features of a hardened criminal, he needed to partake in it himself. He ran over to the prone Jew and trampled him with his own feet. He then bashed him over the head with a truncheon. And while this was happening he taunted the Jew, ***"Where is your God now; why isn't he helping you?"***

Such "punishment" exercises would occur twice daily for 6-7 hours. When they were over we dragged our exhausted bodies back to the block. We could hardly move. But then we were ordered to clean up the barracks and scrub the floors as if nothing had happened. Exercise days were usually accompanied by a couple of deaths. In the mornings we would carry Jews unable to get out of bed to the camp hospital. The Polish medical staff made no attempt to save them. They left them in beds to starve to death. The Block Master supervised the taking of sick Jews to the hospital. He mockingly apologised for those who died yesterday and in the same breath promised to deliver more carcasses tomorrow.

This torment repeated itself nearly every day for three weeks. It produced many invalids. All were sent to the camp hospital. Not one returned.

To describe the Stutthof Concentration Camp hospital as executionary is to be generous. The doctors and paramedics were all Poles. On one occasion, when Jews was brought to the hospital, the first question asked was, ***"Are you Jews and where do you come from?"*** One of the Jews said he was a Bialystoker and a doctor admitted to being one too. The doctor said, ***"Your houses have dominated our streets for too long. But that is a thing of the past, and will never be allowed to happen again."*** The other Poles applauded him and the doctor enjoyed their enthusiasm. These Polish medicos provided no assistance. They added to our injuries. Patients, who couldn't stand, seldom lasted two days. Starvation and beatings helped accelerate their departure.

Jews who could stand were subjected to even greater cruelty. They were stripped of their raggy clothes and clogs and thrown out barefoot into the snow. There they would freeze and their fate was sealed.

The S.S. liked to be present at these hospital receptions. These burly thugs seemed to derive pleasure from seeing their Polish minions, who were prisoners themselves, being crueler to the Jews than they were.

DISTRIBUTION OF FOOD.

The handing out of extra food usually caused a commotion. Normal daily rations were 200 grams of bread, a tiny bit of jam or margarine, and a litre of soup; just enough to starve slowly on. If the Room Master announced there was extra soup left, a crowd would shove its way towards the tureen. This gave the Room Master the opportunity to hit Jews over the head with a stool. Despite this deterrent inmates rushed in for more and seldom regretted it. I remember being surprised when Bunim Farbsztejn joined in the fracas. I asked why. He must have known the Room Master was exploiting the situation to crack open a few Jewish heads. Bunim replied that he had trouble coping with his hunger and exhaustion. He had no energy left and his feet were swollen. He tried to get an extra drop of soup in the hope it might help him. If he got it, good and well! If he didn't, perhaps the blow would put him out of his misery. He would never contemplate suicide. That was wrong! Many of us felt as Bunim did. We simply would have liked to go to sleep and not wake up.

WORK IN THE CAMP.

We were registered with the camp's Labour Office. 50 tradesmen were selected for workshops. These were tailors, locksmiths, carpenters and shoemakers, and they received more favourable conditions. The rest of us were subjected to punishing labour. This was the Nazi way of disposing of us.

In a large field by the camp, roots, stumps and logs were piled up ten metres high. Our job was to move them 300 metres. We were overseen by the same tormentors, who had supervised our punishing exercises. Four exhausted Jews would be made to lug a stump, which was heavy work for eight fit strong young men. If they couldn't shift it, the supervisors and their Polish kapos would beat them over the head with sticks, until they dropped into their own secretions. If someone made no attempt to get up quickly, he was stamped on and his testicles kicked. Sometimes the well-fed Polish kapos demonstrated how a stump should be lifted. ***"This is how you should work,"*** they would say, only to promptly drop it. Then they attacked us again with their sticks. And while we lay beaten and bloodied on the ground, they would rush off to administer similar treatment to others. These Polish murderers killed a large number of our brethren.

New forms of persecution were thought of daily. One day we were forced to run across a field carrying heavy logs. Anyone who stopped was beaten over the head and legs with sticks. If he couldn't get up, a foot would crush his windpipe until he had squawked his last breath.

At other times Jews who couldn't run carrying heavy logs, were taken to an S.S. guard post, where savage dogs were let loose on them. These dogs tore large pieces of flesh off them. The rest of us, out of fear, found that little bit extra, which enabled us to run with the logs. It is impossible for people to imagine what we endured. We prayed that the earth would open up and swallow us.

The Bialystok merchant Nahum Karp was torn apart by savage dogs. He suffered terribly for a few days and died.

On another occasion 20 exhausted Jews were made to carry a tree. This feat would have tested 40 fully fit Germans. There was a technique to it. 20 men lifted one end of the tree and placed it on the shoulders of ten more men. Then the manoeuvre was repeated at the other end. The unfortunate ones left to carry the load would often collapse under its weight. Tree and men would fall to the ground together.

This was a signal for the Polish kapos. They would fly into a rage and beat the fallen Jews over the heads with sticks. The Jews would then have to lift themselves up and try again. Jews were made to carry the tree for a total of two kilometres, and along the way blows were delivered to heads and legs. At the end, everyone collapsed. There wasn't one of us, who hadn't soiled himself. Battered, bruised and maimed, and barely able to stand, it took us two hours to return to the block.

In the three weeks we worked like this 20 of us were hounded to death. They lingered in the camp hospital for a day or two without food and treatment and then they died.

AFTER WORK.

After work there was no respite. Exhausted and frozen, still our masters tormented us. We were made to adhere to arbitrary rules which made no sense. ***"Do not sit here! Do not sit there! Do not approach the stove and warm yourselves!"*** Anyone who tried to approach the stove was hit with a stool. Several Jews were injured in this way. If we talked too loudly, we were mobilised onto the parade ground for an extra hour of punishing exercises. We would then return to the barracks sporting more bruises.

We were forced to take freezing cold showers to clean away any sign of mud. A number of men caught a chill as a direct result of this and died of pneumonia shortly afterwards.

Every few days the Block Master and the Room Master would inspect us for lice. This was a frightening experience. If someone was found to carry even one louse, he was beaten to a pulp. Samuel Portnoy was a louse parade casualty. A louse was found on his person and the Block Master beat him mercilessly. He was forced to undress and stand naked in the bathroom, where he was hosed down with icy cold water for fifteen minutes. Then he was left to lie naked all night in the freezing dormitory. He was still alive in the morning, when two Jews were ordered to drag him to the hospital. To everyone's surprise, he lingered on there for a few days.

We did not experience one peaceful day in the block. ***"A bed was not made properly! A floor was not swept well enough! There was something lying on a bed! There was something lying under a bed!"*** We couldn't win a trick. These were all serious crimes which attracted severe penalties.

One day the Block Master decided we were hiding some money. We would not receive any food or shelter until it was surrendered to him. We were made to shiver outside in the cold, because no-one had any money to give. The impatient devil was becoming noticeably nastier and we worried what else he would have in store for us. We were not kept wondering long. He made us form two lines on the parade ground. It was very frosty. He ordered us to strip off our clothing and to stand barefoot in the snow. We stood like this for two hours, while the Polish criminal searched through our garments in the block. Then he decided he would leave us outside longer until someone surrendered the money. We would have spent the whole day naked outside, if not for an SS officer who was passing by. He asked what was going on. Fortunately the SS officer ordered us back inside. It took us many hours to recover from the ordeal.

I don't know how we endured this pain and suffering. By this time, most of us would have been happy to take our own lives. But surprisingly, there were still a few optimists among us. They insisted we try to live as long as possible. ***"We might even surprise ourselves and survive our misfortune,"*** Yudel Gurewich, the editor of the Bialystoker afternoon journal 'Undzer Tseitung,' (Our Newspaper), would say. He deserves special mention. He was our foremost optimist. Late some nights, if we were lucky enough to get a Danzig newspaper, he would read us reports of the war and other news. By this time the Soviet Army had begun to advance rapidly. This resurrected a faint spark of hope inside us. ***"Perhaps Gurewich was right and we would live to see the liberation?"*** This slight hope gave us the strength and courage to persevere.

THE CHOIR.

The Christmas holidays were coming and we greeted them with enthusiasm. Two days had been designated rest days. Perhaps we would be lucky enough to get a breather. On the eve of the holidays the Block Master asked if anyone could sing or play a musical instrument. He wanted ten men to form a choir and entertain the rest of us during the holy days. Choir members were given extra rations of bread at the expense of everyone else. Our lead singer was Bunim Farbsztejn, who chose prayers from the 'Yamin Nora'im' (the ten days from Rosh Hashanah to Yom Kippur - the so-called Days of Awe). When we heard Bunim sing our hearts ached and tears flowed down our cheeks.

WE PREPARE TO LEAVE.

After the holidays we were no longer required to work out on the punishment field. Something new had been selected for us. We learnt that 30 of the 50 tradesmen selected for the camp's workshops, had been deported to Auschwitz. The 20 who remained were highly skilled tailors. We were told that

Stutthof had no need of the others, whereas Auschwitz did, and that this was true for the rest of us. We would be deported to Auschwitz soon. This was confirmed a few days later. We knew that people were sent to Auschwitz to be gassed and incinerated, but by now most of us had come to terms with this. To be liquidated would bring an end to our suffering.

WE LEAVE STUTTHOF.

A week passed, while we waited for our transport. It was booked for January 5th 1944. During this time we wondered whether people were still being gassed at Auschwitz. No reliable information was readily available. Each one of us had a broad red band painted across the back of his uniform. It made us readily identifiable, less likely to attempt escape.

There were a few Bialystokers in the camp hospital. Most could hardly stand. But in accordance with the new edict, which stated that almost every Jew had to leave Stutthof, they were made to join us on the train. They told us how Jews were treated in the hospital and how much they had been made to suffer there.

Our womenfolk were sent on the same transport. They were less pleased about it than we were. They had received much better treatment and were not persecuted. Most had worked in locked barracks peeling potatoes, which they ate. They would have preferred a better diet, but they hadn't been made to suffer the severe cold and none had died.

A few hours before we left Stutthof the Commandant addressed us. He said, *"You are being sent to another workplace. You are good workers and Germany needs you."* He warned us not to attempt escape. We would be shot if we tried. *"I do not wish to lose any of you,"* he added. *"You will be given rations for the four days of your journey."*

THE FATE OF THE TWO EVIL MEN.

Two days before our departure the Block and Room Masters were deprived of their special privileges. They were beaten up and sent to a strict punishment camp. I heard afterwards that the Room Master's corpse was brought to Stutthof crematorium a few weeks later. The Block Master was recognised by some Bialystoker tailors after the war. They turned him over to the Soviet authorities. He was investigated and executed.

ON OUR WAY TO AUSCHWITZ.

After the Commandant's speech, we were taken to the railway station and waited several hours. It was snowing heavily, a cold wind was slapping our faces, and our feet were frozen. Then suddenly we saw our womenfolk approaching. They were made to stop a short distance away. The S.S. conducted an inspection. Some of us had beer bottles filled with water for the journey. They were confiscated. When the inspection was completed we were herded into the open carriages of an empty munitions train. It had just arrived and it was not long before it began to move again.

Night fell quickly and soon it was dark. The wind-driven snow pierced our bodies. We pressed close together to try to keep warm, but this was difficult to achieve in an open wagon. I doubted we could survive like this for four days. I even contemplated jumping off the train. But then it stopped and we were ordered off it. We were lined up and counted, and herded a short distance towards a passenger train.

INSIDE THE PASSENGER TRAIN.

We were told to enter the passenger train, ten to a compartment. This was hard to understand. Why the change for the better? Everybody had a theory, but in the end it didn't matter. These compartments had central heating and our frozen bones started to thaw. There was no longer a risk of freezing to death.

Our train remained at the station for several hours. We were being treated like human beings. It was a mystery, a puzzle! Was this the beginning of the end of our bad times? At 9 a.m. guards brought us rations. We each received 400 grams of bread, a piece of Swiss cheese, and some black coffee. We were advised to try to make the food last all day, but we were famished. Most of us ate everything straight away. Later in the day we felt hungry.

As we journeyed from Stutthof to Auschwitz, the guards continued to give us rations. They were polite and tried to calm us down. They did their best to reassure us that people were no longer being gassed at Auschwitz. We were being sent there to work. Despite the changed demeanor, we had no faith in the guards' assurances. We took it for a tactic. It was easier for prisoners to jump off moving passenger carriages than deadlocked freight wagons, even though there were several reasons why we shouldn't attempt this. We were wearing camp uniforms with red stripes on the backs. This made us readily recognizable. The surrounding fields were covered in thick snow. Our heavy clogs were not conducive to walking through this. Snow stuck to them in clumps. Finally, we were on German enemy soil. There would be no place to hide and no one would offer us food.

We lost our friend Zuckerman on the journey. The popular poet had lived in Bialystok during the war and had been in prison with us. He was feeling weak before we left and deteriorated along the way. Dr. Sonabend tried his best to revive him but to no avail. He stopped breathing as we approached Auschwitz.

WE ARRIVE AT AUSCHWITZ.

It took us three days to get to Auschwitz. The train stopped at a siding closer to Birkenau than to Auschwitz proper. German thugs met us there. They forced us out of the carriages and made us line up in queues. Dr. Sonabend carried Zuckerman's body over his shoulder for a while. Then two Bialystokers came to his aid and carried the corpse to the camp.

We looked back from afar at our womenfolk being driven off carriages, being treated like beasts. It was pitiful to watch. They were beaten over the head with sticks till they fell in a heap on the ground. They then gathered their last ounce of strength and picked themselves up to march to their deaths.

As we neared the camp we saw many Jews, shadows of their former selves, forced to endure torturous forms of hard labour. For a while we wondered whether Jews were still being gassed here, but once we passed the cremetoria and peered in, there was no longer any doubt. Our blood chilled. We lost all hope of survival.

The women were walking behind us. They reached the cremetoria and veered off in another direction. I choked up with tears. I knew they were gone forever. We were herded into a large yard.

THE AUSCHWITZ BATHS.

Mainly Jews met us at the baths, but they treated us like criminals. First they made us stand and wait for several hours. Then some of them started shouting orders. *"Transport from Stutthof, undress!"* The Jews started searching our clothing. Anything they found they confiscated. Jewish barbers clipped our hair with blunt scissors. We were ready for the delousing showers. If we moved too slowly into the showers, we were hurried on with clubs. The water alternated in temperature, boiling hot then icy cold. On exiting the showers, we were doused with vinegar. It burnt as it was rubbed into our skin. We were chased into a large room, where our de-loused garments were lying in a heap on the floor. The windows were wide open and an icy wind blew in. We ran over to the rags and put them on as quickly as we could. Some of us caught a chill and died a few days later.

Next we were registered in the camp's files. This was also done by Jews, but they treated us humanely. After registration we were tattooed. A camp number was engraved on our left arms. We were assured that registration and tattooing were good signs. Jews sent straight to the ovens were spared this. Next we were informed that we would be quarantined for a few weeks. The fittest would then be chosen for hard labour. There was no immediate danger of being gassed.

Several hundred of us were herded into a large room and spent our first night huddled up on a concrete floor. By morning we were broken in spirit and very hungry. At noon some dirty pots of soup were brought in. The soup was terrible. Only extreme hunger prevented it from being inedible. Even so we had to wait in order to partake of it.

The Nazis provided no containers into which to pour the soup. Some Jews poured it into their hats. Others, these were mainly younger Jews, found bits and pieces on the floor, which they used to imbibe small quantities of soup at a time. They drank what they could, and refilled their 'utensils' time and time again. Many older Jews did nothing and starved. This was the level to which the Nazi were prepared to sink in order to degrade us. They created a situation where younger stronger Jews ate and lived at the expense of older weaker bretheren. Later on more victims would arrive. They would be stronger still and they would survive at the expense of those who were stronger now. It was a system to ensure everyone perished.

BLOCK NUMBER 13 AT BIRKENAU.

After 'our meal,' we were taken to a quarantine chamber in Block 13. It was originally built as stables for Polish cavalry horses. The walls had few windows. They were lined with three tiers of wooden cots, enough for several hundred people, but the Nazis made a 1000 share them. They contained little straw and several people had to share a single cover.

The block was filthy and the Block Masters were harsh. They made us lie on our cots all day. Despite the overcrowding we were always cold. There was no heating and icy winds blew in through holes in the walls. Many of us caught kidney chills and needed to urinate every few minutes. Because we were only allowed out at certain hours, it was difficult to control such needs. Some of us sneaked out to have a piss. Others relieved themselves in a corner of the block. Those caught committing such acts were instantly whipped.

At noon watery soup was brought in for ten people at a time. No spoons were provided. We would drink it and lick the bowl clean with our tongues. When the first ten finished, more was delivered in the same dirty containers. This continued until a 1000 were fed.

In the evenings we would receive 200 grams of bread, a bit of margarine or marmalade, and some tea or coffee. Our diet was so poor, and we were so starved and weary, that everything was an effort. Many developed dysentery and were taken to the camp hospital, usually a one-way trip! Herschel Sofer, his son, and his son-in-law, died in this manner. Our proverbial optimist Yudel Gurewich met with a similar end. Bunin Farbsztejn, whose legs were already grossly swollen in Stutthof, was admitted to the hospital and passed away a few days later.

After spending a few days in Block 13, most of us were moved to Block 14. The two blocks looked exactly the same. We were addressed by the Jewish Block Master, a Nazi collaborator or kapo! He warned us this was no vacation - people don't live long here - the block must be kept clean - noise is not tolerated - and in particular he didn't want to hear a whimper out of us. If we disobeyed rods would be broken over our backs, and we would have no chance of getting out alive.

This Jewish criminal left us in no doubt that our days were numbered. These collaborators behaved like underworld figures. The Block Master was a Godfather figure with several henchmen. His mafia had no conscience. It made a special point of trying to destroy the finest and gentlest of us. They would starve such people and beat them mercilessly. They caused many premature deaths. The Birkenau barracks reminded me of the slaughter houses I had read about in Upton Sinclair's famous novel, 'The Jungle.' But here it was Jews not animals being led to the slaughter.

Early one morning, on January 19th 1944, I heard the Block Master calling my number. I was half asleep in a daze, but I registered it, jumped up, and ran to him as fast as I could. He ordered me to shave immediately. I had been selected to work as a printer in the 'Publishing Barracks.' I ran over there and arrived breathless. Other prisoners were already waiting, but before we could speak an elegant car pulled up. Its doors opened, and an S.S. officer and two subordinates stepped out. We stood at attention. The S.S. officer came over and inspected each one of us, from head to toe. He also questioned us as to our skills. If we passed the test, he ordered the barrack secretary, also a Jew, to write down our numbers. If we failed we were dismissed and chased away by his subordinates. The S.S. criminal chose 12 fortunate men. I was one of them. That is why I am able to tell my tale today, but only just!

The S.S. officer chatted with the Jewish barrack secretary for a few minutes. Then he and his aides returned to the car and drove off. The secretary informed us that we would not be returning to our former barracks. We would be sent to Special Transport Block instead. When we arrived there, we were told that the 700 inmates were about to undergo a selection process; who would live and who would die! The Selection Committee arrived shortly after we did. It comprised the doctor in charge of the block and some Block Masters. Every Jew in the Special Transport Block was ordered to undress. The temperature was very low, close to zero. We shivered and trembled, more from fear than the cold. I was standing there naked in a queue together with the 11 other chosen print workers. The Selection Committee approached us. They wrote down my number and directed me to the sub-group destined for the gas chambers. There were 300 alloted to this group and five of the chosen print workers were among them. The group suddenly became agitated. Many started crying, screaming and shaking. A few hanged themselves on the spot with trouser belts and suspenders. I was in hell on earth. Then suddenly, out of the blue, one of the Block Masters returned and announced that the 12 chosen print workers could return to their former barracks. I ran back as fast as I could. When I arrived there fellow Bialystokers reassured me that the Stutthof transport was not included in the current selection. I didn't believe them. I was in a state of shock. I thought that I was the only Bialystoker from Stutthof who was going to be gassed. Nobody could persuade me to the contrary. I curled myself up in a corner of the barracks and waited for the Nazis to come and drag me to my death.

I remained like this until 8 p.m., deeply submerged in gruesome thoughts. Then I heard my number called again. My heart almost stopped. I was a bundle of nerves, fearful, anxious! It was our block secretary. I dragged myself over to him. He assured me. Everything was fine. I was safe. I should go back to the Special Transport Block, right away! He said I should consider myself very lucky. For some inexplicable reason I started to believe him. I was going to be saved. I did his bidding and ran back to Special Transport Block as fast as I could. When I got there, I was reunited with my 11 chosen companions.

In this new block there were several highly skilled Jews, who had been taken off a transport from Lwow to help with printing and graphics.

Our new Block Master was Fastel, a remarkable Jew! The S.S. had just ordered him to find 30 specialists highly skilled in the manufacture and production of books. Fastel, even in this most gruesome of times, would always risk helping a fellow Jew. He never worried about people's qualifications. He saw his prime role as being able to help save fellow Jews from the gas chambers. After he transferred his 30 extra 'book specialists' to the Special Transport Block, he came and spoke to us. It was 11 p.m. He talked from the heart and was most encouraging. He told us he would return at 5 a.m. and transfer us from Special Transport Block to D Barracks. At D Barracks we wouldn't have to worry about selection processes.

None of us slept that night. We were terribly anxious. Would we ever get out of this hell hole?

Dawn arrived and Fastel returned. He bid us be ready to leave in half an hour. He spoke with great compassion, elevated our mood, and helped re-build our broken spirits. I don't have enough words with which to praise him.

We were led out of Special Transport Block right on time. We walked to the kitchen, where Fastel ordered kitchen hands to provide us with bread for our journey. His word was their command and we received our rations promptly. He bid us Godspeed. The farewell was full of tears. This remarkable Jew had saved us and we prayed that he might survive too!

It was not far from Birkenau to D Barracks. We arrived in an hour and were ushered into Block 11.

BLOCK 11 AT D BARRACKS.

At Block 11, we met with 20 other Jews, also from Auschwitz. Conditions were much better here. It was cleaner. We caught our breaths. We had received a temporary reprieve from the events of the previous day, but not for long! Late that afternoon we were brought back to reality. We heard a loud noise. A large number of vehicles were approaching. We peeked through the cracks in and around doors and through holes in the walls, and witnessed a terrifying sight. Bare Jews were packed tight like herrings into large open trucks. Men, women, and children were being transported stark naked to the gas chambers at Birkenau. It was snowing heavily and their only covering was a blanket of snow. It was a pathetic sight. These Jews were near dead with mental and physical exhaustion. They had no ability to oppose or resist tormentors.

One of us, a young Bialystoker, Sokolowicz, had been selected for the gas chambers. At the time he was beside himself with anguish; so much so that Zishe Bagish, a well-known Bialystoker artist and writer, noticed him. Bagish, his own eyes full of tears, gestured for the younger man to approach him. ***"You are younger and healthier than I,"*** Bagish told him, ***"and I feel I cannot survive the strain of this much longer. I am willing to help you live. When they call you for the transport to Birkenau Gas Chambers, I am prepared to take your place. This will, at least, give me a chance to save a fellow Jew."*** That night, when the Nazi criminals called out for Sokolowicz, Bagish stood up. The two men embraced, said their farewells, and Bagish left for the transport. Sokolowicz survived the war.

WHO WAS IN-CHARGE OF AND RESPONSIBLE FOR ALL THIS CARNAGE?

More than 1,000,000 Jews were gassed and cremated at Auschwitz. How was this organised? Who helped the Nazis carry it out?

In Auschwitz there were several gas chambers. One was very large. It accommodated 3000 victims at a time. Sometimes children were separated from parents, at other times they weren't.

At the entry to the gas chamber there were two doors. One led to showers, the other to the gas chamber. People were ushered into the gas chamber, the door was locked, and gas was introduced.

Jewish commandos or kapos helped oversee the killings.The Nazis liked to use them. It suited their propaganda machine. It helped them argue that Jews were conducting the barbarism.

The pathway from the railway station to the gas chambers was very short. Jewish commandos led their bretheren down it. Many naked Jews led into gas chambers thought they were about to have a shower. This was never the case. They were gassed in newly-built ever enlarging gas chambers, and their remains were incinerated in newly-built ever enlarging crematoria.

About 20,000 Jewish commandos collaborated with the Nazis in the overseeing of the gassings. Few survived. Their tenures tended to be short-lived. Their fate was similar to that of their victims.

ONE OF THE JEWISH COMMANDO COLLABORATORS.

It is estimated that from 20,000 Jewish commandos, only about 20 survived. One watched his own wife and children being gassed. He felt guilty about it. He admitted to betraying his family and the Jewish people as a whole. But somehow he continued to justify his actions. He argued that to disobey the Nazis was to be shot on the spot, even if 35 just men had done so before him. He also argued that if his job had been done by Aryans, he would not have improved the lot of the suffering Jews. The same victims would have been selected on the same day and treated in the same way. All collaborating did was allow him to survive longer, to improve his chances of escaping. He recalled how naked Jews waiting to be gassed, asked commandos to recite the Kaddish (mourner's prayer) for them. The best a commando could do was wink an eye, and hope the victim interpreted it as a 'yes.' No commando dared speak to a victim. Commandos were always being watched by the S.S. These hardened killers wouldn't hesitate to shoot a commando who spoke to a victim. Even to wink was taking a risk. But there were cases where commandos whispered to victims, that since they were about to die, they should try to strangle the Nazi, who was supervising their entry into the gas chamber.

This same commando told us a story about a woman from a night transport, who had escaped with her child from the gas chamber enclosure. They were given food and managed to hide for four days. When S.S. guards finally found them, they shot them on the spot. The S.S. then grabbed some Jewish commandos, and threw them into a gas oven alive.

The S.S. instituted the severest penalties for commandos assisting victims. To shelter or help a victim escape was virtually impossible. Very few Jews escaped from Auschwitz-Birkenau.

RESISTANCE BY JEWISH COMMANDOS.

There were rare instances where Jewish commandos resisted the S.S. On one occasion Jewish commandos forced some S.S. guards into crematorium ovens. As a result the entire Commando Brigade was incinerated alive.

During the spring of 1944, Jewish commandos led by Kaminski, a Jew from Grodno, planned a revolt. They would blow up gas chambers and crematoria as signals that the uprising has begun. This group was betrayed from within by a spy and everyone in it was shot and cremated.

Later that year, Jewish commandos staged a second more successful uprising. This time they blew up the largest gas chamber, the one with a capacity of 3000. Some of the smaller gas chambers were also damaged. At the time 10,000 Jews were awaiting execution in nearby barracks. Some threw caution to the wind and joined the commandos. Once again all the rebels were shot dead and their bodies cremated.

LOLA LIPMAN - JEWISH FIGHTER AND HEROINE.

Among the more than 1,000,000 Jews, who perished at Auschwitz-Birkenau, there are some instances of extraordinary bravery. Lola Lipman, a beautiful Jewish actress from Warsaw, is one such case. S.S. General Schlesinger ordered Lipman to undress herself in front of him. Finding himself sexually aroused he decided to finish the job himself. Lipman taunted him by saying she could never bring herself to have sex with such a beast. Schlesinger started to tear off her clothes. Lipman suddenly pulled a gun out of Schlesinger's hip pocket and shot him dead. She also shot and wounded two of his adjutants who rushed in. She then stated, ***"I now have peace of mind and can readily accept being burnt alive in the gas ovens."*** The bravery of Lola Lipman was praised by thousands of Jewish prisoners throughout the camp. Her determination and heroism were applauded.

THE GREEK BOAT CAPTAIN ALEKER.

Aleker, a Greek Jew, who had been a ship's Captain, worked as a Jewish commando in the Auschwitz crematoria. After a while he could no longer emotionally cope with the task of processing tens of thousands of Jewish corpses through the ovens. He had organised for three other Greek Jews to become his helpers. All four of them transported human ash in horse drawn carts. They collected it at the camp and dumped it into a nearby river. Their trump card was that when they spoke Greek the Germans could not understand them. Aleker formulated a plan of escape. The four Greek Jews would have to overpower their two S.S. guards. It was not long before their first opportunity presented itself. The horse drawn carriage approached the river and the two S.S. officers alighted from it. One of the guards walked down to the water; the second one stood by the cart. Aleker addressed the S.S. guard by the cart in German, and when he turned around thumped him on the head with a heavy shovel. The S.S. officer was knocked unconscious and before his companion could respond, Aleker attacked him too. A life and death struggle ensued. Both men fell into the river. Aleker overcame his enemy and drowned him. Meanwhile the other guard regained consciousness, pulled out a gun, and started shooting at Aleker, who was swimming across the river. Aleker had gestured to his companions to take on the second S.S. officer, but all three of them had frozen in fear. The S.S. officer roared at them to raise their hands and they all obeyed him. Then a third S.S. guard arrived in response to the shooting. He rounded up the three Greek Jews and took them back to the camp. Aleker made it across the river, entered a nearby house, and threatened its occupants into giving him a gun, bullets and some food. He then ran out of the house into the forest.

This incident set off an alarm, and before long a platoon of machine gun carrying S.S. killers arrived at the camp with hunting dogs. They immediately set out after Aleker and the dogs soon picked up his scent. Despite the overwhelming odds against him Aleker put up a mighty fight. He killed a number of the S.S. officers before firing his last bullet into his mouth. His body was brought back to the crematorium. In reprisal the Germans announced they would execute ten Greek Jews. A Jew, who had been a Major in the Greek army, spoke out against this. He said that Aleker had acted as an individual, and that other Greek prisoners should not be held collectively responsible or punished for his actions. The Greek Major was ordered to lift Aleker's corpse and then forcefully dump it onto the ground. He lifted the body up high, but then lowered it gently to the ground in tribute to the dead Captain. The Germans retaliated by executing the Major and all the Jewish crematorium commandos and incinerating their bodies. The inmates of the camp regarded Aleker as a monumental example of a defender of the Jewish faith.

It is important to realise that Jews who went quietly to the gas chambers, seemingly offering no resistance, were also heroes. They acted that way because they were mentally and physically exhausted. They had had all the stuffing knocked out of them. I remember a particularly striking Hungarian Jew. He was tall, handsome, and possessive of a magnificent physique. On arrival he was aggressive and not afraid to speak his mind. ***"Are we really going to be gassed?,"*** he asked of us. ***"If death is inevitable we should kill a few of these S.S. barbarians with our bare hands before they put us away."*** By the time his turn arrived, the stuffing had been knocked out of him. He accepted his fate with more passivity than most.

It wasn't just Jews, who were brought to Auschwitz to be murdered. There were Poles, Germans, and from time to time other European nationals. They tended to be strong heroic persons, who had politically opposed Nazism. But by the time they reached Auschwitz, they too were mentally and physically exhausted. They were led to the slaughter like blind sheep, offering no resistance, no semblance of their former opposition.

There was one strikingly beautiful Hungarian Jewess, very strong and healthy. So much so she survived her gassing. Her body showed signs of life when she was pulled out of the gas chamber. A German barbarian came over and poured cold water on her. She regained consciousness and mental awareness. He then shot her sadistically in each breast, and when this failed to kill her he also shot her in each eye.

THE CORRECT AND FITTING END OF A TRAITOR.

These events exacted a terrible toll on us. Our minds were a constant conveyer belt of suffering, moving continually, never-ending. We became impatient and started to hope for the inevitable day when we could exchange the horrors of the camp for the finality of the gas chambers. So when January 25th arrived, and we were transferred back to Special Transport Block at Birkenau, we were ready and willing to go.

On the way back we drove past the corpse of a man shot by the road. We recognised him as the hated Jewish Block Master from Block 14 at Birkenau. He had asked some senior S.S. officers to help him escape. They shot him for his trouble and left his body rotting by the road, a fitting end for a wretched collaborator, who lacked any sense of personal dignity. He deserves to be cursed forever.

I SURVIVE A THIRD TIME.

There were 60 of us from Block 11 at D Barracks. We were deloused and made to wait standing for several hours for a medical examination. Suddenly two S.S. doctors appeared. They divided us into two groups, 28 who were physically weak, and 32 who were strong enough to work. I was considered physically weak. My heart started to pound. I was sure my miserable existence was about to end. The S.S. doctors phoned Berlin to pass on the details of their examinations. Berlin Command told them to ignore the examinations. They wanted all of us for a special work assignment. I had been selected to survive yet again.

BERLIN.

We were ordered to dress, taken to the railway station, and put into passenger carriages. The guards treated us well. They didn't try to make us miserable and they served us adequate rations. We felt fortunate to be leaving Auschwitz-Birkenau and wondered what was awaiting us in Berlin.

We arrived at Berlin Central Railway Station one and a half hours later. Our guards told us to wait on the platform. The people there seemed interested in us. Most were polite, even sympathetic. A little later we were directed down some steps and along a tunnel to an underground station. A train to Oranienburg was awaiting us there. One of our very young guards, recently recruited from the Hitler Youth, even managed to tell us he was one-quarter Jewish. He became ill and required assistance, but he was not allowed to leave us in such a busy crowded station.

CHAPTER 10.

INSIDE THE CONCENTRATION CAMPS OF SACHSENHAUSEN, MAUTHAUSEN AND SCHLIER.

SACHSENHAUSEN.

It took us less than an hour to travel from Berlin to Oranienburg. From the station we were marched to Sachsenhausen Concentration Camp. We were led through tree high gates into a compound. Our first impression was better than in any other camp we had seen. We were ordered to stand close to the wall of a large building and face it. It was the Camp Commandant's quarters. We remained there for several hours. Then we were led off to well-equipped baths. Everyone was behaving humanely, nothing like Stutthof or Auschwitz. We wondered whether humans were still valued to some extent in this camp. After washing we were taken to an office to register.

The workers in the office were Frenchmen and they were kind and friendly. One of them mentioned there were two Jewish Work Commands in Sachsenhausen. One employed 40 watchmakers, the other one employed printers, but the printers were locked away and isolated from the other inmates of the camp. We were assured that conditions were better here than in other camps and that there was plenty to eat.

The knowledge that the printers were constantly locked away and we were to join them, tainted the bit of joy we had felt till now.

Our Block Master was an elderly German, a communist, and had been a prisoner here for eight years. He led us to Block

18 which was near Block 19, where we were destined to work. Before starting work we would be quarantined for three weeks, in case we were incubating diseases.

OUR FIRST ENCOUNTER WITH FELLOW COMPOSITORS.

The other half of Block 18 was being renovated by its inmates. They had arrived earlier and were already working secretly in Block 19. They were always guarded to ensure they wouldn't speak to us.

The next day I saw my friend Moshe Kozak entering Block 18. I got a good look. There was no mistaking him. I called out, *"Moshke, Moshke,"* but he didn't respond and ran out of the building. I wondered whether I was wrong, that it wasn't Moshke afterall. I knew that six Bialystokers had been sent here several months before the liquidation of the ghetto. Their families had received mail from them. I wondered why Moshke ignored me, why he was forbidden to speak to a future co-worker.

Next morning I saw him again, close up. There was no mistaking him. I ran over to him and offered my hand. ***"How are you?"*** Once again he pulled away and ran off. This time I was profoundly affected. Why couldn't Moshke answer such an innocuous question? Later on I found out that in the printing section it was a capital offence to talk to someone in a different work command.

A few days later both Kozak brothers - Hershke, the father of Nahum, my son's best friend, and Moshke - entered a washroom in which I was standing. They had managed to sneak away from their escort on the pretence that they needed to wash their hands. We had a short but hearty conversation. I asked them for some food because we were suffering the effects of starvation.

The next morning I received some bread and a packet of low grade tobacco. I shared the bread with my closest companions. This made me some enemies amongst the others, because everyone in our block was starving, desperate for a piece of bread. When no one was looking I distributed three quarters of my tobacco among the whole group and kept a quarter for myself.

We were impatient for our three-week quarantine period to end. We wanted to start our secret work, no matter how bad working conditions were. We wanted to work because we wanted to eat. That is how hungry people think. Starving people, even cultured ones, can forfeit their humanity and chase food as aggressively as a wild animal.

In quarantine three of us developed typhoid and one died. Our quarantine was extended from three to seven weeks. Our comrades in Block 19 helped us through this trying time, by providing extra food on several occasions. This gave us extra sustenance, but more importantly joy and gratitude. For the first time in a long while we didn't feel alone in the world.

BLOCK NUMBER 19.

In quarantine we were visited several times by Sturmbanfuhrer Kruger, the head of the enterprise which had recruited us. He was a sly, wily, smiling intriguer of about 50, who had been in the Secret Service since the days of Kaiser Wilhelm. He did not seem to dislike or have any special enmity for Jews. He promised to help us from time to time, but we soon realised his word couldn't be relied on. He consoled us by saying that once our quarantine was over and work commenced, we would regain full strength in six to eight weeks.

We eventually adapted to being in quarantine. We even accepted the poor food supply. Now it was the thought of total isolation that started to worry us. We began to hope quarantine would be extended again, because in quarantine we had more freedom and were not as isolated as the Block 19'ers.

After seven weeks our quarantine ended and we moved to Block 19. A friendly meeting took place between the two groups. It was great to catch up with old friends from Bialystok; Yechiel Platz; the brothers Herschel and Moshke Kozak; Leib Ziberski; Isaac Sukenik; and Naum Zakrzewski.

A few hours later Sturmbanfuhrer Kruger arrived, and we new arrivals were herded into a large workroom to hear him speak. ***"You have been brought here to perform extremely confidential work. We are at war and all means are justified in wartime. Your task will be to forge various English pound notes and other documents. This must be done diligently and with great precision. You are strictly forbidden to make contact with or speak to anyone who is not in your work command. Your work is secret and you must keep it secret. If you betray this secrecy you will be dealt with harshly. I think you understand exactly what I mean by this. You bear responsibility not only for yourself, but for the group as a whole. Your destiny is in your own hands. As long as your work is of good quality I will be with you. As long as I am with you, your lives are safe."***

Kruger's speech had its intended impact. We understood the nature of our work, and like it or not, we made peace with the fact that we were isolated.

Kruger allotted each of us to various foremen and left.

THE COUNTERFEIT MONEY FACTORY.

States can easily counterfeit monies and documents, because all resources are readily available to them. States have little difficulty aquiring machines, papers, inks, and any numbers of skilled tradesmen.

The counterfeiting of other nation's money has always been considered a serious breach of international law, but during World War II the warring parties had little respect for each other and did it freely.

The counterfeiting factory operated in two blocks at the back of Sachsenhausen Concentration Camp. These blocks were completely surrounded by dense barbed wire, on all sides and also from above! This was out of bounds to everyone, including the Camp Commandant. 18 Secret Service men were the only others allowed to enter. The workers inside the block were all Jews. Jews were the best security, because they were dispensable. The day the job was done the Jews could be murdered and there would be no witnesses.

There were 140 Jews in the Counterfeit Work Command. They had been brought there from various camps and ghettos. The largest group was the Polish Jews but there were other Jews from Germany, Czechoslovakia, Hungary, France, Belgium, Holland, Norway and Denmark and even two Jewish Russian prisoners of war.

One of the 140 Jews was the famous German painter Peter Hirsch, who was strictly speaking only half Jewish. Before the war Hirsch had been commissioned by the Pope to paint an important picture in St. Peter's Basilica in Rome. On his return home he was lauded by Propaganda Minister Dr. Josef Goebbels and they were photographed together. But after the war started Hirsch was accused of "racial shame" and interred at Sachsenhausen. Our work command also contained famous photographers, first-class engravers, excellent printers, bookbinders, electricians, chemical engineers, paper experts, bookkeepers and two doctors. These experts produced the counterfeit money, ran the office and managed the accounts.

The 18 Secret Service guards were only concerned with security. They were there to ensure we didn't communicate with other people in the camp. They didn't supervise the actual work itself. The Jewish foremen bore full responsibility for all of that. Their lives depended on it.

The production team was divided into the following work groups: engravers; printers; artist-painters; photographers; specialist light printers; bookbinders; money sorters; those who divided the sheets of money; and those who aged the money.

We received closed boxes, containing between 100,000 and 150,000 sheets of paper. This paper was stamped with the appropriate watermarks. A sheet of paper would yield eight notes. We printed different denominations: five, ten, 20 and 50 pounds. We were counterfeiting close to 10,000,000 pounds sterling a box of paper.

A team of engravers would prepare the plates and place them in the printing machines. The machines were geared to produce at least 2000 pieces per hour, but we limited our production to 500. This allowed two printers to stand continuously by the machine and check constantly that the process was in order.

We would print the English notes three times. The first time the fives, tens, 20's and 50's were thinly imprinted, the second time they were made bolder, the third time the serial numbers were added.

In England sheets of paper currency were separated by hand not by machine. We were obliged to use a similar technique. After each printing the notes were left to dry on special racks for three days. After the last print run the sheets were handed to a special team, who tore them in quarters. The quarter-sheet containing two notes was cut by a knife into single ones. Because it was essential for the notes to appear hand torn, we would put them into a hand press and file them down until they looked like proper English notes. The money was printed according to the Bank of England's blueprint, which the German Secret Service had somehow managed to obtain.

When the notes were finally satisfactorily separated they were stacked in numerical order. They were then sent to a "Money Store," where the foreman passed them on to sorters for checking.

There was a special brigade of 40 sorters, who answered to a foreman and a senior controller. They used specially designed light boxes, which were illuminated both from above and below. Whenever I watched them work, I was reminded of a scene from the well-known German movie about money forgers, "Dr. Mabuse."

The completed notes were classified into five categories: first class; second class; third class; rejects; and totally unfit. Third class was good enough to be circulated. Most of the acceptable notes were classified third class. Sorters rarely classified a note first class or second class. To do so was to take on too much responsibility. Sorters would generally disqualify 75% of the notes. The senior controller would reject a further 5-10%. From 100 notes probably 15 were deemed suitable for circulation.

The notes that were demarcated 'unsuitable for circulation' were registered, bundled, and packed into boxes.

The good notes were handed over to a team of agers. Their job was to make the notes look old. They would handle them, crease them, and perforate them with pins, which was a known English habit. A note from an earlier year of issue would be given more perforations than one from a later year.

After creasing and perforation the notes were re-assembled and pressed. Notes of different years of issue were mixed together, so as not to give a clue that they may have been recently printed.

When this was done, it was time for the 'finding check.' Some genuine notes were inserted in amongst the counterfeit ones and the sorters had to find them. They seldom did, due to the high quality of the counterfeit notes.

We also counterfeited some Yugoslav currency, and during our final six months we started work on American 50 and 100 dollar notes. It took a long time to satisfactorily copy American notes, and by then it was too late.

We also printed false documents for use in Nazi espionage and millions of English postage stamps. One set of stamps featured Stalin's face with a Star of David above it. Presumably these were made for propaganda purposes.

Occasionally we would run out of paper. When this happened it could take some time for new supplies to arrive. We worried about this. We worried about outlasting our usefulness. There was one particularly worrisome period, when we received an order from Berlin to suspend printing. Some of our money had been detected as being counterfeit. At this time we all shared a single thought. Our workshop could close and we would be made redundant. Jews, who worked for the Nazis, knew well the meaning of the word "redundant," but in our case, thank God, the suspension of printing was short-lived. When work began again, we all breathed a sigh of relief.

SABOTAGE.

As a rule we tended to work as slowly as was tolerated. Our excuse was that our work was extremely precise and did not lend itself to hurrying. Sturmbanfuhrer Kruger accepted this point of view. Many times the notes we rejected were not worse than those we accepted. It was our way of limiting German Secret Service funds as much as we could. Until July 20th 1944, we worked two shifts of eight hours a day with Sundays free. On that date ten hour shifts were introduced and Sunday rest was partly abolished. We counteracted these measures by doing less work in ten hours than we had previously done in eight.

LIFE IN OUR CAGE.

Sturmbanfuhrer Kruger and his philosophy were good for us. He believed that the best way to squeeze the maximum amount of precise work out of a highly skilled slave labourer was to treat him well. The regime he set for us was relatively mild. At no time did we feel we were suffering.

The work was not physically demanding and the workshop was warm. There was no standing in the cold for hours before sunrise. There was no walking for kilometres to and from work. We received the same food as Aryan inmates and the Block and Room Masters never stole any. Our bread and other provisions were adequate to quell hunger. In addition 50 members of our work command were half-Jewish, and had parents or wives who sent weekly food packets into the prison. These were divided among all of us.

We were permitted to write a 25 word letter every two months. We wrote to Jews and half-Jews in Prague. At that time the Jews of Prague were still free and they were more than happy to provide us with aid. They would send us a couple of kilograms of bread, some biscuits, onions and other small items. We were really grateful to these wonderful Jews of Prague. They gave of their best in terrible times, and contributed significantly to our survival.

Our standards of hygiene were better than in other parts of the camp. Every week we received fresh underwear, a clean shirt and a new towel. Each one of us had a straw pillow and slept on a separate wooden bunk, covered with at least two blankets. Some of the older workers had three blankets. We had access to running water and clean toilets. We shaved twice a week and on Sunday mornings we took a bath. The bathroom was always clean. Before the bath we were lined up and searched to see if we were carrying any documents. After the bath we were taken back to our cage.

If a worker fell ill, a security guard would escort him to the camp hospital. The patient was not allowed to communicate with anyone except the doctor, and then only to describe his symptoms. If the patient was seriously ill he was not allowed to be admitted. He was treated by a private doctor back in Block 19.

During the 30 months that our work command functioned, six seriously ill patients were taken to the camp hospital for a lethal injection of petrol. Several others died in the barracks. We lost a Bialystoker at Sachsenhausen. Isaac Sukenik, aged only 23 years, was shot dead in January 1945, because he was in the final stages of Tuberculosis.

At work the German radio was always playing. We were allowed to listen to the official German news relating to military matters at the front. The announcer was Lieutenant-General Ditmar. We would talk about these events at night. Sometimes we were fortunate enough to hear British broadcasts too. These radio reports offered us some hope.

THE BEST TIMES.

The best times started when we heard German radio broadcasting, *"Attention, attention! Fighter aircraft are attacking southern Germany."* Then again a bit later; *"Attention, attention! Severe attack on south-west Germany!"* And then again a bit later still; *"Attention, attention! Heavy air fire over Hannover and Braunschweig!"* A few minutes more and we could hear the hum of four-engine American fighter planes directly overhead. Air-raid sirens had started to wail all over Sachsenhausen Concentration Camp.

On June 21st 1944, we witnessed a giant blitz by 2000 American bombers. It lasted six hours. After a deluge of bombs had fallen on Berlin, German radio reported that the planes had flown east towards Russia. We learned later that they had flown to airstrips, near Poltava, in the Ukraine.

Two days later the German Wermacht announced that yesterday morning the Soviet Army had commenced its long awaited summer offensive along a line from Orsha to Vitebsk. The great blitz of Berlin had heralded the beginning of the offensive. 2000 American bombers had lent support by landing behind the Russian front line.

That same night British bombers flew over Berlin; very fast and very high! There must have been 50 or 60 of them. The Germans offered little resistance. They seldom fired on them. The German press labelled these planes "Mosquitoes," and they considered them very dangerous.

Dresden was also being bombed. The radio announcer spoke of streams of bombers flooding the skies, all the way from the French border in the west to Dresden in the east. All of Germany was being attacked. The radio also warned of 'sky divers,' who flew their planes so low over roads and railway lines that they could shoot at anything in sight.

We felt privileged to be able to witness these events. They gave us the strength and the courage to continue our struggle.

At 5 p.m. on July 20th 1944, we heard some exciting news. Someone had tried to assassinate the Fuhrer. We were overjoyed with this. We hoped the assassination might lead to our liberation; but this was wishful thinking. Later on there was a follow-up announcement to say that the Fuhrer was unharmed. Then, at 10 p.m., we heard that Hitler was to address the nation in two and a half hours. We waited up to listen to the greatest mass murderer in the history of humanity. He spoke briefly, in a rather broken voice, but managed to still express a vehement hatred of Jews. Any hopes we had for a speedy deliverance quickly evaporated.

Our block had a small library. It contained books in German, French and Czech, Berlin newspapers, a chess set and other games. After work we enjoyed using these facilities, but because the guards couldn't bear to watch us relax, they often took us out into the yard to participate in physical activities.

Our guards also made us stage theatrical events. These took place in the block hall on Christian holidays. There were in among our number some talented directors, actors, singers, violinists and harmonica players. They were made to perform and recite. We were made to watch them. Our guards enjoyed these shows more than we did. We were upset because of the way we had been manipulated into it.

Towards the end of the summer of 1944, a van that was fully laden with documents arrived at our camp. Some of these documents were foreign office material from Russia, Poland, Czechoslovakia and Yugoslavia. The rest was Gestapo material from Paris, Brussels, Antwerp, Amsterdam and Rotterdam. These documents arrived at a time when we had run out of paper and could not print banknotes. We were asked to sort them into categories and staple them together. Some required cleaning by our experts. Some had photographs clipped on to them.

The photographs were heart-rending. They were of young Jewish men, women, and children, who had been murdered by the Nazis. We were so distressed by this work that we found it difficult to look our companions in the face. This situation became even worse, when several of our number came across photographs of relatives. One man saw photographs of his brother, his sister-in-law, and their child.

Wilde, a member of our work command, became so distressed that he started tearing up his documents. The chief supervisor Werner noticed this and challenged him. Wilde replied that he could not remain silent any longer. He would not look at photographs of dead Jews. Werner was not used to such outbursts from Jews. He had Wilde removed from the room and thrown into a dungeon. When Werner returned he noticed that all of us were very distressed, so he returned to the dungeon to speak to Wilde. Wilde told the chief supervisor his entire family had been murdered, he was all alone in the world, and that when he looked at such photographs he broke down and couldn't work. Werner had no wish to aggravate the situation further. He released Wilde and found him other work.

At about the same time an American plane dropped a bomb on Block 17. The heat generated by the flames was so intense that windows in our block shattered and our roof caught fire. We were evacuated into a little yard behind the block. Most of us were stunned, but a few braver ones sprang into action. They took hoses onto the roof of Block 18 and showered water onto our roof. The flames were extinguished and Block 19 was saved.

On another occasion we were moved into this yard, so that guards could search our barracks. They came back and searched us also. Some five pound notes had gone missing. They continued the search for several hours, but nothing was ever found. The chief supervisor warned us that the disappearance of the notes could have dire consequences. We had already spent half a day in the yard and everyone was starting to worry. Nobody could understand what had happened. ***"Why would one of us do something to endanger everyone?"*** Pessimists argued the story was a fabrication to give the Nazis an excuse for killing us. Optimists argued that there was still a lot of work to do and the Nazis would keep us busy. We stood in the yard until nightfall, hungry, distressed, dejected! Then we were told to return to our barracks. Further investigations laid the blame on a German Jew. We were told he confessed to burning the notes the previous night. Why he did so remains a mystery? The Nazis tortured him for several days and then shot him. They spared the rest of us. This could only mean they needed us. Their usual ***"all for one"*** principle would have normally demanded more victims.

In 1944, we even managed to celebrate the Jewish High Holy Days of Rosh Hashanah and Yom Kippur. I should add that this was not without danger. We organised a secret minyan (the Jewish quorum of ten adult males required for communal prayer).

EVACUATION.

On January 12th 1945 the great Soviet winter offensive started. In less than a month the Soviet armies had reached Kostrin (Kostrzyn), 70 kilometres east of Berlin. Now that the Russians were only 100 kilometres from Sachsenhausen, the German Secret Service made a decision to move our operations to a more secure location. This move took nearly a month to complete, despite long hours of very hard work on our part.

On February 27th 1945, we were given provisions for three days. We were told to consume them frugally, because our journey might take four days. Then almost immediately we were marched to the camp gates, where our regular guards handed us over to Sachsenhausen Camp guards, who would take us to our destination. Our regular guards, many of whom suffered from disabilities, were not fit enough for such a task. The Sachsenhausen Camp guards were forbidden to discuss our work with us. While we were walking out of the camp, a column of cars full of overfed Gestapo approached us. At first we thought they might have come here to dispose of us, but they drove by and we breathed freely.

Our mood was down again. We wondered whether the Nazis would really be able to establish our factory elsewhere. If they couldn't, we would all be made redundant, and we knew the meaning of that!

A train was waiting for us at the station. 16 of its carriages were still being packed with paper, presses and banknotes. We were huddled up into three freight cars, given heaters, and left there all day and into the night.

GERMANY AT THAT TIME.

Our railway journey proved very circuitous. Because many railroads had been bombed we travelled around Berlin for a day. Our journey took us through Dresden immediately after an air-raid. Fires were raging there. Other cities and towns along the way had also been heavily bombed. We started our journey hungry for revenge, but after we saw the bombings our appetites were quickly satiated.

We passed through some wonderful countryside, natural beauty enhanced by careful, arduous tending of the land. We travelled with a sense of almost feeling the end of Nazi Germany at our fingertips. Everywhere we looked civilians and military personnel were weary and resigned to defeat. People started expressing personal opinions without worrying about the consequences. Some of our guards openly cursed Hitler and his regime to our faces. They comforted us, urged us not to lose faith, and told us that we would soon be liberated. These attitudes were increasing in prevalence all the time.

MAUTHAUSEN.

The journey from Sachsenhausen to Mauthausen was over 1000 kilometres, and it lasted four days. We arrived at Mauthausen Station, at 4 p.m., on Friday, March 2nd 1945. From there we were marched over tracks through the hills up to the camp. The sight of its fortress-like walls terrified us and filled our hearts with fear.

We were taken straight to a special isolation block, normally reserved for people sentenced to death. For once we were not deloused. An S.S. guard forbade us to look out the windows, told us we must remain quiet, and warned us that we would be shot if we ventured out of our cell block.

We soon realised that we had been brought to a terrible camp and our spirits bottomed out. This was the pits, the end of the road! How would we ever get out of here? The walls of our compound reinforced our fears. They were bullet-riddled and many victims had scribbled their last testaments on them. We could see their names and the dates they spent their last hours there. But despite ours fears we were dead tired and we soon fell asleep.

Our personal guards were very unhappy at Mauthausen. They didn't want to unload the paper and presses off the train. But the railway authorities objected to a loaded train being left on the tracks, so before long the work of unloading began. The hard physical side of it was our job. The guards only supervised us. We lifted these heavy loads off the train, and lugged them on our backs up the hill to the camp.

Once again we suffered from hunger and fatigue. But far worse than the heavy loads we carried were the tragic scenes we witnessed. One by one we passed many trolleys packed brim-full with corpses being sent to the crematorium. From a distance we could hear the dull thud the corpses made when they were emptied out of the trolleys onto the crematorium's concrete floor.

The crematorium burned day and night. Smoke was always blowing from its chimneys. The air was always polluted with an odour of burnt human flesh.

The inmates, who pulled the trolleys, were barely alive themselves. Another day or two and another labourer would be loading their bodies onto a trolley and taking them to the crematorium. So it went on, day in, day out! The contrast between the starved inmates and their obese cruel guards brought a cringe to our spines. It filled our hearts with terror.

During these weeks, some of us unloaded printing presses into a silo next to the railway line. This gave us the opportunity to smuggle back some wheat to the camp. We ground the wheat into flour with a hammer. The more religious ones among us swapped some of their bread for the flour. They wanted to collect enough flour to bake matzos (unleavened bread) for Pesach (Passover).

On the first two nights of Passover, when the guards left the barracks, we set up two tables in the washroom. We covered them with white paper and lit two small home-made candles on them. Each prisoner who participated in a seder, was given a small piece of matzo. Our service leader read from a Hagadah, hand-written from memory. He recounted the exodus from Egypt. The rest of us listened. Every so often his voice broke and we all shed a tear.

We endured the terribly harsh conditions of Mauthausen for nearly six weeks.

SCHLIER.

After Passover the Nazis decided to re-establish our work command at Schlier Labour Camp. This was close to the railway station at Redyl-Zipf. With great haste and renewed enthusiasm, we reloaded paper, printing presses, and our many money boxes onto a train. The thought of being able to leave hellish Mauthausen behind us was itself a breath of fresh air. The relief it brought was unimaginable. We felt blessed to be able to allow the wonders of nature to fill our hearts with joy. It was the beginning of Spring, trees were budding, the grass was a rich green, birds were chirping, there was a cheerful breeze. Our will to live soared again. It become stronger than it had been for ages. We longed to see the end of this terrible war. We knew it was close-at-hand.

Schlier was only 90 kilometres from Mauthausen, but the local railway lines had been badly bombed. This was particularly the case around Linz and Wels, and lengthened our journey to thirty-six hours. The damage we witnessed from the train pleased us. It helped re-inforce feelings that the end of the war was near.

We arrived in Schlier in the early hours of the morning. The camp made a good first impression. It had a sense of freedom about it, as much as one could expect from a concentration camp. It had no concrete walls, just a barbed wire fence. We never felt as free in a camp as here.

The day after we arrived we commenced the rebuilding of our little factory. To our surprise civilians from town had been conscripted to help us. They had been warned not to speak to us, but they did from time to time. Some offered us words of consolation. Others encouraged us that liberation was close at hand.

Then all of a sudden Sturmbanfuhrer Kruger appeared. We hadn't seen him for eight weeks. We were pleased to. We had him to thank for rebuilding our factory here. It was a decision that helped save our lives.

Sturmbanfuhrer Kruger was in no great hurry to complete the rebuilding of the factory. We got the impression that he wanted to prolong it for as long as possible. I guess the longer we took the less chance he would be sent to the front. I should mention that he was never badly disposed towards us. If he wanted to he could have easily had us murdered.

Kruger was joking with two German Jews from our work command. He laughed. *"In a week's time, when the factory is completed, I'll organise a celebration for you. Who knows? By then you might be the owners of this camp, and I may be dancing to your tune."* His words served to inspire me. I became even more impatient for the day of liberation.

While the factory was being constructed, we were visited by some Nazis in civilian clothing. They ordered us to sort through the bank notes and pick out the good ones. The ones we rejected were burnt on the spot.

Once again we became anxious and began to worry. If the Nazis were destroying all evidence of our work, would we be next? We could only wait, see and hope for the best.

Supervised by guards, we burnt the rejected notes in three ovens. The ovens operated by day and night. The ashes were buried in deep pits. If a guard noticed a bank note was only partially burnt, he brought it back to the ovens. No trace of our work was going to survive. We worked hard for a week, burning hundreds of millions of counterfeit English pounds, and many boxes of forged documents.

The local civilians who worked with us became a source of sensational news. The Soviets had reached the outskirts of Berlin. British and American forces were 80 kilometres away. Field-Marshall Goering and Grand Admiral Doenitz were the new leaders of the German Government.

THE DEATH OF THE MURDERER.

On Wednesday afternoon, May 1st 1945, the Nazi flag above the Commandant's office was lowered to half mast. We asked one of the civilians, ***"Why?"*** He told us that Hitler had died in the fighting for Berlin. A Danish Jew in our work command approached an S.S. guard. He asked him if it was true. The guard confirmed Hitler's death.

We remained somewhat skeptical about this. We had been conditioned to believe if Hitler died we would be taken out and shot. But nothing happened. Everything continued on as before. We hoped for the best and awaited developments.

ANTICIPATING THE WORST.

At 6 p.m. Hauptscharfuhrer Werner announced he was coming back to the block at 9 p.m. He wanted to discuss important matters. When he arrived his voice was different. It was charged with emotion. He told us the front was closing in on Schlier and we were retreating into the mountains. We were being sent there in three groups. The first group would leave at 9 a.m., the second at 1 p.m., and the third tomorrow evening. We would leave our machinery and paper behind. The 100 odd boxes of viable bank notes had already been sent to an unknown destination.

This announcement, like previous ones, stressed us greatly. Our brains were conditioned to pessimism. We thought we were being taken away to be shot. Nobody wanted to be in the first transport, but our Block Leader offered us little choice. The Bialystokers had been selected to go first at 9 a.m. His closest friends had been selected for the last transport. We lay awake all night worrying.

At 9 a.m. on Thursday, May 2nd 1945, we were bustled towards a waiting motor vehicle. We took some meagre possessions along, but the vehicle was too small to accommodate them. Hauptscharfuhrer Werner ordered us to leave our belongings behind. They would be sent to us later. No one stirred. We were paralytic with fear. The fact that luggage was not allowed was a sure sign we were being slated for death. Werner ran up to us swinging a truncheon. He chased us onto the vehicle one by one.

The vehicle drove off. A strong wind was blowing and snow began to fall. Some Austrian Jews were well acquainted with the area. They were certain we were being sent to Mauthausen to be murdered. When the van passed the Mauthausen turn-off they told us to relax, maintain courage, and hope for the best.

EBENSEE.

At 2 p.m. we arrived at Ebensee, a subcamp of Mauthausen. There a series of hidden passages and bunkers had been tunnelled into a mountain, to create a secret rocket manufacturing and research facility. We were told to wait by the camp's gates. There was no attempt made to integrate us with the inmates of the camp. After a while we were led into the ante-room of the camp's baths. This was located near the S.S. barracks.

Our comrades in the second and third transports were sure we were being sent to be shot. When they saw our luggage loaded onto a wagon, they thought it was a trick to fool them.

At 1 p.m. the second transport was sent out from Schlier. It arrived at Ebensee in the evening. The Jews on the second transport were delighted to see we were alive. They told us the latest news from Schlier. The Americans were expected any day. Civilians had broken into the ammunitions armory. The remaining Jews had decided to resist Nazi evacuation.

Once again nerves stopped us sleeping. Dawn broke and we peered out of the ante-room's windows. The sight was horrific. The camp's yards were full of naked, emaciated, half-dead slaves. Most were Jews. They were hanging on to each other, a chain of living skeletons dragging each other along.

CHAPTER 11.

JOYOUS NEWS.

On Saturday morning, May 4th 1945, an older German guard from Sudetenland, who had always treated us well, spoke to a Czech Jew in our work command. He had worried for days we were going to be sent back to Mathausen to be murdered. But now things seemed better and he hoped we would be free in a day or two.

Other guards started saying similar things. To quote one: *"This bloody epoch, which started with Hitler and his devils burning the Reichstag, would end soon with fires consuming the whole of Berlin."*

And then we heard an announcement over the camp speakers. It was repeated 15 minutely. The local Nazi leader, the Gauleiter of Upper Austria, would address us at 12.30 p.m. We waited impatiently for his important message.

At 12.30 p.m. an eerie silence held sway. Then the Gauleiter started. Everyone's nerves were stretched to the limit. *"The Americans are fast approaching Linz. To minimise suffering I have ordered that bridges over the Danube should not be destroyed. We will not conduct`battles here. Military units located here will be transferred to fight the Soviets elsewhere."*

The speech was strong in capitulation. It elevated our spirits. Our hearts began to beat a little faster. We were joyful with the anticipation of impending liberation.

THE NAZIS RETREAT.

During the next couple of hours Ebensee was furiously evacuated. Nazis packed their belongings, abandoned their barracks, and scurried off with rucksacks on their backs.

Our supervisor Oberscharfuhrer Yansi had a change of heart. He realised that his reign of terror was over and that he better be nice to us. He offered us bribes. Every half hour or so he would return to give us gifts he had found in the deserted S.S. quarters. Later that evening he informed us that two of our colleagues selected for the third transport from Schlier, had tried to escape. One died and the other was hospitalised. He warned us not to do the same. We might regret it. This news saddened us, but we brightened up soon after when we heard it wasn't true. Both colleagues had escaped unhurt.

Because we were sad we slept poorly that night, but we lightened up with the dawn. Most of the S.S. guards had fled by then and our own special guard was about to do the same. Oberscharfuhrer Yansi tried to dissuade him, but to no avail. The guard simply stated he was a war invalid, and it was time for him to move on. He had arranged with the Commandant for our group to be moved into the general camp. We would now meet the other inmates.

A WHITE FLAG ADORNS THE CREMATORIUM'S CHIMNEY.

An hour later, Oberscharfuhrer Yansi came running into our room. An elderly S.S. man followed him. They ordered us into the courtyard and told us to stand there in rows of five. It was immediately obvious we were witnessing an historic event. A white flag was hoisted onto the crematorium's chimney. This was tantamount to an official surrender. We yelled out loud - ***"May freedom live"*** - at the top of our voices - *"may freedom live!"* Our joy was boundless. We grabbed each other's arms, kissed each other's cheeks, wished each other mazel-tov (good luck)! Tears rolled down our faces.

We were moved into a block with 600 other prisoners. At 1 a.m. the new Camp Commandant visited us. He announced our food allowance was about to be be doubled and by the end of the week there would be plenty to eat. This bulletin was music to our ears. We were on edge all night with suspense. It was impossible to relax let alone sleep. We were waiting for things to happen, for the light of day, for the sound of advancing American troops on their way to liberate the camp.

FREEDOM.

It was dawn Sunday May 5th 1945. Everyone was up. All public areas were packed with people. At 10 a.m. everyone started to converge on the roll-call area. From there one could see tanks in the distance. They were rumbling towards us and were soon at the camp's gates. Thousands of starved slaves spontaneously erupted into a display of emotions. They cheered with joy. They climbed onto tanks. They hugged and kissed tank personnel. The atmosphere was electric! American soldiers were dragged out of tanks, carried on shoulders, tossed into the air like footballs. Everybody wanted to get in on the act. Thousands did what thousands of others had done only minutes before. Thousands of shadow-like skeletons were repeating the same acts. Joyous emotion flooded out. It spread wildly everywhere, even up into the heavens. It was amazing, awesome, incredible, overwhelming! People were suddenly free!

The welcome continued for more than two hours. The camp was a big party. People, never expecting to survive, were rejoicing! People, certain they were destined for the ovens, were embracing. People kissed each other, left, right and centre. Rivers of tears flowed down thousands of cheeks. Initially they were tears of joy, but then people stopped to think and others appeared. These were the tears of grief shed in memory of loved ones, who had not survived to see this day.

There were 20,000 prisoners at Ebensee, who avoided death two days earlier by taking a brave and determined stance. Camp Commandant S.S.-Hauptsturmfuhrer Anton Ganz addressed an assemblage of prisoners on the roll-call field. He warned them that a fierce battle for the camp was about to rage and that their barracks would be prime targets for enemy fire. To ensure their safety they would be hidden in the tunnels in the mountains. The prisoners knew the murderer Ganz well. He was no friend of theirs, not the sort of person who would ever have their interests at heart. With liberation close-at-hand, they were no longer frightened and replied in a single voice, ***"No!"*** They would not enter any tunnels under any circumstances. Later on it was discovered that a locomotive, left at the entrance to Tunnel 5, had its water tank filled with explosives. Ganz had planned to blow up the tunnel with the prisoners inside it.

REVENGE.

When the heartfelt welcome for American troops died down, the prisoners disarmed the camp's guards. Most were Austrian civilians, who had volunteered to keep order after the Germans left until the Americans arrived. At the same time more aggressive prisoners sought out inmates, who had collaborated with the Nazis. Their hour of judgement had arrived. They were murdered all over the camp.

A new camp leadership was formed immediately. Those who sought active positions tended to be political prisoners from countries Germany had occupied. They elected some of their number to a 'Disciplinary Council,' whose job it was to pass judgement on inmates who had collaborated with the Nazis. They delivered sentence that same night. *"Prisoners, who collaborated with the Nazis, would be burnt alive."* There were a number of Jews in amongst them.

Nobody slept again that night. We just couldn't. We sat huddled together, spilling out our hearts. We dwelt anew on the numerous tragedies that had befallen us. We thought about dead loved ones and the loneliness we would have to bear. We pondered over our future and wondered what it would hold.

At 2 a.m. a fire broke out in the S.S. barracks. There were munitions stored there and when they exploded it shocked everyone. We thought a battle had broken out between the Americans and some S.S. troops. In reality an accident had caused the fire, and by 4 a.m. it was quelled. At dawn birds heralded in a new spring morn with a lullaby. We lay back on our beds and rapidly entered a soothing deep sleep. It was a reward for having waited so long to be liberated.

ARMISTICE.

On the morning on May 8th 1945 many factories commenced work with long drawn-out blasts from their sirens. At first we failed to appreciate the significance of this, but then we wondered whether it was a sign that something important had happened. Was the war over? Had the slaughter finally ended? And then some Jews came up to the camp from the town of Ebensee. They told us the armistice had been signed and buildings in town were flying Austrian flags. Great joy broke out. We wanted to leave the camp and search for surviving relatives.

THE MASS GRAVES AT EBENSEE.

Ebensee was a subcamp of Mauthausen Extermination Camp. Even though it was meant to be a work-camp, tens of thousands of prisoners, not only Jews, were systematically murdered and cremated there. Slave labour at Ebensee was particularly harsh. The inmates were forced to dig deep tunnels into the mountain to establish sites for secret factories. They lugged heavy rocks and stones and were frequently beaten in order to hurry them along. And after a long drawn-out day of this, rations were only 100 grams of bread and some watery soup. No wonder they died like flies. The local crematorium could not service the number of corpses.

When the Americans entered the camp, they found 500 bodies stored in the "Death Barracks." They photographed them and insisted the local civil authorites bury them. The Americans wanted the bodies buried in a prominent part of the town of Ebensee. The Austrians obliged them within a few days. Different nationalities and faiths were laid to rest together in mass graves.

CHAPTER 12.

THE DESTRUCTION OF THE LAST REMNANTS OF BIALYSTOKER JEWRY. (This is based on evidence obtained from a number of survivors.)

THE LAST DAYS OF NAZI RULE IN BIALYSTOK.

The Soviet Army's westward thrust slowed down near Slonim. This gave Nazis left in Bialystok time to loot the town and destroy it. They emptied factories of machines, raw materials and manufactured goods. Anything of military significance left behind was destroyed. Special demolition squads blew up industrial sites, administrative offices and entire streets of private housing. Jewish Bialystok was reduced to ashes and rubble.

BIALYSTOK IS LIBERATED.

Soviet troops entered burning Bialystok on the morning of July 22nd 1944. A large contingent of Vlasov's troops met them there, and a fierce battle ensued near the railway station. Vlasov was a former Soviet army officer, who had been captured by the Germans in July 1942 and persuaded to change sides.

The Soviets called for re-inforcements to come help them at the station. When the re-inforcements arrived, it was much easier to surround Vlasov's troops and bombard them with heavy fire. After noon Vlasov's men were massacred and the Soviets re-captured Bialystok.

This was the cue for a few Jews, who had hidden away for nearly a year, to come out onto the streets. The Okun brothers, textile workers, were two such Jews. Local Poles made no attempt to welcome them back or support them. This attitude even extended to nuns. Some Jews were noticed by Polish nuns, when they passed by the orphanage. The nuns made no attempt to approach them. Instead they were heard complaining to each other, ***"Look, there are still some Jews left here!"***

One dishevelled Jew walked out of a hiding place and onto Mazowiecka Street. He wanted to welcome the liberating Soviets personally, and ran up to a mounted trooper and kissed his horse. The Russian was startled by this behaviour. He might well have wondered whether he was being attacked, and even shot the Jew. Fortunately passers-by explained the situation to him. A tender scene ensued as the Russian soldier and the Jew embraced each other in a brotherly fashion.

AUSCHWITZ-BIRKENAU.

Very few Jewish men from Bialystok survived Auschwitz-Birkenau. They were part of a group of 100 Jews, who were transferred from Birkenau to the nearby slave labour camp at Buna Monowitz, in early 1944. They were starved, poorly clad, and forced to walk around barefoot. When the Soviets liberated them, less than half were alive. The Soviets then marched them, still barefoot, through hundreds of kilometres of snow, to other camps. Little wonder less than 20 survived. That in itself was a miracle.

Dr. Katzenelson, who cared for the 1200 Jewish children in Bialystok, worked in the hospital at Birkenau. He disappeared when Birkenau was evacuated. He was most likely shot dead together with thousands of other Jews.

Most Jewish women, sent from Bialystok to Auschwitz-Birkenau, were instant victims of Hitler's final solution. From the few chosen to work in factories in Auschwitz or its various sub-camps, about 20 survived.

My beloved only daughter Nehama Rajzner died after having worked for a while in a sub-camp of Auschwitz-Birkenau. She was subjected to starvation, hard labour and physical abuse. She passed away during the first days of the Hebrew month of Elul in 1944.

Engineer Barasz's wife, who also cared for the 1200 Jewish children in Bialystok, died of typhus in Birkenau.

Nerita Kaplan (Pesach Kaplan's youngest daughter) and Isaac Markus' daughter were sent to Birkenau via Majdanek. They were gassed and cremated shortly after arrival.

BLIZYN CONCENTRATION CAMP.

Most of several hundred Bialystoker Jews working in Blizyn Concentration Camp died during a typhus epidemic. This included A. Kniazew, the former Director of the Jewish Hospital; Dr, Adamowicz; Dr. Nunberg, a surgeon from Warsaw; Plonski, a well-known women's tailor and his son; Melnicki, of 39 Kupiecka Street, also a women's tailor; A. Tyktin, who sat on the Judenrat Finance Committee and his son; and the two Blum brothers, both tailors. The few Bialystokers, who survived the typhus epidemic, continued to work at Blizyn. When the Soviets drew near, the Germans evacuated the camp. They force marched the starved, poorly clad inmates, barefoot in the cold to a railway station 70 kilometres away. They were then railed for 14 days. Miraculously a few survived.

PLASZOW CONCENTRATION CAMP.

Several hundred Bialystoker Jews were working in Plaszow Concentration Camp near Krakow. Conditions there were better than in many other camps. When the Soviets approached these prisoners were railed to Austria. Nearly every one of them perished. Some starved, some died of cold and exhaustion, some were shot.

STUTTHOF CONCENTRATION CAMP.

When we left Stutthof Concentration Camp for Auschwitz-Birkenau, 20 master tailors from Bialystok stayed behind. Fortunately nearly every one of them survived.

THE BIALYSTOK PRISON.

When we were evacuated from Bialystok Prison, 85-90 Jews remained behind. More than 60 were men and 25 were children, under 15 years, who had been forcefully separated from their mothers.

The men remained in the prison. One-third already worked outside for an S.S. General. The remaining two-thirds were held in prison pending further work duties.

Polish prison guards had volunteered to give the children one third of their food rations. They gave this food to the group of 20 workers each evening, as they returned back from their day's work. A kind act, it was to no avail. A little while later, on a Friday winter's morning, the children were led to a black van parked in the prison yard. When they saw it they started wailing. They knew full well what was in store for them. The group of 40 prisoners who were still awaiting work, heard the racket and ran to their cell windows to see what was happening. They watched the children being forced into the van. Those who resisted were thumped over the head with rifle butts. The van was locked and shortly afterwards it drove off. It returned with the children's clothing 30 minutes later. The brutality of this episode horrified the men who witnessed it. For weeks they could think of nothing else.

Then the day of pending work duties arrived. The 40 men were now led out each morning by 30 armed Gestapo guards. Their duties were horrid and sinister. They dug up and burnt thousands of Jewish corpses, scattered throughout the various fields and locales around Bialystok. These exhumations and cremations were a means of destroying evidence. The Nazis wanted to ensure that nobody could bear witness to their abominable crimes. Most of the corpses were in an advanced state of decomposition, but the Nazis still insisted they be laid out on biers and burnt. One cannot imagine to what extent these men were physically exhausted and spiritually defunct, when they returned to the prison each night.

More Bialystoker Jews were continually brought to the prison. Some were flushed out of hiding places. Others were denounced by Polish neighbours. Their stay in prison was always short. They were led out and shot in a day or two.

In February 1944, a typhus epidemic swept through the prison. The two Jewish work groups were evacuated immediately. The 20, who worked for the S.S. General, were accommodated in a house close to work, now converted into a small prison. The 40, who dug up and burnt corpses, were housed in a prison on Kraszewskiego Street near Gestapo Headquarters. Both groups never returned to the prison.

Once the work of exhuming and cremating thousands of Jewish corpses was nearing an end, the group of 40 men started fearing for their lives. Each day they expected to be taken out and shot. There was no way the Nazis would spare anyone, who had witnessed such barbaric crimes. The men decided, no matter what, they must attempt to escape! If only one of them succeeded it would be worthwhile.

By July 15th 1944, the 40 men had completed all their exhuming and cremating. At 10 a.m. they were rounded up by 40 armed guards, and marched back to where they had last been working. Sensing danger they suddenly scattered in all directions. The Nazis started shooting as soon as they could, but nine Jews managed to escape unharmed. A tenth was seriously wounded, but he still made it to the forest. He was sent to Moscow and recovered from his injuries.

Those who escaped unharmed were (1) Simon Amiel; (2) Moshe Gershum; (3) Samuel Wrobel; (4) Israel Felder and (5) Zalman Edelman (all from Bialystok); (6) Zev Schiff (from Jasionowka); (7) Abraham Isaac Lew (from Sokoly); (8) T. Rabinowicz (from Lodz); and (9) Sheima Lipetz (from Grodno).

Those who were shot included (1 & 2) Mezhibowski and his son; (3) Arke Lew; (4) Aronchik Zubowski; (5) Meishel the glazier; (6) Jehuda known as Yolke Lew; (7) Azriel the son of the porter; (8) Abramel Karaschek; (9) Reuben Perlstein; (10) Joel Samolski; (11 & 12) the two brothers Abram and Berel Botschkowski; (13, 14 & 15) the three brothers Jehuda, Joske and Isaac Lipschitz (from Grodno); (16) Nissell Wolf (from Hrubieszow); (17) Shlomo Rosenblum (from Sarnaki); (18 & 19) the two brothers Zaidke and Chaim Zvi Rajchkowski (from Sokoly); (20) Lewitanski (from Suwalki); (21) Furmanski (from Warsaw); (22) Gwiazda a carpenter (from

Bialystok); (23) Borer (from Grodno); (24) Owsejewicz (from Wilno); (25) Abramowicz (from Slonim); (26) Chaim Berel Kirszenbaum (from Grodno) and (27) my dear only son Samuel Rajzner.

Abram Klyatchko and Shlomo Gelman both died of tuberculosis in Bialystok Prison.

As mentioned earlier the great Soviet summer offensive began across a line from Orsha to Vitebsk on June 22nd 1944. The Red Army advanced rapidly and quickly captured Mohilev, Bobruysk and Minsk. The speed with which this happened greatly alarmed the Germans.

The 20 Bialystoker Jews, who worked for the S.S. General, realised that the Germans were distracted by these events. They planned an escape, three weeks before the Soviets entered Bialystok. Their three weeks in hiding proved difficult. They were hungry and frightened to seek help from Poles, lest they murder them or hand them back to the S.S.

THE PARTISANS.

Among the Bialystokers who survived with the partisans were Dr. Simon Datner; Herschel Dinerman; Israel Felder; Chaika Grossman; Israel Kot; Jehudah Medownik; Israel Prensky; and Mottel Tcheremoshnie.

THE JEWISH SURVIVORS.

Less than 1000 Bialystoker Jews (<2%) survived the Holocaust. Over 200 survived in concentration camps, 50-60 survived with partisans, and 600-700 were repatriated from the Soviet Union.

Most survivors are now scattered throughout the four corners of the earth.

Only a handful of Jews remain in Bialystok. They have inherited the painful ruins, which litter a soil saturated with blood. They are a living memory to our martyrs. They plan to dedicate their lives to the rebuilding of a new Jewish Bialystok.

Rafael Rajzner,
Melbourne, Australia, 1948.

Rajzner's Last Paragraph Was Wishful Thinking. The Jews Who Stayed In Bialystok Are Now Dead. They Failed To Re-Build A New Jewish Bialystok. Like The Hebrew Temple In Jerusalem, It Can Never Be Re-Built!
ALL WE CAN DO IS REMEMBER IT!

Henry R. Lew,
Melbourne, Australia. (October 2007).

EPILOGUE

Rafael Rajzner (Bialystok 1/1/1897 - Melbourne 6/4/1953) died prematurely. He was only 56 years old. He survived liberation by less than eight years. He lost his wife and his only daughter and son. It therefore pleases me to be able to write that he did not die alone.

After the war Rafael met and married Gusta (Gitl) Schnall in Rome, Italy in 1946. Gusta, a widow, had a son David Schnall, who similarly met and married a young woman, Danuta Löven, after the war. All four were survivor-victims of Nazi concentration camps.

Rafael and Gusta came to Australia in late 1946, David and Danuta followed in early 1948.

Danuta calls Rafael "Uncle." She speaks of him with great love and respect. She remembers him sitting by a window in a sunny room in Rome, surrounded by writing pads and pencils, very absorbed in his work. He had started writing shortly after the war ended.

Danuta mentions Rafael's great love for the Yiddish language. At first she would speak to him in Polish and he would answer in Yiddish. ***"I wanted to please him so I tried to learn to speak Yiddish. He would smile at my first attempts. He realised it was very hard for me, a teenage survivor of the camps, to learn Italian and Yiddish at the same time. When I tried his pleasure was obvious, and the more I tried the more he encouraged me. Today I speak a very passable Yiddish."***

In Italy Rafael helped manage the Jewish paper in Rome and in Melbourne he worked for the Australian Jewish News. Danuta recalls Rafael's phenomenal memory, and how the cottage in which they lived, at 75 Lee Street, North Carlton, was full of Bialystokers. ***"Their conversation on occasions was sad. Tears would stream down their faces as they reminisced about loved ones they had lost and atrocities they had seen. But more often they discussed politics, Russia and happier matters and their pleasure in each other's company was obvious. Everyone was working hard and trying to achieve. We were very happy to be alive and able to partake in a homely atmosphere with cherished family members and friends. For me it brought back the security of the family home I had known before the war. It helped us all to heal our minds."***

Henry R. Lew,
Melbourne, Australia. (October 2007).

INDEX OF NAMES

A

B

C

D

E

H

I

J

K

L

M

N

O

P

Q

R

S

T

U